THE SEARCH FOR FRANKLIN

THE SEARCH
FOR FRANKLIN

LESLIE H. NEATBY

WALKER AND COMPANY
New York

First published in the United States of America in 1970 by
the Walker Publishing Company, Inc.

Published simultaneously in Canada by The Ryerson Press, Toronto

ISBN Number: 0–8027–0317–8

Library of Congress Catalog Card Number: 73–99977

Printed in Great Britain

Contents

	List of Illustrations	6
	Acknowledgements	7
	Introduction	9
	Prologue	10
1	Early Approaches, 1576–1818	17
2	The Breakthrough	32
3	Prelude to Disaster	65
4	Fruitless Search from East and West	98
5	The Search in Barrow Strait and Beyond, 1850–1851	118
6	Kennedy and Bellot in Regent's Inlet	143
7	Cruise of the *Investigator* – Northwest Passage Discovered	159
8	The Belcher Expedition and the Rescue of McClure	195
9	The Voyage of the *Enterprise* and the Committee's Award	220
10	The Americans in Smith Sound	230
11	Success at Last	243
	Bibliography	271
	Index	273

Illustrations

Photographs
  (between pages 160 and 161)
Captain Sir John Franklin, R.N.
Lady Franklin
H.M.S. *Erebus* and *Terror* in the Antarctic pack ice
Captain Sir Robert McClure, R.N.
Johann August Miertsching
S. G. Cresswell and J. A. Miertsching sledging from
  Banks to Melville Island
H.M.S. *Investigator* in danger at Ballast Beach, Banks
  Island
Admiral Sir Leopold McClintock, R.N.
Dr Elisha K. Kane, U.S.N.
The *Fox* at Beechey Island
The Franklin record
William Gibson surveys the remains of some of Franklin's
  men
The Arctic Council, 1848–9

Maps
General map of Canadian Arctic, showing the routes of
  Parry to Melville Island, Franklin, McClure and
  Collinson, as well as Sir John Ross's voyage down
  Regent's Inlet   18
Area of Franklin's first overland journey   36
King William Island area, showing James Ross's sledge
  journey from Felix Harbour, and Franklin's last voyage
  up Wellington Channel   71
This is the Arctic as known when McClure came in from
  the west   99
Smith Sound and Kane Basin   231

Acknowledgements

For aid in the preparation of this work the author's thanks are firstly due to the Ohio University Press and the Macmillan Company of Canada for waiving their claims and permitting him to produce this book for the present publishers. Special thanks are owing to Macmillan of Canada for granting permission to use material from J. A. Miertsching's *Frozen Ships;* to Longmans Canada for a short extract from his book *The Link Between the Oceans,* to Niels W. Jannasch of Seabright, Nova Scotia, to use the photograph of his great grandfather, Johann Mierstching, and for supplying the water colour by Lt S. G. Cresswell; to the National Maritime Museum for the photograph of H.M.S. *Erebus* and *Terror;* to Hodder and Stoughton Limited to use the photograph of Lady Franklin from *Portrait of Jane – a Life of Lady Franklin* by Frances J. Woodward; to John Murray to use the photograph of Captain Sir John Franklin from *The Life of Sir John Franklin* by H. D. Traiil, and material from *Life of Admiral Sir Leopold McClintock,* by Sir Clements Markham; to the Hudson's Bay Record Society for permission to use their sixteenth volume as the source of Rae's reports of his journeys of 1851 and 1853–4; and to Her Majesty's Stationery Office for permission to use Parliamentary Papers as reference in Chapters 4, 5 and 9. The author tenders thanks to Rear Admiral P. W. Brock, C.B., D.S.O., R.N. (retired) and to Mr A. G. E. Jones of Tunbridge Wells, England, for directing him to material; to Dr Terence Armstrong of the Scott Polar Research Institute, Cambridge, England; to the Photographic Service of the British Museum; to Mrs Erika Parmi of the Stefansson Collection, Baker Library, Dartmouth College; to the Library, Department of Northern Development, Ottawa; to the staff of the Shortt Collection, University of Saskatchewan Library; to the *Beaver* organ of the Hudson's Bay Company, Winnipeg; to the Canadian Archives, Ottawa, and to the Royal Ontario Museum, Toronto.

He is obliged to the Medical Services, University of Saskatchewan Hospital, for reproducing illustrations, and to Miss Martha Pankratz for typing the manuscript.

Special thanks are due to Professors W. O. Kupsch, Department of Geology, and K. I. Fung, Department of Geography, University of Saskatchewan, for providing the maps.

The author also wishes to acknowledge that the Samwell story is derived from *The Journals of Captain Cook: Volume III, The Voyage of the 'Resolution' and 'Discovery' 1776-1780*, edited by J. C. Beaglehole.

Lastly the writer apologizes to any whose names may have been inadvertently omitted from the above list.

Department of Classics,
University of Saskatchewan
16 July 1969

Introduction

With all its shortcomings the nineteenth century was a brave and generous epoch, and nowhere is this more evident than in the field of geographical discovery. Its adventurers braved incalculable dangers by land and sea in all quarters of the globe, not for gain, but in the unselfish expression of scientific curiosity or of missionary zeal. Dignity of purpose lent a sort of grandeur (conspicuous also in Robert E. Lee) to many of the Victorian travellers, but none of them, not even David Livingstone, has so captured the imagination of posterity or commanded such a perennial interest as Sir John Franklin. This was not due to his personality, which was more solid than brilliant, but to his varied and sensational career. He learned his trade by survey and shipwreck on the coast of Australia, and fought at Copenhagen, Trafalgar, and New Orleans in three of the bloodiest naval engagements of the period. By novel methods and immense labour he laid bare half of the vast and until then inaccessible Arctic littoral of North America, and when the fate which he had so often challenged overtook him he became the object of the longest and most expensive manhunt in history. The mystery of his fate, never wholly solved, remains to tantalize the polar expert and keep the memory of the old sailor green.

A*

Prologue: The *Erebus* and the *Terror* Sail

On a June day, near the middle of the last century, off the North Shetland island bearing the mournful name Rona, two sailing ships cast off the steam tugs that had aided them so far on their northward course. The agile steamboats put about and, with the easy manoeuvrability their power conferred, ranged alongside first the one and then the other of the two ships and with rousing cheers bade them a joyous farewell. That done, they steamed away over the southern skyline leaving the others to labour on through the North Atlantic rollers.

That parting was doubly symbolic of the end of one epoch and the beginning of another. The steamboats, vulgar and assertive parvenus, bore the appropriate names *Rattler* and *Blazer*. At a time when the comparative merits of propulsion by paddle wheel and propeller were hotly debated, they had proved the efficiency of the screw by the ease with which they had tugged the deeply laden ships of Sir John Franklin through the rough and tide-vexed waters north of Scotland. Bearing the grim names *Erebus* (Erebus was the hell of the Ancients) and *Terror*, Franklin's ships were the last of the old age, as the steamers were the first of the new. They were bluff-bowed, stocky little three-masted vessels, rigged as barks – ' bombs ' built during the wars of Nelson to harass enemy coastal installations with mortar fire. As floating gun platforms they were of sturdy construction, and well-fitted to resist pressure in the ice fields to which they were bound. They symbolized the end of an age in discovery as well as in naval architecture. For 270 years (or for over 300 if one admits the pretensions of Sebastian Cabot) English seamen had ventured their lives to find the Northwest Passage, an ocean channel leading around the North American continent to the waters of the Pacific. The *Erebus* and the *Terror* were to settle that question once and for all.

Travel was difficult in those days, and the newspaperman was not the roving fellow he is today. The Crimean War and the first great war correspondent lay several years in the future. But by a singular piece of luck this voyage, destined to have a special interest that the passage of a century has hardly dimmed, *was* reported in its first stage by one who, with his powers of observation and his knack as Charles Dickens put it of ' conveying the results of that observation plainly, unaffectedly and truly,' had all the marks of the travelling reporter. This was Commander James Fitzjames of the *Erebus*.

Fitzjames might have been called a supernumerary. Apart from him, each ship bore a staff of senior officers ample for vessels of their size: a captain (Sir John Franklin in the *Erebus*, F. R. M. Crozier in the *Terror*) and three lieutenants apiece. But to relieve Franklin of routine duties and free him for the general direction of the expedition and supervision of the geographic and other scientific inquiries to which his life had been dedicated, Fitzjames had been appointed as chief executive officer on the commodore's ship. The captain of a man-of-war is, almost of necessity, aloof and withdrawn. But Fitzjames, while exercising some of the captain's functions, possessed none of his dignity. Off duty he moved among the officers as no more than an equal, chatted, observed their ways, and entered what he heard and saw in a journal that was to be sent home from Greenland on the supply ship for the entertainment of Mrs Coningham, the wife of a lifelong friend.

Both officers and men were full of the liveliest optimism. Eager to come to grips with the ice of the northern seas, they saw the towboats off with a sigh of relief, and not a doubt of success existed except perhaps in the mind of him who led them. Sir John Franklin was one of the few men on the two ships who knew what the ice was like. Furthermore, he had had so many hairbreadth escapes that he must have wondered when his luck would run out. He had come unhurt through the two bloodiest sea fights of the Napoleonic wars, Copenhagen and Trafalgar; he had been shipwrecked and marooned for weeks on a sandbank off the Australian Great Barrier Reef. He had come away alive from sanguinary defeat at New Orleans. Then he had tried to chart Arctic shores by canoe and had almost starved in the Canadian tundra. He nearly met the same fate when, as a colonial governor of the age of fifty, he had gone tramping in the bush of Tasmania. His departure on this new cruise had been clouded by an ominous incident. While he was reclining on a couch, Lady Franklin, thinking that he was cold, spread over his feet the British Ensign on which she was working. The sailor sprang up with the angry expostulation: 'Don't you know that they lay the Union Jack over a corpse?' While some hoped that the expedition might be over in one year, he cautioned his wife not to be uneasy if it was absent for three.

Not at all depressed by the unfamiliar dangers which lay ahead, Fitzjames gave his attention to the peculiarities of his brother officers. With the reporter's instinct for the odd and newsworthy, he first fixed his notice on James Reid, ice master. This rank existed only in the polar service. The ice-master was usually an experienced skipper, drafted from the Greenland whaling trade to advise the naval captain on the problems of navigation in the ice pack.

James Reid was an old captain and a Scot, and in neither character easily impressed by authority and protocol. He sometimes forgot that he was not still captain, as, when observing Franklin's steward towing a salted fish overboard, he shouted: 'What are you making faces at there? That's not the way to get the sarlt oout . . .' and proceeded to deliver a harangue on the proper treatment of salt fish to the impatient and resentful serving man. Though junior by several grades of rank to Commander Fitzjames, he hailed him with cheerful familiarity as 'Mr Jems.' When Fitzjames expressed some nervous apprehension, as an executive officer well might who is entering the ice for the first time, Reid instantly reassured him:

'Ah, now, Mr Jems, we'll be having fine weather, fine weather, sir. No ice at arl about it, sir, only the bergs, which I like to see. Let it come on to blow, look out for a big un. Get under his lee, and hold to him fast, sir. If he drifts to land, why, he grounds afore you do.'

Fitzjames, with all his ease of manner, felt some awe towards his captain, an earnest man, nearly double his age, and with the prestige, shared only with Captain Crozier of the *Terror*, of a veteran of the Napoleonic wars. This restraint was dispelled at their first private meeting. He admired the old sailor's frankness and directness and found that, contrary to report, he was not stubborn, but open to reason, 'unless he has already made up his mind.' Franklin won the confidence of the other officers with equal readiness. At a conference he explained the scientific aims of the expedition, urged the need of instantly recording any detail of scientific interest, and emphasized the value he placed on their individual observations. To a devoutly religious temperament, Franklin added the less common gift of making it palatable to others. Fitzjames was much impressed with his sermons: 'I defy any man not to feel the force of what he would convey . . . he has real conviction.'

Fitzjames is much more hesitant in his appraisal of the surgeon-scientist Dr H. D. S. Goodsir. 'I can't make out why Scotchmen just caught [an allusion to Samuel Johnson, who held that the congenital defects of the Scot *could* be corrected by an English education: "Much may be made of a Scotchman, if he be caught young"] always speak in a low monotonous tone of voice. . . . This is, I believe, called "cannyness". Mr Goodsir is "canny". He is long and straight, and walks upright on his toes. . . . He is in ecstasies about a bag full of blubberlike stuff which he has just hauled up in a net – and which he is examining with a *mee*croscope.'

Below deck sharp contests of wit occur between the two Scots, Goodsir 'matching his learning and his science' against the 'north-country wit' of the barely literate Reid. The wardroom of the *Erebus* was a type of the true democracy, now perhaps vanished forever, where genuine equality thrives with no semblance of conformity in manner or outlook.

Purser C. H. Osmer joins the portrait gallery. An elderly man, he had promised his wife that he was leaving home for the last time. 'At first I was inclined to think that he was a stupid old man' – there is something incurably boyish about Fitzjames, despite his thirty-three years – 'because he had a chin and took snuff; but he is as merry-hearted as any young man . . . always good-humoured.' And so he goes on to sketch the other officers with liveliness and perception never tainted with malice. 'The dead and gone come back to us,' Charles Dickens, who was to review the journal, comments, 'for a little while from the icy keeping of death.'

Fitzjames is equally pleased with the men: 'Fine hearty fellows, mostly north-country men, with a sprinkling of men-of-war's men.' He affords us a pleasing instance of his own relations with those he commanded. The night before the ships left their last home port, Stromness in the Shetlands, old Captain Crozier, fearing that some of his crew would have second thoughts about a voyage of such great length and uncertain duration, refused to grant shore leave to the men of the *Terror*. Undeterred by the example of one much his superior in age and experience, Fitzjames granted the usual liberty to the crew of the *Erebus*. All came aboard at the stated hour; but four, 'who had probably taken a *leetle* too much whisky,' got hold of a small boat and stole back to land. One of them was an old sailor who had not been home for four years. They were quickly missed, and all were rounded up by the third lieutenant and brought aboard by 3 a.m. The commander believed that they had had no intention of deserting, but would have come back on their own.

No one could have blamed Fitzjames had he been provoked to punish the defaulters with all the severity in his power. He had 'stuck his neck out' by granting a privilege an older officer had judged it prudent to refuse. These men had repaid him by an act of gross disrespect and had placed him, young as he was, in an embarrassing and humiliating position. 'According to the rules of the service,' writes Fitzjames, 'these men should have been severly punished. . . . It struck me, however, that punishment is intended to prevent misconduct in others and not to revenge their individual misconduct. Men know very well when they are in the wrong, and there is clearly no chance of any repetition of the offence until we get to Valparaiso or the Sandwich Islands.' So he merely sent the sergeant of marines to gather up and throw overboard all the unauthorized liquor (the cause of the offence) that could be found on the lower deck. 'They evidently expected a rowing, and the old man with the wife looked very sheepish and could not look me in the face, but nothing more was said, and the men have not behaved a bit the worse ever since.'

They ran into rain, gales, and fog off Iceland, and had trouble in keeping company with one another and with their transport, the *Baretto Junior*. On 17 June, 1845, a cloudy night, a glow appeared in the sky to the northeast. First Lieutenant Gore, who had wintered in the north, told the younger officers that it was the aurora borealis. Ice-master Reid politely but firmly corrected him: it was the ice blink, a reflection from ice fields near at hand. On the eighteenth they installed the crow's-nest, a barrel lashed to the masthead from which the ice-master could obtain an extended view of ice pack and water lanes. Reid, accustomed to the thrifty practice of the whalers, censured the navy structure as 'very expensive'. Soon the ships are weaving their way through broken pack and around lofty icebergs, 'huge masses of pure snow, furrowed with caverns and dark ravines' – sixty counted at one time.

One night they are becalmed in a great pond in the heart of the ice, with the water so calm that the mastheads of the *Terror* are mirrored in the water near the rails of the *Erebus,* though she is fully half a mile away. Fitzjames wanders into the officers' ward-room and there finds Reid and Osmer, relaxed and drinking the toast to 'wives and sweethearts' in a leisurely manner. Fitzjames will not share in the toast. He has no wife, he says, and no wish for a sweetheart – one wonders if some frustrated romance had impelled the restless adventurer to go sailing steamboats on the Euphrates, warring in the China seas, and was now driving him to adventure in the polar ice – but he sits down with them like a good fellow and drinks a whisky and water to his own speedy promotion.

And now they are nearing the west Greenland port where they are to anchor while the *Baretto Junior* tops off their supplies and collects their letters for home. On Sunday, 6 July 1845, Fitzjames concludes his diary and bids Mrs Coningham farewell: 'Your journal is at an end, at least for the present. I do hope it has amused you, but I fear not; for what can there be in an old tub like this with a parcel of sea-bears to amuse a "lady fair"? . . . God bless you and everything belonging to you.'

Almost his last words. Fourteen years later, Lieutenant W. R. Hobson of the Royal Navy, sledging with his crew of five along an Arctic shore – rocky, wind-beaten, and utterly barren – came to a low headland. He mounted it – with difficulty, for scurvy had gripped him. At the summit he came upon a crumbled pile of stone and, groping in the rubble at its foot, found a metal cylinder and in it a printed naval form, written around its borders in ink:

25 April 1848. – H.M. Ships *Terror* and *Erebus* were deserted

on 22nd April, 5 leagues N.N.W. of this, having been beset
since 12 September 1846. . . .

James Fitzjames,
Captain, H.M.S. *Erebus*.

The rest is silence:

For never yet from out that waste of snow
Came the far footsteps of the weary brave;
The drifting sleet, the bitter west winds blow,
To hide their grave.
– Unknown. Probably Clements Markham.

1 Early Approaches, 1576-1818

The quest that lured the crews of the *Erebus* and the *Terror* to the Arctic was an old one, dating back for centuries. It was a direct and almost immediate outgrowth of the vision of Columbus. He had sought a short route to the Indies by sailing west and found his way blocked by America. John Cabot and others met the same obstacle at somewhat higher latitudes, but the seamen of Europe went on probing farther and farther north for a gap in the barrier which America set up between Europe and the Orient. Sebastian Cabot has made a claim, vaguely expressed and without supporting witness, to have passed, in about 1509, through a strait (Hudson's) into a larger sea beyond. For the first half of the sixteenth century the Portuguese were active along the Labrador coast and perhaps in Hudson Strait. For fear of helping trade rivals they observed strict secrecy, and no one knows the extent of their discoveries. The only evidence of their achievement is in contemporary maps, and these probably owed their form as much to the mapmaker's imagination as to fact. Not until the enterprise of Martin Frobisher do we have a voyage to the northwest fully, clearly, and credibly recorded.

In 1576 Frobisher sailed from London to discover a short route to China by passing north of the Americas – the Northwest Passage. He made his landfall on lower Baffin Island at the entrance to Frobisher Bay and sailed some distance up what he supposed was a strait, with America on his left hand and Asia on his right, before returning home. He came back with samples of ore, which hopeful but prudent analysts declared 'showed promise' of gold. Consequently, his succeeding voyages, in 1577 and 1578, degenerated into gold hunts that brought undeserved discredit on their leader, loss to their promoters, and achieved nothing useful except a brief excursion into the fogbound Hudson Strait.

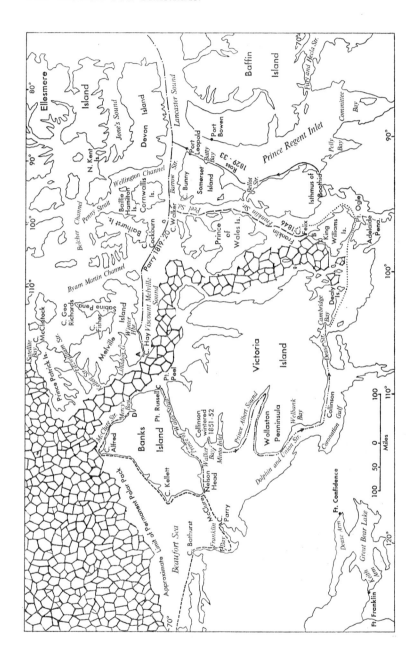

Frobisher was a bold and enterprising sea fighter but an indifferent navigator. His successor in the polar field, John Davis, was a professional seaman and a superbly skilful one. (In 1818 John Ross found that Davis had placed Cumberland Gulf on his chart more accurately than later surveyors who tried to improve on him.) In three voyages – 1585, 1586, and 1587 – he searched the shores of Labrador and Baffin Island for the western passage and obtained, as Frobisher had not, an accurate fix of the entrance to Hudson Strait. Most important for the furtherance of his search for a passage was his 1587 voyage up the west Greenland shore.

Davis's course was directed by the theory, devoutly believed in his time, and not wholly disproved until the late nineteenth century, of the 'Polar Basin' or the 'Open Polar Sea.' According to this hypothesis, seawater froze only near to land, where its salinity was reduced by the inflow from freshwater rivers. Far from land, whatever the latitude, the navigator could be sure of plain sailing in ice-free seas. Hence the belief that at the top of the globe lay a basin of unfrozen brine, which one could follow, as a traffic circle, to make his desired easting or westing. Fitzjames is said to have favoured this notion, and at a somewhat later date the Americans Kane and Hayes certainly did. In 1587, Davis tried to reach this basin and thought that he had succeeded. He set a course up the west shore of Greenland and on June 30

General map of Canadian Arctic, showing the routes of Parry to Melville Island, Franklin, McClure and Collinson, as well as Sir John Ross's voyage down Regent's Inlet. The permanent polar pack is shown thrusting an arm of very heavy ice through McClure Strait, Viscount Melville Sound, and McClintock Channel to pile up against King William Island, and so blocking the passage of Parry and Franklin from the east; of McClure and Collinson from the west.

Dotted line to east and south of King William Island shows route recommended by McClintock and successfully followed by Amundsen forty-three years later. It can readily be seen why McClintock declared this to be the only practicable passage – an opinion which remained valid until the appearance of the icebreaker.

(The *Manhattan* is going in by Lancaster Sound to Banks Island, and down Prince of Wales Strait – McClure's attempted route in reverse. Prince of Wales Strait is deep and far safer than the waters around King William Island.)

passed beyond ice-infested waters into what he describes as 'a great sea free, large and very salty, and blue, and of unsearchable depth'. This point was marked by a great Greenland cliff, 800 feet high, which he named Sanderson's Hope, after his patron and backer, the merchant Sanderson. With a small ship and short of supplies, he could go no farther. On returning to England he wrote joyously to his patron:

Good Mr Sanderson, with God's great mercy I have made my safe return in health, with all my company, and have sailed three-score leagues further than my determination at my departure. I have been in 73 degrees, finding the sea all open, and forty leagues between land and land [Greenland and Baffin Island]. The passage is most probable and the execution easie, as at comming you shall fully know.

Yesterday the 15 of September I landed all weary; therefore I pray you pardon my shortnesse. . . .

John Davis.

Davis had passed right through his strait into the broad basin later to be named after William Baffin. However, he was given no chance of improving on his success. London merchants were diverting their capital to more profitable enterprises – raids on the Spanish trade routes and the East Indian trade by way of the Cape of Good Hope.

Early in the seventeenth century the promoters of discovery turned their attention again to America. In 1609 Henry Hudson went up the Hudson River as far as Albany, looking for a western passage; in 1610 he sought it in the innermost recess of Hudson Bay, where he was marooned and left to die by his rebellious crew. The brave but unpractical visionary had become in a sense a founding father of New York State and of the Hudson's Bay Company, but he had failed in his life's purpose. In 1615 his former officer, Robert Bylot, and his pilot, William Baffin, proved with tolerable certainty that there was no outlet from the bay leading to the Pacific. Their promoters – the London merchants and gentlemen Digges, Smith, Jones, Lancaster, and Wolsten-holme – refused to give up, and as a last resource sent them up Baffin Bay in the track of John Davis.

This 1616 cruise of the *Discovery* was the greatest polar voyage made by the school of seamen bred under the great Elizabeth I. Bylot and Baffin went up the Greenland shore to Sanderson's

Hope and, finding impenetrable pack to the west, went on past the dense ice field spawned in Melville Bay into open water beyond. Passing Wolstenholme Sound and Peary's future base of Inglefield Gulf, they made out land to the north, reaching beyond the 78th degree of latitude – two opposing headlands (later named Capes Isabella and Alexander by John Ross) that enclosed a strait or bay, which they named Smith Sound. But their intended course lay not north but west, so circling to the west, they coasted down the eastern shore of Ellesmere Island, passed the majestic entrance to Jones Sound, with Coburg Island in the foreground, and arrived at 'another great sound in the latitude of 74° 20''. This was Lancaster Sound, the true gateway to the fabled Northwest Passage. 'Here our hope of a passage began to lessen every day.' The sound was full of ice, and a northeast gale was threatening to drive them on to its unyielding barrier. The men, too, were growing sick and exhausted. Bylot struck across to the Greenland shore, where he restored their health with rest and boiled scurvy grass, and sailed for home.

In their circuit of Baffin Bay the discoverers had done all that could be done with the means their age afforded. Though the 55-ton *Discovery* was handier in the ice than the unwieldy *Investigator* and *Resolute* of a later era, her cruising range was restricted by the limited quantity of supplies she could stow. In addition, quarters on board were so narrow that we find the careful Bylot continually on the lookout for a secure harbour where he could rest and relax his crew. Successful penetration of Lancaster Sound could have resulted only in detention for the winter and extinction of the crew by cold and scurvy.

The basin thus surveyed was called Baffin Bay after the pilot of the *Discovery*, who was the scientist and historian of the expedition. The name has 'stuck,' although it is not a true bay, having three outlets – Smith Sound to the north (Peary's 'American Route') and Jones Sound and Lancaster Sound to the west. For two centuries mapmakers assumed these to be closed channels and showed Greenland arching over the top of the bay and joined to America by continuous land. Historians and geographers, prejudiced perhaps by the ambiguous part he played in the marooning of Henry Hudson, have accorded insufficient honour to the memory of that aloof but extremely competent executive officer, Robert Bylot.

Baffin's report on his bay did not encourage further efforts there, and for a long time British-American enterprise was concentrated on Hudson Bay and the fur trade for which it was the channel. About the middle of the eighteenth century, in a brief flurry of activity, attempts were made to find a channel leading from Hudson Bay to the Pacific. Surveys reaching up to Repulse Bay proved that Baffin had judged correctly that no such channel existed.

This seaborne search was supplemented by two important land journeys. From 1770 to 1772, Samuel Hearne, a trader of the Hudson's Bay Company, travelled overland with an Indian escort and descended the Coppermine River to its mouth. There, on 14 July 1771, 195 years after the voyage of Frobisher, he became the first white man to gaze upon the American Arctic Sea. In 1789, Alexander Mackenzie, of a rival firm of Montreal traders, explored the great Mackenzie waterway down to tidewater. These were isolated endeavours, reaching far ahead of the most primitive settlement. When Franklin arrived in that region in 1820, the remotest trading post lay on Great Slave Lake, 400 miles south of the Arctic shoreline.

It was in the latter part of the eighteenth century also that resources of the Royal Navy were first systematically used to further geographical knowledge. In 1776, Captain James Cook, world-famous for his work in Australasian and Antarctic waters, was sent with the *Resolution* and the *Discovery* to attempt the ocean passage north of America from west to east by way of Bering Strait. The British Parliament offered a bounty of £20,000 for its successful achievement and, prompted doubtless by the 'Polar Basin' theorists, voted an additional £5,000 to the crew which should come within one degree of the North Pole. It is not likely that Cook, the first man to cross the Antarctic Circle, and familiar with the ice fields there, was much encouraged by this offer. He came up from Tahiti, discovering the Sandwich (Hawaiian) Islands on the way, and converted the partial and incoherent Russian observations about Bering Strait into a complete and accurate chart of both Alaskan and Siberian shores. In attempting to climb out of the strait into the true Arctic, he was stopped by impenetrable pack ice in latitude 70° 44', near Icy Cape, and returned south to meet violent death at the hands of the natives of Hawaii.

By extending the chart to Icy Cape, Cook had finally set the stage for the great period of British polar discovery (1818–1859), which had as its climax the voyage of the *Erebus* and the *Terror*, and as its finale the long-deferred revelation of their fate.

At the beginning of the nineteenth century a map of North America representing firm knowledge only and omitting unfounded conjecture would have resembled a wineglass or the mature bloom of a lily. It had no top. Except for the isolated points where Hearne and Mackenzie had just reached the margin of salt water, the map of America's Arctic shore was a blank from Repulse Bay to Icy Cape. The extensive archipelago to the north was unknown save for a few tracings of the east shore of Baffin Island. Continental lake and tundra were lost in the same obscurity, in some areas far south of the Arctic Circle.

In forty years all this was changed, and the frontier of the unknown was rolled back 1,000 miles to the 77th degree of north latitude. The story of the journeyings by which this was effected is given unity by the name Franklin. While he lived Sir John Franklin was foremost in the assault upon the frozen stronghold. Dead, his image brooded like the ghost of Caesar over the strivings of those who sought to rescue him or to learn his fate.

The story of the search for Franklin is easily understood if one is familiar with the map of the American Arctic, with its climate and ice pattern, and with the early voyages into the ' Polar Sea ' of which Franklin's last venture was the climax. To the south the archipelago is bounded by the ocean channel, which extends along the continental shore from Hudson Bay to Alaska, but is interrupted by the Boothia Peninsula. Further north it is split from east to west by a broad sea corridor extending from the top of Baffin Island to Banks Island, where it merges with that part of the Arctic known as the Beaufort Sea. This channel consists of Lancaster Sound, Barrow Strait, Viscount Melville Sound, and McClure Strait. From it there are several exits on either side. Wellington Channel, passing between Devon Island and Cornwallis Island to merge with the inner waters of Jones Sound, is the only northern branch to figure much in the history of the search. To the south there is Prince Regent (or simply ' Regent's ') Inlet between Baffin and Somerset Islands – a false lead for anyone looking for a Northwest Passage, as it is a dead end and cut

23

off from the west by Boothia. To the west, Prince of Wales Strait gives an exit to the southwest, and has become the most convenient route since icebreakers have been introduced strong enough to plough through the heavy ice which clogs its northern end. In the heart of the islands, Peel-Franklin Straits and McClintock Channel extend south on the east and west sides respectively of Prince of Wales Island and converge on King William Island near the continental shore. Early expeditions sent to Franklin's rescue judged both Peel Sound and McClintock Channel to be permanently ice-choked and quite impassable to ships, and so did not suspect that that wretched little outcrop of rock held the key to his mystery.

The physical geography of the Arctic, the pattern of land and sea, presented no unusual obstacle to the seaborne discoverer. It was the climate which made the search for a Northwest Passage so protracted and costly. Winters at that high latitude were sunless for months and marked by a length and intensity of cold which Europeans had never experienced. The salt water froze annually to a thickness of seven feet. In the straits of the archipelago, where tide and current ran strong, this ice would break up during the summer months into fragments varying in size from great floes measured in miles to small pieces which a moving ship could brush aside. The ice in Barrow Strait and Lancaster Sound tended to drift east into Baffin Bay and then south to the Atlantic, affording a ship in the months of August and September an uncertain and dangerous navigation. In a windswept sea the navigator might find a large expanse of open water; his ship might be 'beset,' imprisoned in a dense ice pack; she might be gripped between converging floes, heaved up, and borne away on a cradle of ice – or, if she failed to rise to the pressure, she might be 'nipped' and sunk. The Arctic navigator was sometimes reduced to a practice which, in the open seas, he would of all things avoid, that of creeping along shore between land and the floating ice, taking his chance of striking rock or sandbank and, if the wind shifted and the ice moved in, of being pushed clean ashore by the remorseless pack. Even this difficult navigation was possible for only two months out of the twelve. During the remaining ten, the men might make lengthy journeys by land and frozen sea dragging their supplies by cart or sledge, while their ship was locked immovably in some bay or cove. And here there lurked another danger. A harbour was chosen to give the ship protection from gale and ocean swell. But when the ice began to rot in the summer sun, gale and ocean swell were needed to shatter it, and make navigation again possible. A ship was usually detained in harbour long after the open sea had become navigable. Sometimes the crew freed her by sawing a canal through the harbour ice; when too deeply embayed for this, they might be imprisoned for two or more seasons until compelled to desert the ship and make their getaway on boat or by foot. A forlorn hope this – for so desperate a remedy was usually avoided until the company was too much reduced by hunger and sickness for it to offer much chance of success.

By way of compensation for these extraordinary hazards, the familiar risks of the salt-sea gale were much reduced in the ice-strewn seas of the far north. There was less danger of a ship's foundering in foul weather or driving on the shore. Swelling seas were smothered by the pack. Crews often might saw out of some stout old floe a space the size and shape of their ship, and in the security of this 'ice dock' ride out the gale as easily as if moored in their home port. When driving on to a lee shore, a ship could, as Reid explained to Fitzjames, harness herself to a large ice piece, which, with seven-eighths of its bulk submerged, might be trusted to 'take the ground' in a depth which gave a handsome margin of safety to any ship attached to it. At the worst, the ice which crushed the ship would give its crew a temporary refuge and a chance of reaching land. An extraordinary example of this was furnished when nineteen crew members of the American *Polaris* drifted on an ice floe from the top of Baffin Bay to lower Labrador, kept themselves alive by catching seal, and were picked up by a Newfoundland sealer with their numbers undiminished.

With the guidance of his ice-master, the Arctic captain soon learned how to protect himself from the normal dangers of the ice pack. But in the depths of the Canadian Arctic there lurked a trap which brought destruction to Franklin and his crews, and almost extinguished his would-be rescuer, the bold McClure. As mentioned, the ice bred among the islands tended to dissolve or drift away before the second season added to its thickness, but west of the islands, in the Beaufort Sea, where tide and current had less disruptive power, the ice grew year after year to a thickness of fifty feet or more. A stream of this tremendous polar pack squeezed into McClure Strait and flowed on through Viscount Melville Sound and McClintock Channel to pile up against the northwest shore of King William Island. Thus, from Banks Island to King William Island it set up a normally impenetrable barrier. However, a gap could occur. With luck McClure might have got through in 1851. With luck the police boat *St Roch* did get through in 1944. In 1956 the high-powered icebreaker *Labrador* ploughed through it at a rate of a little more than a mile per hour. But an old-fashioned sailing ship entering it was courting destruction.

Such were the hazards awaiting the unsuspecting mariners of England when, in 1818, the British Admiralty, prompted by its Secretary, John Barrow, resumed the North American survey, which had been discontinued during the Napoleonic wars. But first brief notice should be taken of the Admiralty itself and the character of the officers in its service.

In early times, when the King of England was also her chief executive, he entrusted naval affairs to some eminent person with the title of Lord High Admiral of England. As the service expanded and grew too sophisticated for a nobleman or a prince of the blood, the English, with characteristic reluctance to alter avoidably an existing institution, did not abolish or redefine the office of Lord High Admiral. They simply omitted to appoint one, transferring his functions to a board of three 'Lords Commissioners' of the Admiralty, who were subject to the general direction of a member of His Majesty's Government, the First Lord of the Admiralty. (Winston Churchill held this post at the commencement of both World Wars.) The Secretary of the Admiralty, when a person of originality and force of character, could exert considerable influence on policy and method. One such secretary was that amorous diarist Samuel Pepys. Another was the grim puritan John Barrow, whose services to discovery are justly commemorated in the name of Barrow, Alaska, the northernmost non-military settlement of the United States.

Barrow had an easy task in promoting the Arctic voyages on which his heart was set. From the time of Elizabeth I the mystery of the Northwest Passage had haunted the English people, and now, proud in the thought that it was their navy which had 'stood between Napoleon and domination of the world', they were troubled by a jealous fear that some intruding foreigner might snatch the honour on which England had expended so much effort, a motive recurring constantly until Franklin's final voyage. The expedition of the Russian Otto Kotzebue into Alaskan waters had caused uneasiness – Russia bore the same perplexing and vaguely sinister aspect to Western Europe in the early nineteenth century as she does in the mid-twentieth century. Then, when the post-war lassitude had worn off, the Admiralty were desirous of maintaining morale and exercising the daring and skill of their seamen by some notable adventure. There was pressure, too, from the savants of the Royal Society, for scientific discovery of which the Arctic was an untapped and promising source – in winds, tides, climate, astronomy, geology, plant and animal life and, above all, magnetism. As the Admiralty would by no means consent to enrol a naturalist – a title which embraced all the natural sciences – as an officer on a man-of-war, they would enrol him as surgeon or assistant surgeon. One wonders if the medical colleges assisted these aspirants by granting special degrees to get them aboard. As will be seen, they rendered distinguished services of all sorts.

The officers by whom the exploration of the north was to be carried, though seldom derived from the high aristocracy, were a privileged class. A boy would commonly need 'interest' to get aboard a man-of-war as a cadet, and his advancement could depend on influence and favouritism as much as on merit. But merit could mean a great deal, and one advantage which patronage had over the more equitable system of the present day was that extraordinary gifts could be recognized and promoted with a rapidity no longer possible. Nelson was a post captain at an age when a young man of today is just graduating from the naval academy. James Cook, of humble birth and with little formal education, gave up his post as mate in the Baltic trade to join the navy as an able seaman. Yorkshire friends of his poor but respectable parents approached their Member of Parliament; the M.P. wrote to the influential Captain Hugh Palliser, and in sixteen years Cook was a captain in the Royal Navy, known all over the civilized world for his scientific achievements. The naval captain of the French Revolutionary period has been portrayed as a cold-blooded sadist, and it cannot be denied that he could play that role if he chose. Afloat in isolation for months with a rough, illiterate crew, some of them pressed men filled with new Republican ideas, he embodied in himself all available authority and means of coercion, and he had to be given despotic powers which were liable to abuse. There was the case of the insanely brutal Captain Pigott of the *Hermione*, who was stabbed and flung, still breathing, in to the sea by his infuriated crew. But there was also the case of the unknown seaman who, at the height of the Great Mutiny scare, dropped a note on the quarterdeck of the *Theseus*, stating that no disloyalty need be feared on a ship commanded by Rear Admiral Nelson and Captain Miller. Common sense and the general efficiency of the navy justify the inference that Captain Miller – a New York Tory who had chosen to follow King George III – was more typical of the service than Pigott. The melodramatic version of Captain Bligh is a sad misrepresentation; Bligh was a good officer in a narrow sense, but no gentleman. His punishments were neither frequent nor excessive; he took good care of his men in a teasing, nagging way, but exasperated his officers by his coarse and bullying disposition. It was an officer who instigated the *Bounty* mutiny.

Any rational officer, desirous of promotion, would try to promote the contentment and physical well-being of his men. The long, tedious blockades of the French wars taught him to provide also for their mental health by dramatic and other entertainments.

The officers of the Arctic service, inaugurated in 1818, worked in a happier and more relaxed environment than their wartime elders. Fears of mutiny and revolution had subsided; their men were all volunteers whose zeal was stimulated by double pay and the promise of a liberal bounty in event of success.

The plan for discovery in 1818 provided for four ships, making up two distinct expeditions with the same ultimate purpose – arrival at the Pacific by way of Bering Strait. Commander David Buchan in the *Dorothea*, with Lieutenant John Franklin in the *Trent*, was directed to sail up the east coast of Greenland and set a westerly course past its northern extremity. Commander John Ross, who more by character than by achievement was to be a prominent figure in the Arctic record, was appointed to the *Isabella*. Seconded by Lieutenant W. E. Parry in the *Alexander*, he was to go west of Greenland up Davis Strait, and when he had obtained a good offing by passing well to the north of America, he was to steer for Bering Strait also. The theory of the Polar Basin is reflected in both sets of instructions.

Buchan brought his ships back battered and leaking from the Spitsbergen ice. Ross failed too, but in more dramatic fashion.

With his two ships he entered Davis Strait, and finding it impossible to pierce the ice and reach its western side, he accompanied the whaling fleet up the Greenland shore to Sanderson's Hope and Upernavik, the usual limit of whaling operations. Beyond lay Melville Bay, a shallow depression on the Greenland shore, whose surplus ice annually poured out and fouled the adjacent sea. In a month Ross got past this obstacle and left the whalers behind. At Cape York, on the northern angle of the bay, near modern Thule, he found a hitherto unknown tribe of Eskimos, whom he named the Arctic Highlanders. A century later they were to furnish both Peary and Cook with recruits for their polar journeys. Still heading northward, the two ships passed the ' Crimson Cliffs of Sir John Ross ' (the effect of a minute plant that lends a crimson colour to the snow), identified Cape Dudley Digges, the Cary and Hakluyt islands discovered by Baffin, and crossing the 76th degree of latitude, raised the massive headlands which mark the entrance to Smith Sound, which he named Cape Isabella and Cape Alexander.

Ross was on the threshold of a discovery which would have won him fame and added a whole new province to the map of the globe. Yet he faltered on the brink and passed it by. ' I considered,' he says somewhat vaguely, ' the bottom of the sound to be about 18 leagues, but its entrance was completely blocked by ice.' Barrow (who had a bitter tongue) subsequently observed that ' if any faith is due to [Ross's] own chart ' he was too far from land for his observations to have any validity.

Ross had been shouldered northward by the ice farther than he wished, and was no doubt in a hurry to get to the more promising west side of Baffin Bay. In his journal Parry noted his approval of Ross's choice here, though less sure than his chief that Smith Sound was closed. Wheeling away to the southwest down the east shore of Ellesmere Island, they passed Jones Sound, which Ross, deceived by mirage, reported to be closed by a range of mountains. On 29 August they were standing in towards the gap in the coastal barrier called by Baffin after his patron, Sir James Lancaster. It was a majestic opening, forty-five miles across. Parry was hopeful and buoyant as they sailed up the inlet; Baffin, he was convinced, *could not* have seen its bottom, and the swell setting from the northwest continued strong. On the thirty-first, with the wind light and variable, the *Isabella* drew eight or nine miles ahead of her sluggish consort. In the afternoon, Ross reports, the fog 'completely cleared for about ten minutes, and I distinctly saw the land, around the bottom of the bay, forming a connected chain of mountains with those extended along the north and south sides . . . At a quarter past three, the weather again became thick and unsettled; and being now perfectly satisfied that there was no passage in this direction, nor any harbour into which I could enter, for the purpose of making magnetic observations, I tacked to join the *Alexander,* which was at a distance of eight miles; and having joined her a little after four, we stood to the south-east . . . The weather appearing more unsettled, it became advisable to stand out of this dangerous inlet, in which we were embayed, being within it above eighty miles.'

Parry saw it thus:

'About three o'clock in the afternoon, the *Isabella* tacked, very much to our surprise indeed, as we could not see anything like land at the bottom of the inlet, nor was the weather well calculated at the time for seeing any object at a great distance, it being somewhat hazy. When she tacked, the *Isabella* was about three or four [not eight] miles ahead of us. . . .'

It is an odd reflection that, but for Ross's appalling blunder, the immortal Parry might have lived his life a respected, competent, but obscure member of the naval forces of his country.

Ross's premature withdrawal from Lancaster Sound may have been dictated in part by his belief that Davis's Cumberland Gulf was a more promising opening. But the date of his arrival there (1 October) was the day fixed by the Admiralty for his withdrawal from the Arctic – unless he had achieved the object of his search. So home he went, having added little to the work of Baffin except a rough and, in Parry's opinion, a careless and inexact chart of the east Baffin Island shore.

Ross was unpopular with his brother officers and detested by the all-powerful Barrow. Consequently, the error of converting an Arctic mirage into what he called the Croker mountains and so closing Lancaster Sound has been treated with undue severity.

Only those who have been in the north can understand how easy it is to make such a mistake. Nevertheless, the mistake was Ross's, and his alone. In his just, but perhaps over-emphasized apology for Ross, Ernest S. Dodge writes: 'One of the most baffling aspects – certainly the most damaging to Ross in the discussion – was the way in which his officers changed their minds about what they had or had not seen in Lancaster Sound.' Even if the change of mind was as pronounced as Ross would have us believe, it admits of a ready explanation. The commanding officer had reversed the normal procedure of a council of war by revealing his own opinion before asking that of his juniors. Ross had ordered the ship about on his own authority without consultation; an individual officer would naturally concur in an order already given – dissent would be insolent and presumptuous – until he learned that his doubts were shared by others. Years later, Ross asserted that Parry had committed an impropriety in not communicating his doubts if he had any. Parry declined any controversy, stating privately that he had offered to search the sound more closely by boat and had been told in reply that Captain Ross, not he, was in command of the expedition. By suggesting in extenuation that Ross 'had the good sailor's shyness of land,' Dodge concedes Barrow's point that Ross was a good sailing master but unfit for hydrographic work.

2 The Breakthrough

If Ross's officers had changed their minds about Lancaster Sound, they at least convinced Barrow and the Admiralty Lords that the change was sincere. Preparations were at once begun for a fresh expedition, directed specifically at Lancaster Sound. In addition, plans were drawn up for a secondary Arctic survey, by a method new to the British Navy, though it had been used by the Russians on the North Siberian shore. Like Russia, Canada possesses a rich system of inland waterways, giving access to all parts of the sub-continent. By means of this, it was proposed to send a party overland to survey the American Arctic shore by boat or canoe. Command of the seaborne expedition was given to Parry; Lieutenant John Franklin, late of the *Trent,* took charge of the boat party.

At the time of this appointment, William Edward Parry was twenty-seven years of age. He had no 'family' or naval background, and his career illustrates the scope for advancement afforded by the relatively liberal class society of the period. His grandfather, a person of obscure origin, had made good as a popular preacher in a nonconformist sect. His father, Caleb Parry, obtained a good education and became a fashionable physician. One of his patients was a niece of Admiral William Cornwallis, old 'Billy-go-tight', who had avenged his brother's defeat at Yorktown by the capture of the French admiral who had helped to bring it about. Through the agency of Miss Cornwallis, Parry, at the age of thirteen, obtained a berth as First Class Volunteer on her uncle's flagship. He saw active service in the Channel, the Baltic, and on the North American station, where he took part in a raid by boat up the Connecticut River. The end of the war threw him out of employment; but in the meantime the studious young officer had produced a treatise on 'nautical astronomy', which caught the eye of the all-powerful Barrow.

Hence in 1818 Parry was appointed as second to Ross, and in 1819 was chosen to succeed him.

The vessels selected for Parry's command were the 'bomb' vessel *Hecla* of 375 tons, and the gun brig *Griper* – an unfortunate choice, for she proved slow and unhandy. With Parry sailed Captain Edward Sabine of the Royal Artillery, an expert on magnetism, and Ross's nephew, Midshipman James Clark Ross, a young man destined to do great things at both extremes of the globe. Lieutenant Matthew Liddon took command of the *Griper*.

Parry's orders were to make for Lancaster Sound, and if he found it a strait leading to the westward, to do his utmost to pass through Bering Strait and leave dispatches with the Russians at Kamchatka for transmission overland to London. Their Lordships realistically stipulated that his proceedings 'must be regulated chiefly by the position and extent of the ice'. In late June the two ships were between the Greenland coast and the endless ice field of Baffin Bay.

In the summer the ice sheet of Baffin Bay detaches itself from the land and drifts southward – like a finger withdrawn from a glove – leaving at its northern end fairly open sea, the North Water. The usual route of the discoverer making for the Canadian Arctic was that of Baffin and John Ross: up the Greenland shore – despite the difficulty of getting past Melville Bay, across the North Water, and down to Lancaster Sound. But the moving pack, the Middle Ice, when worked on by wind or current, opened lanes which might afford passage to a ship. Parry resolved to attempt this short cut, and he was one of the few who succeeded.

He spent the month of July making his crossing of the bay. At times the ships made sail freely in relatively open spaces; at others they were immovably beset by the ice. Sometimes, in pools too restricted for manoeuvre under sail, they made headway by 'warping' or 'tracking'. The former operation consisted of carrying hawser and ice anchor to a floe ahead and winding the ship up to it on the capstan. If, as sometimes happened, the ice-piece was lighter than the ship, it, not the ship, would move in, much to the frustration of the sweating crew. In a narrow lead of uniform width, the crew would disembark on either side of the lane and tow, or 'track', the vessel like barge horses. In the calm water of an ice lagoon it was possible to hoist out the boats to take the ship in tow, but this method, 'the work of galley-slaves', was seldom employed except in an emergency, to get clear of a threatened nip. Parry describes a typical day's work in this dreary navigation:

'On the 22nd the wind was light from the eastward, and we made very little progress. We had occasionally to heave the ship through with hawsers, between the heavy masses of ice, which became more and more close as we advanced till, at length towards the evening, we were fairly beset, there being no water in sight from the masthead in any quarter of the compass. Some hands were kept constantly employed in heaving the ship through the ice, taking advantage of every occasional opening which presented itself, by which means we advanced a few hundred yards during the night.'

On the twenty-ninth, they felt the ships pitch – a sure sign of open water close ahead; two days later, skirting the high, snow-clad peaks of Baffin Island on the left, they entered the blue and ice-free waters of Lancaster Sound.

Was the sound a strait or a bay? The question would soon be answered. Urged on by a stiff breeze from the east, they drove ahead, the unending daylight showing no trace of land to the west. Parry observes: 'It is more easy to imagine than describe the almost breathless anxiety which was now visible on every countenance' ... 'A crowd of sail was set to carry us with all rapidity to the westward.' Forgetful of form and order, officers and men jammed the mastheads, raking the horizon with telescopes. The south shore of the sound began to recede; to the north lay continuous land, Devon Island. And now they had run in 100 miles, with uninterrupted sea still ahead. The more hopeful of the young officers were beginning to calculate 'the bearing and distance of Icy Cape as a matter of no very difficult or impossible accomplishment'.

They were hoping for too much. On 3 August, they became aware of a considerable surf ahead, rolling on a 'compact and impenetrable body of floes', and hauled to the wind for fear of being embayed and cast up on the ice. Finding passage to the west completely closed, Parry turned into open water to the south, Regent's Inlet, and ran down it 120 miles. There again they ran into compact ice, and lost in fog and rain – for in the vicinity of the Magnetic Pole the compass is no guide – they anchored themselves to a floe until the weather cleared.

They were off the inner shore of Baffin Island with land, Somerset Island, distantly visible to the west. Fearing that he was in a mere bay on the American shore, Parry reversed his course, crossed Lancaster Sound to the north, and began to work his way west along the Devon Island shore. 'The wind and sea increased on the 19th,' he recorded, 'with a heavy fall of snow, which, together with the uselessness of the compasses, and the narrow space in which we were working between the ice and the land, combined to make our situation for several hours a very unpleasant one.' It was an unpleasantness to which the Arctic navigator soon became accustomed.

Thus working his way ahead Parry soon arrived at the western end of Devon Island, marked by the 'noble' northward-stretching Wellington Channel, 25 miles across at its mouth. On the east side of this entrance, almost touching Cape Riley on Devon Island, lay the islet of Beechey, narrow in circuit, but shooting up to a height of over 600 feet.

Crossing Wellington Channel to Cornwallis Island, they continued westward along the north side of Barrow Strait. In the far distance on its southern side land was made out, high and bold and terminating in the blue headland of Cape Walker. This important landmark was the last land sighted to the south for 300 miles.

In his historic run from Cornwallis to Melville Island, Parry was less hampered by ice than by fog and used some novel methods to make up for lack of a compass bearing. Observing that the wind generally blew up or down, seldom across, Barrow Strait, he gave orders to steer by the wind. 'It was amusing, as well as novel, to see the quartermaster conning the ship by looking at the dog-vane,' he wrote. On one occasion he kept the ships on a steady course by ordering the steersman of the *Hecla* to keep the *Griper* dead astern, and the steersman of the *Griper* to keep the *Hecla* straight ahead. By these means Bathurst Island and Byam Martin Island were passed and Melville Island sighted on 1 September. Barrow Strait was held to end at Bathurst Island, and the waters on which they were now sailing were named Viscount Melville Sound.

The government had offered a reward of £20,000 to the first crew to make the Northwest Passage, with a consolation prize of

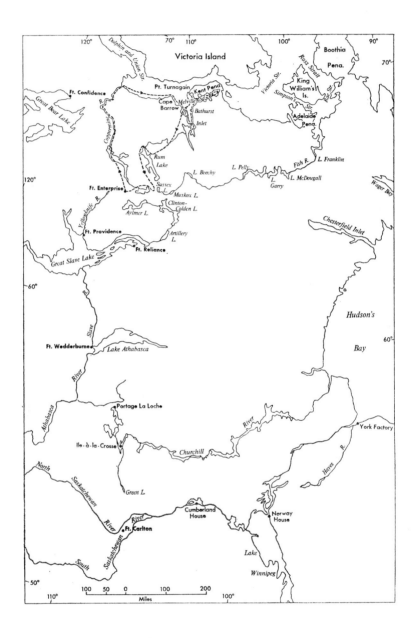

£5,000 if it should reach latitude 110 degrees west. A little way down the Melville Island shore, close to a cape appropriately named Bounty, this zone was crossed. Since at least a year must elapse before the reward was collected, Parry solemnized the event by granting an extra round of grog to all hands.

The adventurous ships, now 500 miles west of Baffin Bay, were groping their way between the shore and the ice stream flowing in from the Beaufort Sea. On 20 September, the *Griper* was pushed ashore by the moving pack. She floated off at high tide, but Parry was taking no more risks with winter near at hand. He turned back a short distance to berth for the winter. A bay was found with its sheltered waters already frozen to a thickness of seven inches. Officers and men spent a busy three days sawing a canal two and one-third miles long, and the ships found a secure anchorage in Winter Harbour, Melville Island. Topmasts were sent down, a magnetic observatory set up, a canvas housing spread over the upper decks, and all was ready for the winter.

Never before had civilized people spent a winter in conditions of such remoteness and inaccessibility as Parry's crews on Melville Island. They had passed the bounds not only of the inhabited but of the known world by 500 miles. Except for isolated trading posts the nearest settlement was 2,000 miles away. They were fixed there for ten months, including a long period of extreme cold and darkness. Theirs were the first naval ships to winter above the Arctic Circle. They had no tested means for combating failure in health and morale. One advantage of their situation was that game, musk oxen especially, was more plentiful there than in many parts of the American Arctic.

Parry's epoch-making voyage had had a large element of luck, as the fortunes of later expeditions (including his own) were abundantly to prove. His methods for maintaining health and good cheer through months of cold and gloom were all his own. He enforced his dietary regulations not, as Cook had done, by harshness, but by unremitting supervision, which was less irritating to the crew as officers and men were treated alike. He warred especially against dampness and frost in living quarters and conferred daily with the surgeon on conditions and their possible

---

Area of Franklin's first overland journey. Route from and back to Fort Enterprise marked

improvement. He cultivated mustard and cress with some success as an antiscorbutic. He ensured the co-operation of all officers in theatrical performances by actively participating himself. Captain Sabine edited a journal to which all were invited to contribute. Thus the winter was passed in good cheer, and symptoms of scurvy were promptly suppressed.

On 14 February two marines were flogged for drunkenness, the only punishment of its kind inflicted on board the *Hecla* on this cruise. Parry punished a later serious breach of dietary regulations merely by placing a ridiculous placard on the offender's back. In this instance, he observed, the crew were on his side, and no harsh example was required.

It was not then realized that the season for land travel in that latitude was April to June, when daylight has returned, the cold is endurable, and the snow still hard and dry. Parry postponed his extended journey until 1 June, when the snow was beginning to fade from the sunlit slopes. Then, with a party of ten, dragging its supplies on a cart, he set out northward and in five days crossed the island to Hecla and Griper Bay. It is characteristic of the unvarying monotony of some Arctic landscapes that the explorers were not *sure* that they had reached the sea until they had bored through fourteen feet of ice and found the water salt. In the journey across the island they noted the remains of dwarf willow, sorrel, and poppy rooted in decayed moss and sand. The interior of the island was cut up by ravines, and contained boggy flats, still hard frozen. In one place Parry found pieces of coal and noted that stones bruised by the cart wheels emitted a strong, fetid smell. He had found the first traces of petroleum deposits on Melville Island. Returning by a more westerly route, they reached Liddon Gulf, where the cart broke down – McClintock found its wreck still lying there thirty years later – and they packed the supplies on their backs for the last leg of the homeward journey.

June was spent in hunting game, July in watching the slow dissolution of the ice in the sheltered waters of Winter Harbour. The surgeon, J. Fisher, carved the names of the ships and their captains on a large sandstone rock on the beach, Parry's Monument, a famous landmark in the years to come.

Though Parry was growing impatient in the last days of July, he was luckier than most in the date of his release. The ice moved out on 31 July, and the ships resumed their course to the west. On 7 August, they were stopped by ice at Cape Hay. Lieutenant Beechey mounted the cliff, and made out land across the strait from WSW to SSW. He distinguished three capes at an estimated distance of forty to fifty miles. Parry confirmed the find and gave it the name Banks Land – not 'Island', since for all he knew it was joined to the continent.

A few miles past Cape Hay the voyage ended. The ships were at the point where Viscount Melville Sound narrows into the strait later named after McClure. On the one hand lay a rugged pack with pieces up to forty-two feet thick; on the other rose a bold coast which offered no protection should a southerly gale drive the ice in. Taking note of Cape Dundas, the last headland visible to the west, Parry put about. He spent ten days squirming out of the intricate channel into which he had thrust his ships; from Winter Harbour east, he found easy and rapid sailing. As the ice stream still thwarted his purpose of steering south for the continental shore, he passed out of Lancaster Sound, checked Ross's survey of the Baffin Island shore, and sailed for home. Although this tame finale may have seemed to him an anticlimax he had in fact made the most successful of all Arctic journeys by sea, except perhaps Franklin's last voyage, of which no record has survived.

Parry had no great desire to lead a second expedition into the Arctic. He had had exceptional luck on the first; by a second attempt he would only hazard the reputation he had won. But John Barrow would not take no for an answer, and Parry fell in with his wishes. As the Melville Island ice had proved an impenetrable and probably permanent barrier, it was resolved to look for a more southerly passage from the north end of Hudson Bay. The *Fury* and the *Hecla* were made ready for the service in the usual manner by fixing sturdy braces within the hull and extra sheathing outside. Parry took command of the *Fury;* Lieutenant G. F. Lyon, a newcomer to the polar service, was appointed to the *Hecla*.

Lyon was an original character, yet not untypical of his time. The general disbandment of Great Britain's armed forces at the close of the French and American wars had turned adrift a number of young men with a taste for adventure which they could

39

no longer satisfy in the service of their country. A number of these migrated to the New World and fought with distinction in the Latin American wars of liberation. One unlucky adventurer espoused the cause of the Seminole Indians in Florida and was shot as a spy by Andrew Jackson. Before joining the *Hecla*, Lyon had nearly lost his life on a diplomatic mission in Tripoli. After his Arctic adventures, he took part in speculative commercial ventures in Mexico and the Argentine, before dying, widowed and heartbroken, at the age of thirty-seven. He was a hearty fellow, full of sympathy and kindness.

The years 1821 to 1823 were spent on this expedition. To some extent Parry's luck held. He passed through the tide-vexed Hudson Strait, safely navigated the notorious Frozen Strait past Southampton Island, and after surveying Repulse Bay found a winter anchorage at Winter Island. There Lyon entered wholeheartedly into the social life of the Eskimo settlement on the shore. He was accepted by the natives, as the following anecdote, recorded by Lyon, proves:

'Visitors to the huts found all the men absent, and the women at high romps. Fourteen of them voluntarily exhibited some very curious dances and contortions for nearly three hours, till at length their gestures became indecent and wanton to the highest degree. This was the first instance of any exhibitions which had the slightest indelicate tendency and might be accounted for by their being uncontrolled by their husbands. As a proof that they were perfectly conscious of the impropriety of their conduct, a little boy was stationed as sentinel at the door, and a woman occasionally ran out to see if any of the men were returning home.'

The next day Lyon and his associates were at a gathering where natives of both sexes were in attendance. Lyon continues:

'Affairs were in this merry train, when unfortunately one of the party of the *kabloona* [Europeans] asked for the closing dance of the preceding day. The men laughed, but the women looked very serious, conceiving such a request as a breach of confidence. They instantly began in a hurried manner to leave the hut, and in half a minute the whole company was dispersed.'

The most entertaining of Lyon's friends was the magician Toolemak, who had profited by his gift of ventriloquism to gain a reputation as a medium and faith-healer.

'In the evening,' says Lyons, 'Toolemak rolled very jovially into my cabin, telling me that having drank [sic] four glasses of 'hot water' at the *Fury,* he was come to do the same with me. He was immediately accommodated, and together with what he obtained from the officers, as well as myself, in about ten minutes gulped down five glasses and a half of raw rum, which he designated as above. Nine glasses and a half of spirits were however too much for him, and in a short time he became most noisily drunk. Mr Fife, who had been a little unwell in his stomach, quite delighted the old fellow by asking his assistance as conjuror, and being shut up in a dark cabin, he made the ship echo with his bellowings and exorcisms. All his familiar spirits were summoned in a bunch, and I could not but observe that the sage immortals were as drunk as the potent *annatko,* who constrained them to answer for themselves. In fact, poor Toolemak was so overcome, and so little aware of it that he made some curious mistakes and betrayed all the secrets of his art which I had in vain tried to learn in his sober moments . . .

' . . . All these exertions made him so thirsty, that the most wonderful exhibition yet remained, which was, that as fast as he could be supplied, he drank eleven pints and one gill of water! At each tumbler, and they amounted to seventeen, he proudly patted his belly, exclaiming, "Annatko ooanag" ('I'm a conjuror') – which no one could now for a moment doubt. When absolutely filled to the throat, and unable to pour down any more, his countenance fell, and in a desponding tone he two or three times beat his breast and acknowledged himself vanquished: "I'm no conjuror, I can drink no more " . . . I sent to enquire after his health on the following morning, and he was found well and merry, without the slightest headache or sickness.'

Lyon's intimate and sympathetic study of Eskimo life was perhaps the expedition's most valuable achievement. In the summer of 1822 they made their way to the top of Melville Peninsula and wintered at Igloolik. A channel was found to the west, Fury and Hecla Strait, dividing the continental Melville Peninsula from Baffin Island and leading, as was conjectured, to Regent's Inlet. It was frozen and impassable to ships. Of greater significance was a map traced for Parry by the natives, showing that the base of Melville Peninsula was a narrow isthmus, separating by only some fifty miles the waters of Hudson Bay from those of the Arctic.

This second cruise was notable for Parry's experiments with specialized Arctic clothing and with the dog sledge, and also for the school for seamen conducted during the winter. The latter was so successful that there was not a man on board who did not learn to read his Bible.

In 1824–5 Parry with *Hecla* and *Fury* (under Captain Hoppner) headed a third attempt at navigating the Northwest Passage. His instructions were to sail down Regent's Inlet (not then known to be a dead end) and feel his way west along the continental shore. This time Parry met with blank defeat. In a rough passage through Baffin Bay the *Hecla* was nipped and thrown on her side. Both ships were beset in Lancaster Sound and carried some distance back with the moving pack. On obtaining release, they barely clawed their way into Port Bowen, at the top of Regent's Inlet, before the onset of winter. In the next summer Parry made his way across the inlet and worked his way down its west side (Somerset Island) almost to Cresswell Bay.

There both ships were pushed ashore, and the *Fury* so badly damaged that she was given up as a wreck. Her stores were stacked on the beach and both crews carried home in the *Hecla*. All that had been accomplished had been the establishment of a 'wreck cache', which was later to save the lives of John Ross's men, and, but for a sad misunderstanding, might have preserved Franklin's also.

In Parry's opinion, 'the only wonder' was to have escaped shipwreck for so long. The Admiralty agreed, and for many years gave no more thought to the Northwest Passage.

While Parry had been burrowing into ice-clogged channels among the islands, other naval units, with equal danger and much more personal hardship, were charting the north shore of the mainland. This work was directed by one who, not so much by his personal achievement (though that was extensive enough) as by the quality of 'colour', has come to personify British Arctic endeavour, John Franklin.

Born in 1786 to a middle-class family with no naval tradition, young Franklin secured his parents' grudging consent to his enlistment in the Royal Navy, then grappling with the forces of Napoleon. At the age of fourteen he witnessed the bombardment of Copenhagen – except for Trafalgar, the bloodiest naval action of the war. Then, learning that a ship was sailing under the command of his uncle by marriage, Matthew Flinders, to chart the coast of Australia, he obtained a transfer to that vessel. Though the captain's kinsman, he had the tact to win the favour of the first lieutenant also. He struck up a friendship with the ship's surgeon-naturalist, Robert Brown, which was to be decisive in shaping his career and made himself so proficient in astronomy as to aid in the survey. He early displayed the knack of just skimming by the brink of disaster. His ship was wrecked off the east coast of Australia, and he spent weeks marooned on a sandbank among the Great Barrier Reefs. He secured a passage home with the East Indian convoy, and narrowly escaped capture by a French squadron and years of confinement in a prison camp. Posted to the *Bellerophon,* he fought at Trafalgar, and was one of the few left unwounded on the quarterdeck when the action was over. As lieutenant of the *Bedford,* he was wounded in the disastrous attack on New Orleans. The summer of that year, 1815, witnessed the final overthrow of Napoleon. Along with hundreds of others Franklin lost employment and went on half pay.

Although Franklin had served in the preliminary operations at New Orleans with a distinction which would have ensured his promotion if the action had had a happier termination, his ambitions were not those of a combat officer. Some months before the end of the war he had written to Robert Brown, now well known and influential in scientific circles, expressing his wish for appointment to any voyage of discovery which might be undertaken. It was Brown's recommendation, transmitted to the Admiralty by the president of the Royal Society, which procured him the command of the *Trent,* and now of the overland expedition to the shores of the polar sea.

This line of approach was made comparatively easy by the trend of Canada's coast and the pattern of her inland waterways. Hudson Bay, a huge basin scooped out of her eastern shore, brings the waters of the Atlantic into the heart of the North American continent. The salt-water port of York Factory is as far west as St Paul, Minnesota. While the waters from the eastern slope of the American Rockies drain southward to the Gulf of Mexico, the Canadian rivers from the same source which do not flow into the Arctic Ocean drain eastward into Hudson Bay, providing an almost transcontinental system of waterways, navigable by boat or canoe. Furthermore, only a short portage divides the headwaters of the Churchill River, emptying into the bay, from those of the great Mackenzie system, flowing into the Arctic Sea. This accounts for the speed with which British-American fur traders made their way across the continent. They were surveying river routes down the western slope of the American Cordillera when the United States still had the Mississippi as its western border. Alexander Mackenzie reached the Pacific by land twelve years in advance of Lewis and Clark. To the southwest, Canadian fur buyers disputed the possession of Oregon and the Columbia River waterway with their American competitors. To the north-west, in 1819, the year of Franklin's departure, their posts and supply routes extended to Great Slave Lake.

Franklin was therefore directed to the Great Slave region, where he was to hire boatmen and hunters from among the *voyageurs* of the Hudson's Bay and Northwest Companies, and draw on their local factors for supplies in exchange for bills on the British Government. As staff he was given John Richardson, surgeon and naturalist, and two Admiralty midshipmen, George Back and Robert Hood. The two latter were artists, almost indispensable to journeys of discovery until the camera found a place in the explorer's kit.

The party sailed for York Factory on a Hudson's Bay Company ship, calling on the way at the Orkneys to enlist a number of boatmen for the river journey across the continent.

Franklin's orders required him to journey to Great Slave Lake and, having obtained men and the necessary supplies from the fur posts there, to cross the lake, ascend the Yellowknife River, and set up base in the highlands near the headquarters of the northward-flowing Coppermine. In the next season he was to descend that river and explore the coast eastward to Hudson Bay by canoe – for no boat could navigate the Coppermine rapids. Their Lordships knew that the distance from the Coppermine to the bay was 700 miles as the crow flies; and they must have surmised that accidents of geography would make the completion of the task impossible; where conditions were so vague they gave large assignments and were satisfied with very partial fulfilment.

Franklin was furnished with boats at York Factory, and with his crew of deep-sea fishermen plunged into the rock and scrub of the Canadian Shield. The ascent of the Hayes River tried them severely; the unfamiliar hazards of rapids, rocks, and sandbanks being aggravated by heat and swarms of flies. Passing *voyageur* crews greeted the greenhorns with more ridicule than sympathy. One can see them by night camped on the riverside, Franklin seated outside the tent working out sights, Back and Hood finishing sketches and distractedly smiting mosquitoes, the grave Scottish surgeon moving among the rocks in search of specimens, with the vast arching sky of the north shrinking all else to insignificance.

Stubbornly subduing all obstacles, the travellers worked their way west by portage and side stream past the north end of Lake Winnipeg and had reached Cumberland House on the Saskatchewan when the onset of winter ended their voyaging for the season. Franklin could not endure this detention. He had already seen enough to fear that the agents of the fur companies would lack the will, if not the means, to honour the pledges of help given by their superiors in London, and he determined to travel by winter to the Athabaska region and start bargaining at once. With Back and John Hepburn, a Scottish seamen to whom he had become attached, he joined a party of dog sledges journeying to Ile à la Crosse. Richardson and Hood stayed behind to bring up boat, crew, and equipment when the ice went out.

Despite easy travelling up the frozen snow-covered Saskatchewan, the feet of the three sailors were cruelly chafed by the thongs of their snowshoes. Their seasoned companions refused to indulge them by slackening pace, no easy matter, in any case, when following dogs in sub-zero temperatures. They left Cumberland House on 18 January 1820, and reached Fort Carlton on the thirty-first, where they rested for a week. Carlton stands on the northern fringe of the prairies, and Franklin gives an entertaining description of the Indians of the Plains. One old visitor to the fort informed Franklin and the fur factor, Mr Pruden, that the horse-thieving natives of the area were plotting the extermination of the white men and, seeing them undisturbed by this intelligence, added peevishly, ' And a pretty state we shall be in without guns and ammunition you give us ', at which both his hosts laughed heartily.

From there they travelled north back into the country of rock and lake, and on 26 March reached the western end of Lake

Athabasca, where stood the rival forts of Chipewyan and Wedder-burn, the local headquarters of the rival companies on whom they depended for aid.

Here Franklin made diligent inquiry among the native popula-tion concerning the country through which his intended journey lay. From the Indian Black Meat he heard vaguely of the Great Fish River, which after his death was to be closely associated with his name. Beaulieu, 'a half-breed who had been brought up amongst the Dog-ribbed and Copper Indians', told him that his best base would be at the eastern end of Great Bear Lake, whence boats could easily be drawn overland to the lower waters of the Coppermine. The hostility between the fur companies, and the demand for supplies that their fierce competition had generated, hindered the adoption of this sound advice. The local factors would not compromise their trading operations by supplying all the expedition's requirements immediately – in fact they could not. So Franklin was forced to set up base near enough to the fur forts to maintain a continual supply line.

Richardson and Hood reached Chipewyan with the boat crew on 16 July. The crew, except John Hepburn, were paid off and given passage home by Hudson's Bay Company boat and ship. They were replaced by French and half-breed *voyageurs* (river boatmen) recruited from the fur companies, and Frederick Wentzel, a clerk in the Northwest Company, was enlisted as general adviser and liaison officer with the Indians. The expedi-tion went down the Slave River by canoe to Moose Deer Fort on Great Slave Lake, and crossed the lake to (old) Fort Providence, the northernmost outpost of the fur trade. From there they ascended the Yellowknife River in noisy convoy – Franklin and his officers, Wentzel, some twenty *voyageurs*, and Eskimo inter-preters (brought in for the expedition from Hudson Bay), along with Akaitcho, chief of the Copper Indians, his hunters, and their numerous dependants. Quarters were set up in the high-lands at Fort Enterprise on the northern fringe of the forests. Wentzel supervised the erection of buildings, while Back and Hood reconnoitred a route to the headwaters of the Coppermine on the other side of the divide.

Franklin wished to carry a survey down the Coppermine that autumn and rejected the advice of Akaitcho until the old chief admonished him: 'If after all I have said, you are determined to go, some of my young men shall join the party, because it shall not be said that we permitted you to die alone after having brought you hither; but from the moment they embark in the canoes, I shall lament them as dead.' Franklin had rightly despised the traders' contemptuous predictions of disaster, but there was no doubting the sincerity of this earnest admonition, and he resigned himself to wait until spring.

In order to have a sufficient supply of pemmican and other prepared foods, it was intended that during the winter the explorers would support themselves on game provided by their Indian allies. Early in the winter Franklin found himself short of the ammunition required for this purpose and sent Back south with an Indian escort to prod the traders into great liberality.

Many years after, John Hepburn, cruising with Lieutenant Bellot, told him a story which suggests that Back's winter journey was prompted by considerations other than a shortage of tobacco and gunpowder. In the Indian camp was a young woman, Greenstockings, of a beauty which white men as well as red found irresistible. Robert Hood wished to paint her portrait, and did so, despite her mother's objections, who feared ' that her daughter's likeness would induce the Great Chief who resided in England to send for the original '. According to Hepburn, Hood and Back fell out so bitterly over this wench that they arranged to fight a duel at daybreak, but were frustrated by Hepburn, who privately drew the charges from their pistols. If true, this would account for Franklin's subsequent coolness towards the man who saved his life. He might have overlooked the *amour,* but not the irresponsibility which would have wrecked the expedition over a squalid quarrel.

George Back, at any rate, carried out his mission with zeal. After enduring much hardship on the journey to Providence and Moose Deer forts, where the factors could give little help, he pushed on to Fort Chipewyan and Fort Wedderburn. He took up quarters with the Northwest Company men and made his wants known to the rival Hudson's Bay factor at Wedderburn. This man was the formidable George Simpson, soon to begin his forty years of empire over the trading posts of the British American West.

Relations between explorers and traders had been bad from the outset. Few in number and living in scattered outposts, the traders quickly learned the frontier mode of thought and despised those who were unskilled in its ways. The naval officers, for their part, were authoritarian and tactless. Later expeditions were marked by more (though still imperfect) mutual tolerance and understanding. The degree of irritation produced by the explorers is indicated by the gross injustice and ill temper of an entry in Simpson's journal:

'There is little probability of the objects of the expedition being accomplished . . . Lieutenant Franklin, the officer who commands the party, has not the physical powers required for the labour of moderate Voyaging in this country: he must have three meals p diem, Tea is indispensable, and with the utmost exertion he cannot walk above *Eight* miles in one day, so that it does not follow if those gentlemen are unsuccessful, that the difficulties are insurmountable.'

Simpson's bad humour, provoked by Back's lodging with his rivals, was heightened by notes in which the young officer commented on the arrival of shipments at Wedderburn, and solicited a portion for the expedition. Simpson finally retorted with a crushing snub: 'The arrivals you allude to have no connection with the goods expected from Ile à la Crosse and your conjecture that they were not empty is perfectly just, but I presume you will give me leave to know the purpose for which they were intended.' Back returned to Fort Enterprise with his requirements only partially met. The morale of the expedition was damaged by these differences. The *voyageurs* were disheartened by the factors' contempt of the explorers and their predictions of disaster, and the Indians, though still loyal, distrusted Franklin's ability to pay in full for their services. Both had been frightened by rumours of Eskimo ferocity. Anticipating a witticism of Mark Twain's, Back told Franklin that at Chipewyan 'reports were so far in advance [of the facts] that we were said to have fallen already by the spears of the Eskimos'. In view of all these discouragements it is much to the credit of the *voyageurs* that they followed Franklin as well as they did.

On 14 June 1821, the travelling party, with its escort of Indian hunters, left Enterprise and dragged its canoes and equipment through rock and bush, and over the treacherous surface of half-melted lakes, to the banks of the Coppermine. In two weeks they descended the river, and came within sight of the ocean at the Bloody Falls of Samuel Hearne. There, Franklin instructed Wentzel to leave food caches along the route back up the Coppermine and at Enterprise, and gave him and the Indians their discharge. With two canoes and a party totalling twenty officers and men he emerged from the river and steered a course along the coast to the east.

It was a reckless venture. The party was already 300 miles from its base, and supplied for only fifteen days. Nevertheless, the killing of a few deer and a bear, and one good catch of fish, enabled them to prolong their survey for a month. They had to contend with fog (in which offshore islets could only by painful groping be distinguished from capes), with ice, and with a rocky shore affording little protection. The frail canoes were often held up by ice that would have been no obstacle to boats of sturdier construction. Despite all these difficulties, they had completed the circuit of Bathurst Inlet and had crossed Melville Sound (not to be confused with Parry's Viscount Melville Sound), to Point Turnagain, when shortage of food, threatening weather, and the damaged condition of the canoes brought the journey to an end. They had laid down 550 miles of a shoreline so devious that they were only six and a half degrees, little over 100 miles, east of their jumping-off point on the Coppermine.

Franklin had carried perseverance to the point of rashness in the hope of finding an Eskimo settlement where they might pass the winter. Failing this, he was compelled to make the homeward journey overland, for this offered the best chance of killing enough game to ward off starvation. For three days they were held up by gales in the camp near Point Turnagain. On the fourth they crossed Melville Sound through heavy seas and barely escaped shipwreck in the surf on its southern shore. In calmer weather they made the westward crossing of Bathurst Inlet, entered Arctic Harbour and paddled up Hood's River until shoal water brought their voyage to an end. Out of the wreckage of the canoes they put together two light, portable craft for the ferrying of rivers, packed their belongings on their backs, and set out on foot. It was 1 September. They were almost destitute of food, and 150 unexplored miles of rock, lake, and tundra lay between them and Fort Enterprise.

The journey would have been difficult for men who were fresh and well-fed. Buffeted by a fierce wind, the overburdened *voyageurs* staggered in their tracks, and alternately lacerated their feet on sharp stones and drenched their legs in the water of thinly frozen swamps. Before the week was out, the weather turned wintry and they were plunging through three feet of snow. They marched in single file, the men taking turns to break the path, with an officer second in line to keep the leader on course with a compass.

The compass, however, was an unreliable guide. For several days the sun was hidden, and in consequence they strayed off course to the left and became entangled in one of those mazes of rock and lake so familiar to travellers in the north. A week was lost in correcting their error. Just enough caribou and musk oxen were killed to avert starvation. There was great difficulty in cooking these as moss and scrub were drenched and snow-laden. When no game was to be had they fed on *tripe-de-roche,* or rock tripe, a lichen which was edible, but of poor nutritive quality and, for some of the party, quite indigestible. Discipline was dissolving into a clamour of complaint, rebuke, and recrimination. The canoes had been dropped and smashed deliberately, Franklin asserted, by their disheartened and mutinous carriers.

On obtaining true directions from a glimpse of the sun, the travellers got into the clear by scrambling, rather than walking, along a rocky bank that plunged steeply into a lake, and on 26 September they reached the bank of a rapid-flowing river which they recognized as the Coppermine. But it was unfordable and they had no boat. Richardson tried to swim across the freezing waters with a line and was dragged back half dead. Back went some distance downstream but could find no practicable crossing. Eventually an Indian, St Germain, constructed a raft of willows on which the whole party was ferried over. It was a measure of the *voyageurs'* despondency and indifference that eight days elapsed before they employed this obvious device.

Now, with only forty miles of familiar country separating them from Fort Enterprise, the party's strength and determination crumbled away. Franklin ordered Back with three of the strongest *voyageurs* to push ahead to Enterprise and bring back provisions for the rest. In the meantime, he urged his failing band to make what effort it could. All semblance of discipline was gone. In a bitter wind each man hurried ahead to find shelter behind rock or bush while his weaker comrades came up. When he stopped to encamp on the evening of the second day, Franklin was informed that two men, Crédit and Vaillant, had fallen in their tracks and been left behind. Richardson, with a heroism beyond all praise, though still crippled from his Coppermine swim, tramped out to find and encourage them. He came back to report that Vaillant was incapable of further effort, Crédit he could not find, as the track had been covered by drifts. Since their comrades professed themselves incapable of giving help, the poor fellows were left to die in the snow. The fate of Crédit was especially pitiful, for he had been the best hunter of the party and had worn himself out in finding meat to keep the others alive.

Grimmer events followed. At the next encampment, Hood declared himself unfit to go any farther. Richardson refused to desert his patient; the seaman, Hepburn, would not leave a fellow Scot in the lurch, so all three were left in a tent, pitched in a sheltered spot. On the next day's march four *voyageurs* received permission to return to the tent also and await the help confidently expected from Back.

With the five remaining men Franklin tramped on to Fort Enterprise. They found there neither Indians nor the promised store of food. A note left by Back stated that he had gone on to find Akaitcho and his hunters, failing which, he would walk to Fort Providence – a counsel of desperation, for it was 150 miles away. The Eskimo interpreter Augustus and one *voyageur* set out for Providence and, skilled in survival, got through alive. Franklin and the other three tore up the floors of the buildings for fuel and fed themselves on boiled deerskin and a soup of pulverized bone. Temperatures were down to 20 degrees below zero, and the starved men were unequal to the cold and the labour of hunting.

A few days later Richardson and Hepburn tramped in. Hood was dead, they said, and so, as far as they knew, were the four *voyageurs* who had dropped out on the march. Richardson confided to Franklin alone a grisly suspicion relating to the fate of some of the *voyageurs*.

According to his story, two days after their separation from the party, Richardson, Hood and Hepburn had been surprised by the arrival of the Iroquois *voyageur* Michel. He bore a note from Franklin stating that he and Solomon Belanger had permission to return to the tent. (Two other men, Fontano and Perrault, left the travelling party later.) To questions about Belanger, Michel returned evasive answers. He went off into the bush and returned with meat which he asserted to be the flesh of a wolf gored by a caribou. Richardson later supposed it to have been part of the body of one of his *voyageur* companions. Thereafter the Iroquois lounged moodily in the tent, ignoring the peevish remonstrances of Hood, who urged him to help the others to gather fuel and *tripe-de-roche*. On the morning of 20 October, Richardson, out foraging, heard a shot, rushed back, and found Hood lying in front of the tent, shot through the head. Michel asserted that the gun had gone off accidentally with such vehemence that neither Richardson nor Hepburn dared to challenge him. They placed the body in a bush, boiled and ate the dead man's buffalo robe, and set off for Fort Enterprise. On the way the Indian dropped behind to prepare, Richardson suspected, 'for another murder'; Hepburn hastily acquainted Richardson with certain 'material circumstances' that put Michel's guilt beyond doubt. The surgeon stepped behind a bush and, when Michel came up, shot him dead with a pistol.

Fearing the vengeance of Michel's friends and compatriots, Franklin suppressed the facts until returning to England, and even then no disclosure was made beyond Richardson's ambiguous utterance that 'poor Hood fell a sacrifice to the hardships he was exposed to' – until the dead man's relatives had been notified. This temporary suppression of the truth provoked Wentzel to insinuate that Hood's death was due to natural causes and Michel's to murder. In a letter to Roderick Mackenzie, he charged Richardson with 'unpardonable want of conduct', and wondered whether 'it would be proper for me to write everything that I know'. What could he know beyond what Richardson and Hepburn had told him? He quoted Back: 'To tell the truth, Wentzel, things have taken place which *must* not be known.' But Back's statement is wholly consistent with Richardson's published version of what had occurred. If this was false, and he was nursing a guilty secret, Back was the last person with whom he would voluntarily have shared it, for that amiable officer talked freely with the natives and told an amusing story of a drinking bout with his Indian guides. Richardson's whole life contradicts the imputation of crime and he had deserved too well of the *voyageurs* themselves, at the crossing of the Coppermine and later on the march, to have his honour questioned in their name.

The two Scots, who had expected to have their own wants supplied at Enterprise, were appalled at the destitution, filth, and wretchedness that met their eyes. 'Our own misery,' wrote Richardson, 'had stolen upon us by degrees, and we were accustomed to the contemplation of each other's emaciated figures, but the ghastly countenances, dilated eyeballs and sepulchral voices of Captain Franklin and those with him were more than we could bear.' Richardson implored the occupants of the hut to make their voices more cheerful, unconscious, Franklin observes, that his own partook of the same key.

The surgeon had twice already made extraordinary exertions for his comrades' safety; now he did so a third time. He rebuked Franklin for the filth and disorder he was tolerating, made the men roll up their blankets and put the hut in order, enforced daily religious observances, and laid down a system for preparing food and fuel. By these means he barely kept their spirits alive for the ten days of privation that remained. Two of the *voyageurs* died; the third, Adam, was confined to his bed, suffering, says Franklin, from 'gloomy apprehensions of approaching death, which we tried in vain to dispel'. Franklin and Richardson were quarrelling, mutually begging pardon, and quarrelling again, with a sickly peevishness which drew a rebuke from the loyal Hepburn. Hepburn, who had hunted partridge with some success, was crippled with swollen limbs; the supply of bone was exhausted, and boiled deerskin their only resource. One more day, Franklin thought, would have finished Adam, and a few more killed them all.

In the meantime George Back had been striving to bring them help with a resolution equal to Richardson's own. With his three *voyageurs* he had reached Fort Enterprise a day or two in advance of the main party and found it deserted and void of provisions. They revived their strength by gnawing putrid and frozen meat and set out to seek aid from the Indians or, failing them, from Fort Providence, more than 100 miles to the south. The former were not to be found, and the fort was, for the present, beyond their reach. They had not the strength for travelling over rough ground, and the Yellowknife River was not yet solidly frozen. So they crawled about in a feeble and unfruit-ful quest for fish and game. One of the *voyageurs* parted from his comrades and was found next morning dead, his limbs swollen and frozen as hard as the ground on which he lay.

The lives of the others were saved by the discovery of the shrivelled and eyeless heads of several deer, half buried in the snow. While the *voyageurs* devoured all the fragments they could find, Back 'with infinite care and self-denial' collected two packets of dried meat and sinew to support them on the journey to Providence. The *voyageurs*, despairing of meeting the Indians, consented to set out. On the third day they *did* come upon tracks which led them to the camp of Akaitcho. The old chief, who had given the white men up, was full of pity when he heard that they were alive and in desperate straits. Two sledges, loaded with meat, took the road for Fort Enterprise.

The rescuers reached Fort Enterprise on 7 November to find Richardson and Hepburn tearing down an outhouse, while Franklin was lying in bed with Adam to warm and cheer him. 'The Indians,' he says, 'set about everything with an activity that amazed us. Indeed, contrasted with our emaciated figures and extreme debility, their frames appeared to be gigantic and their strength supernatural.' Franklin was struck by their gentle-ness and compassion. Familiar with the effects of starvation, the Indians fed the helpless Adam with caution; the others fell too rashly upon tongue, fat, and deer's meat, and paid for it with intestinal torment. Richardson cautioned them repeatedly to be moderate but, as Franklin notes, 'was himself unable to practise the caution he so judiciously recommended'.

As soon as they were able to walk they were conducted by these friendly guides to Akaitcho's camp and on to Fort Provi-dence. Franklin gratefully acknowledges the kindness shown him both there and at Moose Fort, where he spent the winter. Former ill feelings were forgotten. Wentzel, however, did not share in the otherwise universal reconciliation. Franklin, it appears, spoke harshly of the neglect that had left Fort Enterprise unsupplied, and Wentzel wrote him a coldly dignified letter of explanation. After parting from the expedition, he and the Indians had suffered much from game shortage while reascending the Copper-mine, living for eleven days on *tripe-de-roche* alone; shortage of powder and sickness had made them slack in hunting, and hindered him from depositing meat at Enterprise as ordered. 'These details, Sir, I have been induced to enter into (rather unexpectedly) in justification of myself, and I hope it will be satisfactory.'

Wentzel had his share of impudence to adopt this self-righteous tone to a man whom, although through no fault of his own, he had left to starve. It is true that the expedition might not have returned to Enterprise – it might not have returned at all – and that the Indians, well aware of this, could not be persuaded to exertions for which they might never be paid. Still, Franklin had given strict orders for the provisions to be made, and one would have expected Wentzel (who was paid the handsome sum of £600 for his services), when the Indians failed him, to have made extraordinary exertions to obtain help from the traders before leaving those who depended on him in the lurch. Franklin did not find it consistent with his dignity to engage in any dispute; he put Wentzel's letter in a footnote to his *Narrative* with no comment. Wentzel's anger over this transaction may account for his recording (and possibly believing) his slanderous insinuations against Dr John Richardson.

When Franklin, Richardson, and Hepburn reached Fort Providence, they learned that competition in the fur trade was over and the rival companies amalgamated, and that, owing to the temporary disorganization caused by the merger, the expedition's supplies, from which their Indian helpers were to be paid, had not yet come up. Back had already crossed Great Slave Lake to beg or borrow what he could from the posts to the south in order to make up the deficiency in part. Franklin was deeply hurt at his inability to redeem his promises, but Akaitcho received the unwelcome news with generosity and tact, gratefully recorded by Franklin. '"The world goes badly," he said, "all are poor. You are poor, the traders appear to be poor, I and my people are poor likewise, and since the goods are not come in, we cannot have them. I do not regret having supplied you with provisions, for a Copper Indian can never permit white men to suffer from want of food on his lands without flying to their aid. I trust, however, that we shall, as you say, receive what is due next autumn, and at all events," he added in a tone of good humour, "it is the first time that the white people have been indebted to the Copper

Indians."' The goods did arrive in the spring, not the autumn, of 1822, and Franklin, before leaving for home, arranged with the traders for the payment of his debt to Akaitcho, and the assignment of gifts to all Indians who had aided the expedition, with special reward to those who had been instrumental in saving his life. The officers and Hepburn went by river to York Factory, where they met George Simpson (no doubt, with more mutual respect than before), now governor of all British-American posts, and from there they sailed to England. The expedition had lasted forty-two months.

Though his positive success had been limited, Franklin had, in the face of extraordinary difficulties, achieved a breakthrough which he was to exploit on a grand scale in his second overland journey. The cost was the almost inevitable consequence of attempting a dangerous and wholly novel operation without any preliminary trial runs.

Franklin, in his *Narrative*, has done the *voyageurs* less than justice. It was unfair to expect of them the sympathy and prompt obedience of men who had been trained to the sea. They were men of the forest, river boatmen, strange to the tundra and appalled by the ocean surf. Yet they followed their leader, grumbling but still obedient, as far as he dared to go, and died pitifully for the cause of science, which they could not comprehend. There was perhaps remorse as well as pity in the kindness which Franklin expressed for his surviving comrades, Adam and little Peltier, when they all lay dying at Enterprise.

The achievement of the expedition was small compared with that of Parry's voyage to Melville Island. But the drama of it made Franklin easily the popular favourite. He was pointed out in the streets of London as 'the man who ate his boots,' lionized at social gatherings, and received as a guest at the Yorkshire home of his old commander at Trafalgar. His popularity was more than maintained by the publication of his *Narrative of a Journey to the Shores of the Polar Sea*. With a grave sense of humour, and a sensitivity to atmosphere and circumstance, he produced in a style sometimes ponderous, but quite sincere and unaffected, what still reads as a stirring tale of adventure.

Though modest, and not at all likely to win public favour (except by some lucky accident), Franklin was just the man to keep it. Lady Franklin's biographer, Frances J. Woodward, says that his portraits represent him as a solid, almost bovine personality, and that his written style is platitudinous – as it often is, when he is not deeply stirred. She adds the acute observation that there was fine quality in the man who was attractive to and attracted by two gifted and sensitive women. That quality is not hard to identify.

Though shyness made Franklin awkward and a little pompous in approach, he was full of kindness and good feeling. It was that, more than the commonplace virtues of courage and persistence, that most impressed Richardson and Back. It was particularly noticed by Indians with whom he could hardly communicate. During his term as governor of Tasmania, he and his official party lost their way in the woods, and one of the party's élite suggested that the rations of the convict baggage carriers be cut. Franklin replied severely that if supplies ran short, the men who were doing the work would be the last, not the first, to feel the pinch. Long after he was dead, one of those transported jailbirds composed a letter – a burdensome labour for one of his background – to tell Lady Franklin of his sympathy for her, and his grief for the husband she had lost.

Franklin was deeply and sincerely religious. Both his first and second brides found themselves in the role, very unusual for a wife, of having to curb rather than to stimulate the religious fervour of the male half of the household. But, sincere as it was, his religion had been mellowed on the waterfront, and could be made palatable to other sailors besides James Fitzjames.

He was sympathetic and unselfish. Some other Arctic captains of the period gave offence by trying to take credit for scientific work done by their junior officers. Franklin held that officers whose reputation was established should, as much as possible, withdraw in favour of younger men who had yet to make their way. Nor was this mere pretence. The Appendix to his *Narrative of a Second Journey* . . . contains a table of sound velocities at low temperatures, there credited to Midshipman Kendall only. From the body of the narrative we learn that Franklin shared in the experiments. He said himself that he had no purpose in life but to do his duty, and if that can be reconciled to a love of adventure which no hardship could quench, he spoke no more than the truth.

Shortly after his return he married Miss Eleanor Porden, with characteristic honesty stipulating before the marriage was solemnized that it must be no bar to renewed Arctic endeavour. And he meant it. The union was quickly blessed with a daughter, and shortly after her birth, in 1825, Franklin, Richardson, and Back, with the young midshipman Ernest Kendall, sailed for New York en route to the Mackenzie.

On his second expedition Franklin made good use of the experience acquired on the first. His plan, approved by the Admiralty, called for a more convenient base on Great Bear Lake and the use of the broad and relatively tranquil Mackenzie River as an outlet to the sea. He would thus be able to use boats – small and not the best sea vessels, but a good deal more seaworthy than the canoes in which his first venture had been made. The choice of British seamen to man these was a guarantee of mutual understanding and discipline. Four crews were authorized, of which Richardson was to take two east from the mouth of the Mackenzie to that of the Coppermine, while Franklin surveyed westward in the direction of Icy Cape. At the same time, Captain Beechey in the *Blossom* was ordered up to Kotzebue Sound and directed to send a boat past Icy Cape to meet Franklin and ensure, if possible, a complete survey of the Alaskan north shore.

Richardson's admirable qualities, especially as a scientist, had procured his reappointment as surgeon. With Back the case was different. He had committed indiscretions; he seems not to have been a precise surveyor, and the personal indebtedness, which Franklin cordially acknowledged, did not oblige him to recommend Back (who was already employed at sea) to an important official duty. He therefore chose as his second-in-command Lieutenant Bushnan, a valued officer of Parry's. But Bushnan died suddenly, and Back was recalled from the West Indies to take his place as an officer of the expedition. A hint of his imperfect sympathy with the two older men may be seen in the clause of the Admiralty orders that, if by any mishap to Franklin, Back should become leader of the expedition, he was to make no avoidable alteration in the plans that Franklin and Richardson had agreed upon. A unified Hudson's Bay Company under the governorship of a now friendly George Simpson guaranteed an easy and reliable line of transport and communication. Chief Factor Peter Warren Dease of the company was appointed counsellor and supervisor of Indian and *voyageur* auxiliaries. When the main party arrived he had already chosen a site for the base and begun the accumulation of supplies.

As the sea route to Hudson Bay did not open until July, officers and seamen sailed in February for New York; they then went to Montreal, and from there by river, lake, and portage to Great Slave Lake, down the Mackenzie to Fort Norman, up the Great Bear River to their base Fort Franklin on the Keith Arm of Great Bear Lake.

Arrival early in August permitted extensive reconnaissance of the routes to be followed on the intended voyages of discovery. So, while the popular Back, who chatted readily with native and *voyageur,* aided Dease in putting up buildings and organizing hunting and fishing, Richardson explored by boat the north-eastern (Dease) arm of Great Bear Lake, while Franklin and Kendall went down the Mackenzie to its mouth. And here occurred an example of the stupidity of the British naval officer which his twentieth-century critics have overlooked. ' Some spirits, which had been saved for the occasion, were issued to the men; and with three fervent cheers they drank to the health of our beloved monarch, and to the continued success of our enterprise. Mr Kendall and I had also reserved a little of our brandy in order to celebrate this interesting event; but Baptiste, in his delight on beholding the sea, had set before us some salt water, which having been mixed with the brandy before the mistake was discovered, we were,' says Franklin with rather lumbering humour, ' reluctantly obliged to forego the intended draught, and use it in the more classical form of a libation poured on the ground.'

For the winter fifty men in all were gathered in and around Fort Franklin. Seamen and marines numbered nineteen. Augustus, the Eskimo interpreter of the first journey, had joined the second, bringing with him his compatriot Ooligbuck, with whom Back in his amiable fashion struck up a friendship. The slackness of the native hunters, so hurtful to the previous expedition, caused a temporary reduction of rations, which the men took in good part, being as keen as the officers for the success of the summer voyage. A school was operated, and some total illiterates among the men learned in the course of the winter to read and write with what Franklin thinks 'tolerable correctness'.

As soon as the rivers cleared of ice, the four boats were off,

Franklin and Back with the *Lion* and the *Reliance*, Richardson and Kendall with the *Dolphin* and the *Union*. At Point Separation, at the head of the Mackenzie delta, they parted, Richardson following an eastern and Franklin a western channel. On his way to the sea the ardent Franklin involved himself in a danger that Richardson, on the other side of the delta, judiciously avoided. Seeing a large number of Eskimo tents on the river bank, he turned inshore to make inquiries about his intended route. Both boats took the ground in a maze of shoals and were almost overrun by the natives, who after exchanging some trinkets began a unilateral process of theft. The Europeans shoved them back with all the good nature they could command. They dared not offer violence as long as the boats were grounded, and they had no retreat. Back got the *Reliance* afloat with the help of a well-disposed Eskimo and, by menacing the mob with muskets, frightened the natives away from the *Lion*. Both boats took the ground again 150 yards from the shore. Augustus waded ashore, remonstrated with his countrymen with such effect that he recovered the more valuable of the articles seized. He learned that at high tide, just after midnight, the boats could find a channel by hugging the western shore. This they did until forced to land by a gale. In the meantime, the Eskimos, repenting of their moderation, manned their kayaks in pursuit. Back saw them approaching through the mist and gave the alarm. The weary men dragged the boats down and launched them through the surf, threatened their pursuers with firearms, and so were permitted to escape. This was the only instance of such misconduct on the cruise; natives, frequently met along the coast, treated the strangers with uniform hospitality, tempered by a little pilfering but never by the threat of violence.

The forces of nature were not so kind, and the 350 miles of new coast mapped fell far short of Franklin's previous performance by canoe. The boats were continually being held up, sometimes for days at a time, by ice forced up to the shoreline, by fog and by shoal. They passed the 141st degree of west longitude, which separated Russian (now American) from British territory and gave the name of Demarcation Point to a neighbouring cape. They were held up for several days at Foggy Island in a visibility which sometimes did not exceed forty yards. A few miles brought them to Return Reef, about the midpoint between Mackenzie

River and Icy Cape. It was the middle of August, and orders were to turn back not later than the twentieth, unless certain of reaching their objective, Icy Cape. The certainty was all the other way. Franklin gave the name Beechey to the farthest cape visible to the west (about 149 degrees west), and put about for his base.

More than six weeks had been spent in coming from Point Separation to Return Reef, but they made the return voyage in little more than two. The ice had wasted away with the advance of summer, and they now knew, even in fog, what course to steer. But an ice-free sea has its own dangers for open boats, and on the first stage of the voyage home they barely escaped shipwreck.

'As the afternoon wore away,' writes Franklin, 'gloomy clouds gathered in the north-west, and at six a violent squall came from that quarter, attended with snow and sleet. The gale increased with rapidity, in less than ten minutes the sea was white with foam, and such waves were raised as I had never before been exposed to in a boat. The spray and sea broke over us incessantly and it was with difficulty that we could keep free by bailing. Our little vessels went through the sea with great velocity under a close-reefed sail hoisted about three feet up the mainmast, and proved themselves to be very buoyant. Their small size, however, and the nature of their construction, necessarily adapted for the navigation of shallow rivers, unfitting them for withstanding the sea then running, we were in imminent danger of foundering. I therefore resolved on making for the shore, as the only means of saving the party, although I was aware that in so doing, I incurred the hazard of staving the boats, there being few places on this part of the coast where there was sufficient beach under the broken cliffs. The wind blowing along the land, we could not venture on exposing the boats' side to the sea by hauling directly in, but edging away with the wind on our quarter, we most providentially took ground in a favourable spot. The boats were instantly filled with surf, but they were unloaded and dragged up without having sustained material damage.'

The finding of a strip of sand at the foot of the rocks was another instance of Franklin's luck.

For the rest, the homeward journey was made in safety. The thievish band at the mouth of the Mackenzie had moved on elsewhere. Other natives, without exception, showed the travellers ready kindness. The women of one encampment, observing that the men were footsore from tramping over the coarse gravel and broken rock of the beach, detained them while they sewed seal-skin pads on the soles of their moccasins. Separation Point was passed on 4 September, and on the twenty-first they were back at Fort Franklin.

In the meantime, the boat's crew of the *Blossom*, working from Bering Strait, had, like Franklin, achieved only partial success. On his way up to Alaskan waters Captain Beechey called at Pitcairn Island and interviewed old John Adams, the last surviving *Bounty* mutineer. He berthed his ship in Kotzebue Sound and sent the mate Elson with the barge of the *Blossom* to join hands, if possible, with Franklin. With difficulty, Elson carried his boat as far as Point Barrow, now the northernmost point in the territory of the United States. There ice made further progress impossible, and he had not a little trouble in extricating his boat and getting back to the ship. An unexplored gap measuring 160 miles was left between Point Barrow and Return Reef.

Richardson and Kendall had returned to Fort Franklin on 1 September after fulfilling their mission with comparative ease and complete success. Sailing east with the boats *Dolphin* and *Union*, they fixed Capes Bathurst and Parry, and traced the shores of Franklin and Darnley bays. Proceeding eastward, they gave the name Wollaston to an island of unknown extent that was separated from the mainland by Dolphin and Union Strait, and arrived at the mouth of the Coppermine on 1 August, less than a month out from Point Separation. In that period, 900 miles of new coastline had been laid down.

The outward journey of 1,500 miles was reduced to 500 on the way back by a resource suggested to Franklin by the half-breed guide Beaulieu. The boats were rowed up the Coppermine and cached at Bloody Falls, while their crews tramped overland to the Dease Arm of Great Bear Lake, where Beaulieu met them and carried them by water to Fort Franklin. Richardson promptly went off to join the naturalist Drummond in the foothills of the Rockies. The European members of the expedition wintered over and returned home in the summer of 1827.

An accurately planned expedition had achieved an outstanding success at minimal cost. Two men only lost their lives, one by drowning at a rapids, the other from a tubercular condition. No avoidable risks had been run and no unusual hardships suffered. Together, the two branches of the expedition had mapped 1,250 miles of coast, which, added to the discoveries of the previous journey, made a total of 1,800 miles of coastline, or less than half that distance by crow's flight. Franklin had added more frontage to the map of North America than any other man in its history, and had his career ended when he came back from the Mackenzie, he would still have ranked among the great travellers of the nineteenth century.

From *Narrative of a Second Expedition to the Shores of the Polar Sea in the Years 1825, 1826 and 1827,* by John Franklin, Captain, R.N., etc.

Entry in Journal for 16 August 1826 – describing the end of his westward voyage along Alaska coast at Return Reef:

Between Point Anxiety and Point Chandos, which is eight miles to the westward (from Foggy Island), the land was occasionally seen; but after rounding the latter point we lost sight of it and steered to the west across the mouth of Yarborough Inlet, the soundings varying from five to two fathoms. (Twelve feet of water, when out of sight of land!) The fog returned, and the wind freshening, soon created such a swell upon the flats that it became necessary to haul further from the land: but the drift ice beginning to close around us, we could no longer proceed with safety, and, therefore, endeavoured to find a landing place. An attempt was made at Point Heald, and another at the western point of *Prudhoe bay,* but both were frustrated by the shoalness of the water and the height of the surf. The increasing violence of the gale, however, and the density of the fog, rendering it absolutely necessary for us to obtain some shelter, we stood out to seaward, with the view of making fast to a large piece of ice. In our way we fell among gravelly reefs, and arriving at the same time suddenly in smooth water, we effected a landing on one of them. (Return Reef). A temporary dispersion of the fog showed that we were surrounded with banks nearly on a level with the water, and protected to seaward by a large body of ice lying aground. The patch of gravel on which we were encamped, was about five hundred yards in circumference, destitute of water, and with no more drift wood than a few willow branches, sufficient to make one fire.

Above is the only reference to the discovery of Prudhoe Bay in

Franklin's published account. This extract portrays vividly the conditions in which the first Europeans – travelling in row boats, which were not the best sea boats, having been built shallow to get through the sandbanks of the Mackenzie River – discovered the shore soon to be visited by the 100,000-ton *Manhattan*.

3 Prelude to Disaster

After the spectacular success of his first voyage, Parry had undertaken the second and third with no particular keenness. Such luck, he thought would not repeat itself. Franklin's zest for adventure was, on the contrary, keener than ever; and neither his more than forty years nor his marriage with Miss Jane Griffin (his first wife had died while he was on his second journey) deterred him from making early application for a third Arctic commission. When the Admiralty invited him to draw up a plan for further discovery, he responded with two – both employing the amphibian approach which he had learned to use with such success. The first plan was not new, but had been in the air ever since Parry's voyage to the straits of Fury and Hecla. In 1824, Lyon had tried to apply it unsuccessfully in the wretched little *Griper*. According to an Eskimo map which Parry considered reliable, only a narrow isthmus separated the top of Repulse Bay from the true Arctic. Franklin therefore reintroduced the scheme of berthing a ship in Repulse Bay, hauling boats and supplies across the isthmus, and coasting away to the west. His alternative plan was quite original. On his first voyage he had learned from an Indian, Black Meat, of the Great Fish River, which took its rise in the highlands north of Great Slave Lake and flowed northeast to the Arctic. So he proposed to set up base on the northeast shore of Great Slave Lake, where timber was procurable for boat-building, discover the river's source, build boats and draw them over it, sail down the Great Fish River, and follow the coast east or west according to the location of its mouth. But by the time these plans were submitted, the Admiralty had decided to authorize no more polar journeys; the next three major Arctic expeditions were privately financed.

The first of these was headed by Captain John Ross. Though somewhat discredited by his unlucky mistake in Lancaster Sound,

C

and barred from sharing in official polar enterprise by the enmity of John Barrow, Ross had some original ideas. In 1828 he published a prophetic *Treatise on Steam Navigation* – which probably harmed rather than helped him with his official superiors, who dreaded the displacement of the sailing ship, which had given Britain her maritime supremacy. Ross, however, was not a man who held his convictions lightly. He prepared to prove the advantage of steam power by putting it to the test in the frozen seas. Agreeing with Parry that the Northwest Passage could not be navigated in a vessel of the *Hecla's* type, Ross maintained that it could be done in a ship of shallower draught (and so better fitted for edging between beach and ice pack), and equipped with steam power, giving manoeuvrability in narrow and crooked ice lanes. He proved his sincerity by putting £3,000 of his own money into the venture! Felix Booth, a wealthy distiller, advanced the balance of the £20,000 required. Ross bought the 150-ton *Victory* and fitted her with engine and paddle wheels, which could be hoisted up to avoid contact with the ice. It was a brave venture, but attempted too early in the era of marine engineering to have much promise of success.

Declining the offers of Back and Hoppner, an old officer of Parry's, Ross appointed as second-in-command his nephew, James Clark Ross, who had shared in all four of Parry's Arctic voyages. Two capable seamen, Blanky and Abernethy, were enrolled as ice mates. The always wearisome task of mustering and selecting a crew was enlivened by an incident from which even the dour Ross derived not a little amusement. He had enrolled as cook a man who seemed eager for the service. But he did not appear on the day appointed, and his absence was accounted for by a letter from his wife addressed to Captain John Ross:

9 April 1829

Sir:

I have just found out that my husband has made an engagement with you to join your expedition *without consulting me;* I must beg to tell you, sir, that he shall not go – I will not let him have his clothes ' [a powerful deterrent, whatever the would-be traveller's destination, but especially so when that destination is the Arctic]. He must be mad ever to think of leaving a comfortable home, to be frozen in with ice, or torn to pieces with bears; therefore I am determined he shall not leave Gosport, so I hope you will not expect him.

Mary L.

66

It was Ross's intention to go down Regent's Inlet (still un-explored to the south of Fury Beach) and seek a passage west along the continental shore towards the Point Turnagain of Franklin. He had two reasons for choosing this course. He hoped to avoid the heavy ice which Parry had encountered at Melville Island; and in Regent's Inlet, he had the wreck cache at Fury Beach as a source of supply in event of disaster to the *Victory*.

The voyage to and through Lancaster Sound was no easy one. The *Victory* carried away her foretopmast in a squall, and the engine proved almost useless. It was continually breaking down and seldom propelled the ship at more than a mile an hour. The ice of Regent's Inlet, which had twice baffled Parry, gave Ross no kinder reception, as he graphically records.

They were approaching Fury Beach, and the two Rosses, after forty-eight hours of continuous duty, had gone below, leaving the mate Blanky in charge on deck. 'At two o'clock in the morn-ing a heavy pack of ice, which had been concealed from us by the fog, suddenly made its appearance only three cable's length under our lee, being then only recognized by the tremendous breakers that were surging over it. [It was blowing a gale.] Deciding at once that the only chance for us was to weather the end next the land he [Blanky] let fly the storm trysail sheet, and putting the helm up, gave us notice of the danger, immediately proceeding to hoist the storm jib and reefed boom foresail, which had been kept in readiness for such an emergency.

'We found it nevertheless impossible to keep clear of a piece of ice in wearing [putting the ship about], yet though it gave us a violent shock, it assisted in bringing the ship's head the right way. It was still doubtful whether we could clear the end of the pack of ice which was now on our lee bow, with the sea breaking over it. We therefore set all the sail that we could carry, and at last weathered it only by the ship's length: finding suddenly the most delightful relief in quitting a turbulent sea for one that was smooth as glass: a quiet retreat in which we could venture to finish our night's rest. We were indeed perfectly sheltered from the gale by this great mass which was hourly gaining in size and solidity by attaching the smaller pieces that were floating near it.' Ross warmly praises the 'care and ability' shown by Blanky in this crisis.

On 12 August they reached Fury Beach, where the wreck cache lay, and found the supplies Parry had stacked on the beach generally well preserved. They then pushed on into the unknown waters to the south, groping along the coast for a channel that would conduct them to the 'western sea'.

Such an outlet did in fact exist, if they could have found it. The land forming the western shore of Regent's Inlet, named non-committally by Parry North Somerset Land, consists of two sections: the bulb-shaped Boothia Peninsula and, separated from it by Bellot Strait (only a mile wide at its narrows), Somerset Island. Held offshore by islets and massed ice in Brentford Bay, Ross missed the narrow cleft of Bellot Strait and passed on to find his winter quarters at Felix Harbour in Lord Mayor Bay. He dismantled his useless engine and left the parts on the beach. Some of them have recently been retrieved and now lie in the Citadel Museum, Halifax, Nova Scotia, a memorial to a courageous but unlucky experiment. A school was set up to instruct the men in reading, religion, and arithmetic, a curriculum the dogmatic old captain – he was fifty-two – varied by an occasional lecture on total abstinence. His phenomenal resistance to cold was, he affirmed, due to his abstemious habits, though he had the objectivity and candour to admit that his square and sturdy frame gave him an advantage over men of more slender build.

On 12 January 1830, the ship was visited by Eskimos. Intelligible communication and mutual confidence were quickly established. Perceiving that the white men were strangers to the climate, the natives adopted the same protective attitude that Franklin had noted in Akaitcho. Ross relates that when he had frozen his face on a ramble, his Eskimo companion drew the frost out by applying snow, 'after which he continued always near me, frequently reminding me to put my hand to the same part, for fear of a recurrence of the attack. This was good-natured and aided, with all else, to give us a favourable impression of these people'.

Association with these friendly natives had other results more significant than cultivation of mutual goodwill. Under the guidance and with the help of the Eskimos the Europeans hunted game with such success that they kept scurvy at bay and, after three winters in Boothia, had the strength to travel hundreds of miles on foot and by open boat; and after eighteen months to reach England with the loss of only three men out of twenty-five.

Like the Eskimos encountered by Parry and Lyon, the people of Boothia were excellent geographers and traced for Ross a map from which he learned that he had indeed come to a dead end and was shut off from the western sea by an isthmus, low and cut up by lakes, but an impassable barrier to boat or ship. Bellot Strait was unknown to them. By way of compensation they taught the strangers that they could make journeys of considerable distance by carrying supplies and equipment on sledges, man-hauled or drawn by dogs.

James Ross, the pioneer of the sledging art, later carried to such perfection by McClintock, made one or two trial trips; and then with the mate, Abernethy, four men, sledges, and dog teams, set out to and beyond the western shore of Boothia.

Leaving the ship early in May, James Ross reached the western shore at Cape Isabella (a name to which the Rosses were attached), and was immediately impressed by the difficulty of unravelling land from sea in the panorama spread before him. 'Those unacquainted with frozen climates, like the present,' he writes, 'must recollect that when all is ice, and all one dazzling mass of white, when the surface of the sea itself is tossed up and fixed into rocks, while the land is on the contrary often very level, the two cannot be distinguished with accuracy.' Unmistakable land did lie to the west, so steering in that direction he skirted the northern extremity of Matty Island and came to more extensive land, later indicated on John Ross's map as King William Land. The travellers followed the new coast to the northwest and arrived at its northern extremity, Cape Felix.

Here James Ross took note of a phenomenon which, veteran as he was of no fewer than five Arctic voyages, he found astonishing. 'The pack of ice which had, in the autumn of the last year, been pressed against that shore, consisted of the heaviest masses that I had ever seen in such a situation. With this, the lighter floes had been thrown up on some parts of the coast in a most extraordinary and incredible manner; turning up large quantities of shingle before them, and in some places having travelled as much as half a mile beyond the limits of the highest tide-mark.' Had James Ross suspected that the heavy masses exerting this amazing pressure flowed in, in an unbroken stream, all the way from the

69

Beaufort Sea and Melville Island, he might have altered history.

Beyond Cape Felix the coast trended southwest in the direction of Franklin's Point Turnagain, some 250 miles away. To reach it was utterly beyond Ross's power – rations were already half gone – but it occurred to him that a reduced allowance would enable him at least to lengthen his survey. 'Mentioning my wishes to the mate Abernethy, he informed me that the men had intended, themselves, to make the same proposal to me, and were only waiting for the proper opportunity of transmitting their wishes through him . . . I rejoiced in this generous feeling.' The formality that required the enlisted men in a party of six to communicate with the captain only through the mate strikes one as eccentric, but this anecdote helps to absolve the Arctic officers of the slander that they were inhuman in their relationships with their men.

The survey was thus extended twenty-five miles southwest down the King William Island coast to Point Victory, where a cairn six feet high was built to mark the journey's end. It must have been beaten down by the fierce Arctic gales, for eighteen years later, when Franklin's crews made land there, 'Sir James Ross' pillar' was nowhere to be found.

On his way back to the ship, despite the shortage of rations, Ross made a detour to the south of Matty Island to ascertain whether King William Land was a detached island or joined to the isthmus of Boothia. In poor visibility he thought that he saw a chain of islets to the south, but could not determine whether or not they formed an unbroken coastline. 'To make an actual examination was now impossible' – as it was, the party was indebted to Eskimo help for its safe arrival at the ship.

In consequence, presumably, of these imperfect observations, the map of the expedition's discoveries showed King William Land linked to Boothia by a line of coast, represented, however, by a dotted line, indicating plausible conjecture, not confirmed

---

King William Island area, showing James Ross's sledge journey from Felix Harbour to and beyond Cape Felix, Franklin's last voyage up Wellington Channel, back to winter at Beechey Island, and thence south to his 'rendezvous with Fate' in the polar pack west of King William Island. Dotted line shows course of Thomas Simpson's boats: M is the then location of North Magnetic Pole.

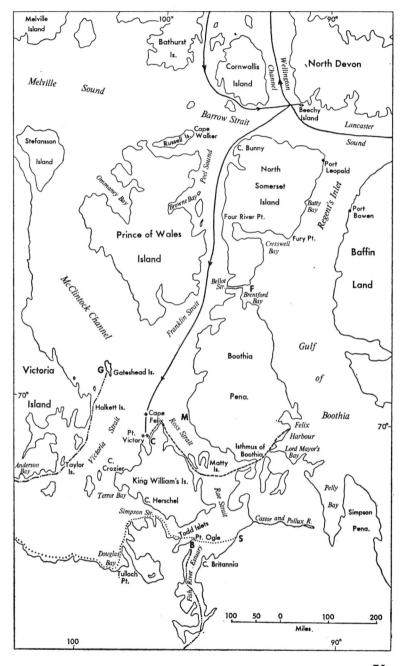

fact. Whether James or John was responsible for this is not known. It seems more like John to add detail to the visionary coast in the shape of Sheridan and Rowley capes and to call the basin which it formed with Boothia and King William Land Proctes's Bay. But it does not matter. If the Rosses believed that there was no through channel between Boothia and King William Land, they were right in saying so. They did not assert it as fact. But in McClintock's opinion it was their supposed land which diverted Franklin from the open strait on the east side of King William Island to the murderous ice on the west.

The *Victory* did not free herself that summer. She was moved only a few miles before becoming icebound in Victoria Harbour, named by the loyal John Ross after the heiress presumptive to the British throne. (He appears to have been the first to place on the map the name of that geographically overpublicized monarch.) In the spring of 1831, James Ross again made the crossing of the isthmus and went north up the Boothia coast to Cape Adelaide, where he fixed approximately the North Magnetic Pole. (It has moved a long way since then.) That summer the ship could not stir; another winter was endured, and in the early months of 1832 John Ross had to make a critical decision: Was he to attempt escape on foot in April and May, the only period when travel was practicable for a large body of burdened men, or to wait for the breakup of the ice, with the certainty of detention for a fourth winter if the ship did not obtain release? He chose to travel.

If they had depended on their own resources the chances of the explorers would have been poor indeed. Three or four hundred miles lay between them and the waters frequented by whaling ships. But the wreck cache at Fury Beach was a halfway house where they could renew supplies and prepare their boats for the voyage to safety.

Doubting the seaworthiness of the boats at Fury Beach, Ross required the men to haul two of the boats of the *Victory* in addition to supplies. Early on the journey the men appealed, through the mate, Blanky, for permission to leave the boats behind. Ross's response was harsh and decisive. If the men were permitted to question his orders when they were fresh and good-humoured, they would tolerate no control when tired and disillusioned. He refused to consider the request and bitterly rebuked Blanky for lending it countenance. The men, doubtless realizing the wisdom of the precaution, took the captain's refusal in such good part that he was offended at their light-heartedness and complained that they left all the worrying to him. This seems an odd reaction for an officer of his experience. In an equally serious crisis, McClintock rejoiced (more rationally, one would think) that his carefree tars neither understood nor cared about the peril in which he had placed them.

At Fury Beach they collected timber and set up living quarters, which the men, with unimpaired cheerfulness, named Somerset House, after the former mansion of an English duke. When the ice permitted they took to the boats and sailed up to Lancaster Sound in the hope of being picked up by a whaler. The approach of autumn compelled them to give up and turn back into the detested Regent's Inlet. The ice grew too thick for the passage of boats; they were secured on shore at Batty Bay; the disheartened crews made their way back to Somerset House on foot. There they spent their *fourth* winter in the Arctic.

The summer of 1833 was their last chance, for strength and courage were beginning to fail. The long tramp from Fury Beach back to Batty Bay where the boats were secured, was a difficult task for the captain, who had to direct the transportation of the sick by comrades who were scarcely stronger themselves. These sick men were a serious threat to their comrades' survival, though Ross later affirmed that the idea of leaving them behind never entered his head. By boat they passed out of Regent's Inlet, along the Baffin Island north shore, and put ashore to the east of Navy Board Inlet, on a coast much frequented by whalers.

Early in the morning of 26 August 1833, a whaler was reported lying to for her boats. She was a great way off and soon passed out of sight. At 10 A.M. another was sighted, and Ross's desperate men manned their boats and set out in pursuit. This ship also made sail to the east and, with a stiff breeze, was drawing away from the boats, when a calm enabled the lighter boats to narrow the distance and at last make their signals observed. The whaler rounded to and lowered a boat to meet the castaways. In reply to Ross's hail the mate in charge informed him that the ship was the *Isabella* of Hull, formerly commanded by Captain John Ross. Ross replied that he was that very man. 'With the usual blunder-headedness of men on such occasions,' he adds, made a little peevish, perhaps, by the frightful suspense of the last hour, '[the

C*

mate] assured me that I had been dead two years.' He soon proved his identity. He and his comrades, 'unshaven, dirty, dressed in the rags of wild beasts and starved to the bone,' were hauled aboard and given the news of the world from which they had so long been exiles. They were told that France had suffered a second Revolution, and that Ross's friend and patron, the Duke of Clarence, had ruled for the last three years as King William IV.

The troubles of captain and crew, however, did not end when they set foot on an English dock. Anticipating a cruise of a year and a half only, Ross had made promises of pay, which he was unable to redeem after a period three times that length. He listened to the reproaches of his broken-down and destitute men with a composure that was all his own. 'I am too well experienced in mankind to be surprised, or to entertain enmity against those who only acted according to their evil natures' – by demanding pay that was their due! He applied to the Admiralty to relieve him of this indebtedness, pleading that the geographical and other discoveries of his expedition were of public value and ought therefore to be charged against the State. The Admiralty, either agreeing to this, or yielding to a public opinion which sympathized with the eccentric but adventurous old sailor, undertook to discharge all claims against John Ross arising from the expedition, amounting to some £4,600. Barrow, Ross's inveterate enemy, informed him of their consent in these terms:

'Their Lordships being ... satisfied of your utter inability to fulfil the engagements entered into by you, and of the destitute state in which these people have providentially arrived in their native country, have been induced under such peculiar circumstances, from a feeling of humanity, immediately to relieve you from your engagement and them from pressing necessity.'

Barrow preferred to ascribe Their Lordships' bounty to 'a feeling of humanity' for 'destitute' persons than to a recognition of services rendered by John Ross. His statement of the situation was correct, and probably copied from Ross's letter of application, but it was neither necessary nor generous to 'play it back' to Ross in this insulting manner.

But the Admiralty had not yet heard the last of John Ross. He had sunk his all in the expedition and, without help, was a ruined man. With characteristic independence and reliance upon his own merits, he declined the help freely offered from private sources. He had served the public – it was for the public to reward him. From the Admiralty he received a tart reminder that it had served him enough by paying his debts and promoting James Ross to the rank of post captain. The last may have been an 'unkind cut' of Barrow's. Ross was growing somewhat jealous of his 'philosophic nephew', who was undeniably more of a scientist and had been made much of by the Royal Society for his magnetic researches. So Ross appealed to the government, and a committee of the House of Commons was appointed to examine and report on his claim to a public grant. The members of this group had plenty of malicious gossip to help them to a decision. Ross was alleged to have organized his expedition from no worthier motive than to retrieve his reputation, which had supposedly been damaged by the Lancaster Sound affair. He was censured for reporting that 'we' did thus and so, in instances where James Ross had been the sole agent – unfair comment surely, for Ross as promoter and commander of the enterprise could claim a share in the credit for whatever it accomplished. It was maliciously reported that he had falsely magnified the number of islets in the Clarence group in order to confer on them the names of the numerous bastard offspring of the Duke of Clarence (King William IV). He was perhaps justly ridiculed for affirming that, owing to the rotation of the earth and the inertia of the sea, the ocean surface was thirteen feet higher on the east side of Boothia Isthmus than on the west. The committee *did* rather mischievously quiz James Ross about this and compelled the embarrassed officer to admit that evidence which his uncle found conclusive might not convince an approved scientist. For the rest, the honest gentlemen (among them Sir Robert Peel and W. E. Gladstone) had fought too many elections to pay much heed to frothy detraction. They found that the *Victory* expedition was a serious undertaking in which distinguished officers like Back and Hoppner had volunteered to share; that it had made important and useful additions to scientific knowledge; and that Ross's maintenance of health and discipline and the unfaltering courage which had brought his crew home were an honour to himself and glorious to his country. They recommended an honorarium of £5,000, which was duly paid. On the now triumphant Ross, King William conferred the knighthood with which both Parry and Franklin had been honoured at an earlier date.

Unsatisfied with these successes, the old warrior reopened the question of Lancaster Sound. In his *Narrative* of the *Victory* cruise, he reasserted that Parry had agreed with him in 'closing' the sound, or had committed 'gross misconduct' in not declaring that he disagreed. Barrow was enraged and even the sober Parry slightly ruffled. 'That foolish man, Ross, is determined *always* to get himself into a Hobble,' he wrote. For a time Parry was inclined to take the advice of the more combative Franklin, and publish a retort; on second thought, he wisely chose to avoid a controversy 'of which one half the world would not understand the real merits, and two-thirds of the other half would not care about it'. Sir John Ross went off to a diplomatic post in Sweden; but the Arctic had not seen the last of him yet. Years after, when Franklin was dead, when Parry, Back, Richardson, and James Ross, all much younger men, had retired, Dr Elisha Kent Kane (unborn when Ross made his first northern voyage) was to meet the septuagenarian rear admiral at Beechey Island, the last anchorage of the *Erebus* and the *Terror*.

On reaching home in October 1833, the Rosses learned that eight months previously a small expedition, led by Commander George Back, had left England to bring them aid by the overland route. Back's descent to the Arctic shore by way of the Great Fish (Back's) River was to gain a celebrity quite out of proportion to its geographical importance. It conducted him to the very spot where the last survivors of Franklin's crews were to perish, and it brought on to the Arctic stage the gifted but ill-balanced Richard King, who was to lead the chorus of public dissatisfaction at the way in which the quest for Franklin was directed.

Early in 1832, with the *Victory* unreported for nearly three years, George Ross, father of James, began to agitate for an expedition to be sent to her relief. As the Admiralty declined to intervene, a committee of naval officers, scientists, and other influential persons was formed to raise money and draw up plans for a private expedition. When Richardson, first choice as its commander, was refused leave by the Royal Navy, the post was given to Back. Dr Richard King was appointed surgeon-naturalist to the party and its only other officer.

The plans guiding its operations were marked by the simplicity and optimism so characteristic of the era. John Ross was known to have relied on the cache at Fury Beach in event of emergency. As an emergency had obviously arisen, it was there he must be looked for. Back was therefore directed to set up his base near the east end of Great Slave Lake and locate the source of the Great Fish River, which by Indian report rose beyond the height of land and flowed northeast, presumably emptying into the Arctic. In the next summer he was to go down the river by boat, and on reaching the ocean, use his best endeavours to bring help to Ross. His journey would measure at least 800 miles by a route entirely unknown except at one point, where it was crossed by the outward track of Samuel Hearne. Back conjectured that the unknown river would, like the Coppermine, be infested with rapids. It is a safe guess that, apart from the immediate relatives of the missing crew, contributors were more hopeful of blazing a trail through the heart of a vast wilderness than of finding the crew of the *Victory* at the trail's end. The government, which had refused full responsibility for the expedition, contributed £2,000 to its cost, and the Colonial Secretary, by signing the committee's orders to Back, gave him the prestige of a public official. The Hudson's Bay Company undertook to furnish whatever aid might be required free of cost.

Back and King sailed for New York in February 1833, with three shipwrights. Boatmen and other helpers were to be recruited on the spot. They made the passage in thirty-five days, travelled to Montreal via the Hudson River, and there obtained boats and crews for the journey west. By way of the Ottawa River, Lakes Huron and Superior, and Rainy River, they came to Fort Alexander on Lake Winnipeg. There they met Governor George Simpson, who confirmed the pledges Back had already received of unstinted aid, and advised him that another old acquaintance, Chief Factor A. R. McLeod, had been appointed as aide to the expedition. They went up Lake Winnipeg to Norway House, where King was sent ahead with boats and cargoes, while Back waited to recruit *voyageurs*. Travelling light by canoe, he overtook him, and together they arrived at Portage la Loche, where a freight road links Churchill River on Hudson Bay basin with the Clearwater River, which drains into Great Slave Lake and the Arctic.

Back never achieved real greatness as a discoverer. But he was an artist, with a gift, never properly appreciated, for describing the peculiar landscape and atmosphere of the American West that would have delighted Theodore Roosevelt.

'After labouring with frequent halts through the thick woods,' he writes, 'we came suddenly upon the spot from which the picturesque and beautiful view from Portage la Loche bursts upon the sight. A thousand feet below the sylvan landscape [the Clearwater valley] lay spread before us to the extent of thirty-six miles in all the wild luxuriance of its summer clothing.

'There is something appalling in the vastness of a solitude like this. I had parted from my companions and was apparently the only living thing in the wilderness around me. Almost unconsciously I reloaded my gun and then stepping cautiously along the narrow ridge of the descent, glided silently into the valley ... It was a positive comfort to hear now and then the hollow tread of the men as they passed rapidly through the thicket which screened them from sight, and when the white tent was pitched and the curling smoke rose through the dense green of the forest, it seemed as if the spell of the desert was broken and the whole landscape was suddenly animated into light and cheerfulness.'

They sailed down the Clearwater and Athabasca rivers to Fort Chipewyan, and on the way were met and joined by Mr McLeod. King was left behind at Chipewyan to bring up the laden *bateaux* or river freighters, while Back and McLeod hurried forward to set up base and locate the unknown stream while summer weather permitted. They reached Fort Resolution on Great Slave Lake on 8 August. On the eleventh Back set out by canoe to discover the source of the *Thlew-eecho-dezeth* – the Great Fish River.

In the years ahead Back was to contribute to the misdirection of the search for Sir John Franklin by his insistence that under no circumstances would his shipwrecked crews have attempted to escape from the Arctic by way of the Great Fish River. It is only just, however, to note that the difficulties of the route, on which his conviction was based, were very real indeed. Under the direction of his Indian guide, Maufelly, he entered the northeast arm of Great Slave Lake, McLeod Bay. After much probing around bold rocks and into green recesses they came to the mouth of a stream, the Hoar Frost River, which Maufelly declared would lead them to their objective in only three portages. It proved to be 'a series of appalling cascades and rapids,' where the labour of portaging was made almost intolerable by intense heat and swarms of mosquitoes. In addition, Maufelly was plainly vexed with doubts that he dared not openly admit, and one of the party was disabled by indigestion:

'The unhappy interpreter,' says Back, 'had been unable to take any share in the work, and was evidently suffering severe pain which he begged me to assuage. I had only a box of common pills and some brandy, neither of which could be prudently applied in a case which seemed to require the skill and attention of a professional man. The poor fellow, however, persisted in his belief that I could relieve him, not doubting that anything under the name of medicine would answer the purpose. I yielded, there-fore, to his importunity, and indulged him, first with the contents of the box, which made him worse, and next with the contents of the bottle, which made him better.'

There was a fund of good humour in the man who, at a time of tension and physical discomfort, could take leave of his brandy so cheerfully.

After four days Maufelly confessed that he had mistaken his stream. Luckily he was not completely lost, and by a series of small, unconnected lakes, causing fifteen portages in a single day, he guided the party to Artillery Lake, a section of the water-way he had missed. From there they passed by water through Clinton-Colden to Aylmer Lake. Over a low ridge lay tiny Sussex Lake, with a northward-flowing stream issuing from it. They traced its downward course until it grew to a size and turbulence which they dared not brave in a damaged and rickety canoe. Back put about satisfied that this was the river he sought.

The party made its way back by the chain of waterways to Artillery Lake and found the river which Maufelly had missed on the way up – the Ah-el-dezeth, linking Artillery with Great Slave Lake. Here again Back reveals his artist's eye in describing the grim effect of an autumn twilight on the ragged expanse of the Canadian Shield:

'It was a sight altogether novel to me: I had seen nothing in the Old World at all resembling it. There was not the stern beauty of Alpine scenery, and still less the fair variety of hill and dale, forest and glade, which makes the charm of an European landscape. There was nothing to catch or detain the lingering eye, which wandered on, without a check, over endless lines of round-backed rocks, whose sides were rent into indescribably eccentric forms. It was like a stormy ocean suddenly petrified. Except for a few tawny and pale green lichens, there was nothing to relieve the horror of the scene, for fire had scathed it, and the grey and black stems of the mountain pine, which lay prostrate in mournful confusion, seemed like the blackened corpses of departed vegetation.'

Having noted to the east of Artillery Lake timber that would serve for the construction of boats, Back went down the Ah-el-dezeth to Great Slave Lake. At the nightly campfires he chatted with his crewmen and visiting Indians, gathering those snatches of Indian thought, myth, and folklore which gave his *Narrative* much of its charm. On the lake near the river's mouth he found Mr McLeod far advanced in the construction of his winter base, Fort Reliance.

In early spring the shipwrights began the construction of the two boats required for the relief of Ross and his crew. But in April a Hudson's Bay courier arrived bearing news of Ross's safe return the preceding October and a chart of his discoveries on and around the Isthmus of Boothia. Back's orders now were to take one boat only down the newly discovered river and chart the coast from its mouth to Point Turnagain.

At the beginning of June, Mr McLeod set out in advance with his hunters to kill and cache game for the main party. Back and King followed on the seventh. Supplies were carried and the boat hauled 200 miles by frozen river and lake past Artillery, Clinton-Colden, and Aylmer lakes to the source of the Great Fish River, and down its melting surface to Muskox Lake, where it became navigable.

Here Back met a party of Copper Indians, and among them poor Hood's old flame, Greenstockings. 'Though surrounded by a family with one urchin in her cloak clinging to her back and sundry other maternal accompaniments, I immediately recognized her and called her by her name, at which she laughed and said, " She was an old woman now," – begging at the same time that she might be relieved by the medicine man for she was much out of health. However, notwithstanding all this she was still the beauty of her tribe and with that consciousness which belongs to all belles, savage or polite, seemed by no means displeased when I sketched her portrait.'

With all his easygoing kindness, Back can hardly have met this poor woman without recalling with some remorse the quarrel of which she had been the cause. Another old friend aroused none but the kindliest recollections. Akaitcho, now old and infirm, came in to bid him farewell and give him a paternal admonition: 'Should you escape from the great water,' said he, 'take care that you are not caught by the winter, and thrown into a situation like that in which you were on your return from the Coppermine, for you are alone, and the Indians cannot help you.' The fondness of the natives for Back offsets the dislike freely expressed by the traders.

The boat party separated from Mr McLeod at Muskox Lake on 4 July, and made the descent to the sea in three weeks. The so-called river proved to be a chain of widely spaced lakes where the travellers were sometimes compelled to portage over ice or open a way with an axe. Time was lost also in prying into bays to find the outlet to the next reach of the stream. At the same time, its pronounced easterly trend aroused fears that the river might not empty into the Arctic at all but into one of the inlets of Hudson Bay. In addition to this, the river was infested with rapids, some so dangerous that only with difficulty could the *voyageurs* be persuaded to make the descent.

Back did not permit the cares of a commander to divert his mind from incident and scenery, which he describes with unfailing force and variety of phrase: 'Early in the following morning we pushed out into the beginnings of the rapids, when the boat was twirled about in the whirlpools against the oars; and but for the amazing strength of McKay, who steered, it must inevitably have been crushed against the faces of the protruding rocks. As we entered the defile, the rocks on the right presented a high and perpendicular front, so slaty and regular that it needed no force of imagination to suppose them severed at one great blow from the opposite range which, craggy, broken, and over-hanging, towered in many-coloured masses far above the chafing torrent. There was a deep settled gloom in the abyss – the effect of which was heightened by the hollow roar of the rapid, still in deep shade, and by the screaming of three large hawks which, frightened from their aerie, were hovering high above the middle of the pass, and gazing fixedly upon the first intruders on their solitude, so that I felt relieved as it were from a load when we once more burst forth into the bright sunshine of day.' At the exit from the lower end of Lake McDougall, 'the space occupying the centre from the first descent to the island was full of rocks of unequal heights over which the rapid foamed and boiled and rushed with impetuous and deadly fury. At that part it was raised into an arch; while the sides were yawning and cavernous, swallowing huge masses of ice, and then again tossing the splintered fragments high in the air.' Cargo was unstowed and portaged and the cataract safely run. Below it the course of the river pointed north. They crossed Lake Franklin and saw, at the top of the rapids at its outlet, an Eskimo encampment on the eastern bank.

The boat drew into shore, and the dialect which Back had learned on the Mackenzie was sufficiently intelligible to the natives for him to soothe their fears and convince them of his friendly intentions. So while the men assisted King and the *voyageurs* to portage boat and cargo past the rapids, the leader mingled with the others, fondled their children, sketched the portrait of one woman and professed himself delighted with the ' sprightliness ' of the rest. They gave him the pleasing intelligence that salt water was only one day's journey away. On the afternoon of the following day, 29 July 1834, 'while threading our way between some sandbanks, with a strong current, we caught sight of a majestic headland in the extreme north, which had a coast-like appearance. This important promontory was subsequently honoured by receiving the name of Her Royal Highness the Princess Victoria. ... This then may be considered as the mouth of the Thlew-ee-choh, which after a violent and tortuous course of five hundred and thirty geographical miles, running through an iron-ribbed country without a single tree on the whole line of its banks, expanding into fine large lakes with clear horizons, most embarrassing to the navigator, and broken into falls, cascades, and rapids, to the number of no less than eighty-three ... pours its waters into the Polar Sea '.

On the way down, Back had observed that the country traversed, though rugged and treeless, was green and fed herds of caribou. It may have been this circumstance which years later induced Captain Crozier of the *Terror* to ' start on tomorrow for

Back's Fish River' instead of retreating to Fury Beach.

The explorers were soon aware that they had emerged not onto an open sea but a long arm of salt water (Chantrey Inlet) infested on its western side by ice which blocked their intended route along the coast to the west. They worked their way to and past Montreal Island to Point Ogle, marking the mouth of the inlet on its western side. An attempt to make a survey in that direction on foot was foiled by rain, fog and mud. To the northeast, Back distinguished Ripon Island, which King declared, rightly as it proved, to be a cape. The sea appeared open in that quarter, and the surgeon urged his commander to sail in that direction, which offered the only hope of constructive achievement. Had Back done so, he might have corrected the error of James Ross and discovered the channel which separates King William Land from Boothia. But it was Ross's error that deterred him from entering what had tentatively been mapped as a bay of no great dimensions. Furthermore, King had a way of pressing his views with an insulting arrogance that would have provoked a milder man than Back to contradict him. Features on the south shore of what later proved to be King William Island were identified, and on the mainland, past Point Ogle, Point Richardson was seen. It was on the island's western side that the *Erebus* and the *Terror* were to come to grief. Had Back complied with King's advice, he might have been the means of the ships taking a safer channel. As it was, he never emerged from Chantrey Inlet, and on 14 August, as health and morale were suffering from inaction and foul weather, he turned back upstream. They wintered over at Fort Reliance with Mr McLeod. In the spring, Back left King to wind up the business of the expedition, and went home to deliver his report.

In fairness to Dr King, his impregnable conceit and exaggerated self-advertisement were founded on personal gifts of a very high order. Back's duties as commander and organizer had frequently required him to leave his surgeon in sole charge of freight and transport, and King, though untrained for the task and new to the country, people, and mode of travel, had discharged his duty with efficiency, and had, green as he was and a stranger to their ways, won the affection and respect of the men under his command. Back warmly praised his zealous attention to the health not only of expedition members but also of all others who needed his help. Dr Richardson, in the Appendix to Back's *Narrative*, spoke highly of his industry and success as a scientific collector. The unlucky surgeon's splendid gifts were marred only by a pitiable deficiency in common sense.

On his return to England, King found himself in competition with his former commander. Back's success, limited though it was, had revived official interest in northern discovery; it was proposed to renew the attempt – made unsuccessfully by Lyon in the *Griper* – to send a ship to Repulse Bay, whence boats could be dragged over the base of Melville Peninsula (now Rae Isthmus) for further exploration of the Arctic shore. King urged that another attempt by way of the Great Fish River would be far cheaper and more likely to succeed. But he could not convince the right people. The 340-ton bomb vessel *Terror* was commissioned for the Hudson Bay route, and Back was appointed to the command.

The 1836-7 cruise of the *Terror* accomplished nothing except to furnish an illustration of the dangers of the pack which voyagers in the ice long recalled with dread. She had almost reached her intended berth at Repulse Bay when, on 20 September, she was beset and suffered a heavy nip. 'The ship creaked as it were in agony,' wrote Back, 'and strong as she was, must have been stove and crushed, had not some of the smaller masses been forced under her bottom, and so diminished the strain by actually lifting her bow nearly two feet out of the water.' The *Terror* was a prisoner, and so remained for almost ten months. She began a slow drift southeast down the shore of Southampton Island. On 20 November some invisible force, a gale, perhaps, working on the open edge of the pack many miles away, drove her inshore, where pressure had forced ice thirty to forty feet up the face of the cliff. 'No art could save us, if we were once exposed to the grinding pressure of the mass against the rocks,' declared Back. To seaward pressure had thrown the level pack up so high that from its summit, Back could look down on the ship's maintop. In successive nips her bow was split and the lower part of her sternpost driven over several feet. The spring breakup brought no relief; the ship was hoisted on a mass of ice, the plaything of wind and current.

Her final release came about in a manner which must be without parallel in the story of the sea. The ice on the sides of the ship, loosened by continual sawing, broke off in a light swell, and liberated the mass under the ship's keel, which began to float upward with a rotary motion. Back describes what followed: 'Then it was that we beheld the strange and appalling spectacle of what may fitly be called a submerged berg, fixed low down with one end to the ship's side, while the other, with the purchase of a long lever, advantageously placed at right angles to the keel, was rising slowly to the surface. Meanwhile, those who happened to be below, finding everything falling, rushed or clambered on deck, where they saw the ship on her beam-ends, with the lee boats touching the water, and felt that a few moments only trembled between them and eternity.' Luckily the weather was calm; boats were stowed and got away, and the ice-saws again brought into action. 'Suddenly there was a perceptible yielding beneath the feet, and before a word could be spoken the liberated ship righted entirely; while the broken spars, the bent saw and the massy berg were all in commotion together.... The good ship was once more in her element and subject to the will of man.'

But once afloat she proved 'crazy, broken, and leaky'. It was a question whether, after surmounting appalling dangers, her crew would ever see harbour lights again. Improvised repairs and constant work at the pumps kept her afloat in a condition so critical that Back gave up all thought of making his home port and set a course for the nearest haven on the Irish coast. In a westerly gale the waterlogged ship was 'so difficult to steer as to compel us to take in all sail off the mainmast and to depend upon a triple-reefed fore-top-sail and foresail, etc.; even then she was so wild as to be scarcely manageable'. Fresh leaks started; First Lieutenant Smyth came to inform the captain that the exhausted men could no longer keep the water down and that the *Terror* was sinking. The stout-hearted Back rallied his crew, as he had his *voyageurs* sixteen years before, to keep the ship afloat, until on the afternoon of 3 September the welcome cry of 'land ho' assured them that their toils were almost ended. It was dark before they neared Lough Swilly; guns, rockets, and blue lights were unobserved by the pilot, so they brought their maimed and unhandy ship in by soundings past the lights of the fishermen's cottages and grounded her on a stretch of sand. Back noted in his journal: 'When morning came with what indescribable delight did we inhale the fragrance and contemplate the beauty of the land. Imagination could scarcely picture a scene so enchanting to our weary and frost-dazzled sight as appeared that soft and lovely landscape, with its fresh green tints and beautiful variety of hill and dale. It was an enjoyment to be felt but once in a life, and how much was that enjoyment enhanced when the wind suddenly changed and blew a gale offshore which a few hours earlier must have driven us back to sea and, in all probability, terminated our labours in a different way.'

So ended Back's polar service. His last two journeys had broken him; he never fully recovered his health, or accepted another seagoing appointment. He had achieved an honourable place in the second rank of Arctic discoverers, and of this medals bestowed on him by the geographical societies of London and Paris, and a knighthood conferred by the Queen, were no more than a fair acknowledgment. But for him semi-retirement would not mean obscurity: a celebrity of a very peculiar kind awaited him.

During Back's absence on the *Terror* cruise, Dr Richard King, brave, capable, and enterprising, wielding a powerful pen but possessing the mind of a child in all that concerned human relationships, had produced his own *Narrative* of the Fish River journey. In this book he solicited support for a second attempt at discovery by the same route and gravely explained to his readers the qualities that ensured his success where 'a Parry, a Franklin, and a Back' had failed. To set off his own merits, he passed some ill-natured censures on Back – for too much familiarity with the men, for imposing on his second-in-command (on his Mackenzie journey Franklin had delegated pretty much the same duties to Back as Back required of King), and for blundering hesitation in the Fish River estuary. For good measure he censured the management of the Hudson's Bay Company, an organization whose goodwill would be very necessary to him should his projected journey materialize, and fixed a vicious and irrelevant slander on Roman Catholic missions to the Indians. King had grasped the principle that a writer can win readers by savaging an individual or establishment, but he lacked the common sense to perceive that the notice which he obtained in certain newspapers was dearly purchased by the offence he gave to the friends and patrons of discovery who were bound by ties of friendship and loyalty to Back. As a result, he did not obtain the necessary funds for his projected voyage of discovery, was snubbed by the Royal Geographical Society, and relapsed into obscurity until the last voyage of the *Erebus* and the *Terror* gave him fresh scope for proving the soundness of his views and his lamentable want of tact in presenting them.

Back and King were vivid individuals who lent colour to events in which they participated out of proportion to their positive contributions. It is evident that they had quarrelled on the Fish River journey. Back's last letter of instructions to King is phrased with a haughty insolence that would have provoked a milder person than the hot-headed and unforgiving surgeon:

'It does not occur to me that I have anything to add, except the tender of my thanks for the uniform attention that you have bestowed upon the health of the people and the general manner in which you have made yourself useful throughout the service.'

'– made yourself useful! –' This to the comrade of many months of toil and hardship, who had spared Back much trouble and responsibility and had virtually shared the command. It was a calculated insult, which King, as he afterward abundantly proved, would be the last man to forgive.

As this was an official document, King violated no confidence in publishing it. Yet it was neither wise nor generous to do so. In his *Narrative,* Back had gone out of his way to praise the character and services of his surgeon, and it was ungracious of King to advertise the quarrel which his commander was willing to forget.

King may have been swayed by the prejudice which the clerks and factors of the fur company had conceived against his commander. Back was popular with all sorts of natives and half-breeds, with whom he talked easily in their various patois. He was popular, according to his own report (which there is no reason to doubt), with all women – Indian, Eskimo, or white. But no Hudson's Bay Company official seems to speak well of him. Shortly after King's return to England a company officer sent him a letter (published by King after the writer's death) in which, alluding to King's plans for his own expedition, he says: 'Peter Taylor is at Lac la Pluie, and fully expects you. Both he, as well as your other companions in adventure, are high in your praise, while Sir George Back is the theme of their aversion and contempt.' Thomas Simpson, who on their first meeting found Back affable, but easy-going and deficient in authority, later described him extravagantly as 'not only a vain, but a bad man'. Other critics expressed the same dislike in more measured language. It seems that Back, courageous and persevering in urgent and demanding situations, was at other times vain, self-indulgent, and patronizing. In a group portrait as late as 1850 he appears with the delicately curled hair fashionable in the era of George IV but not acceptable in the shaggier Victorian epoch. These superficial faults were just the ones to repel the hard-bitten Scots who formed the top echelon of the company's servants, but they do not invalidate the judgment in the *Dictionary of National Biography* that Back 'in bravery, intelligence and love of adventure . . . was the very model of an English sailor'. In 1853, when Dr John Rae left England on his second journey to Pelly Bay, Back entrusted him with a finely mounted hunting knife as a gift to Ooligbuck, his friend on the Mackenzie twenty-seven years before. One can only hope that the fiery King and Back's other critics had as long a memory for an old comrade. There was no vain display here, for if the letter in which Rae mentioned this transaction had not also contained the first authentic tidings of the crews of the *Erebus* and the *Terror*, Back's thoughtful kindness would never have been noticed outside the office to which the dispatch was addressed.

While Dr King was winning favourable comment in the London press, and inaugurating his long feud with the members of the Arctic Establishment, the task of discovery which he coveted so ardently was being carried out by others. The unfortunate surgeon had offended not only George Back, but the far more formidable George Simpson. The Governor wanted no more of King's comments on the way the company did business, and anticipated his return to the Northwest by delegating to his own officers and *voyageurs* the completion of the Arctic coastal chart.

As surveyor-scientist he appointed his own nephew, the gifted, ambitious egomaniac Thomas Simpson, and, to ensure the loyalty of the *voyageurs*, who detested the young man's arrogance, he placed Franklin's old colleague, Chief Factor Peter Warren Dease, in supreme charge of the boat parties. To set a tutor over the key officer in such an enterprise seems an unpromising expedient, but George Simpson knew his men, and it worked admirably. For three seasons Dease, 'a worthy, indolent, illiterate soul,' according to the patronizing Thomas Simpson, kept the men in good humour and responsive to the most exacting demands of his impetuous young colleague.

Their first assignment was completion of the North Alaska chart from Return Reef to Point Barrow. They reached the former point well in advance of Franklin's date, and had come within sixty miles of Point Barrow when, like Franklin, they were grounded by ice. Simpson set out with a small party to cover this distance on foot; when the ice moved offshore he borrowed an Eskimo umiak, reached Point Barrow, and so linked his survey with that of Beechey from Bering Strait.

For the other part of his task, an eastward survey from Franklin's Point Turnagain, Simpson chose a far easier line of approach than Back's Fish River. The explorers set up their winter quarters at Fort Confidence, at the northeast angle of Great Bear Lake. In the spring of 1838 they dragged their boats to the Coppermine and set sail past Bathurst Inlet to Point Turn-again, where they were halted by ice. Again the unwearied Simpson, despite mud, fog, and foul weather, made a survey on foot as far as Cape Alexander. From there the crews returned to winter at Confidence. Dease had by now had enough but, over-ruled by the resolute Simpson, consented to try once more.

In the summer of 1839, after a slow start, they made good progress, and the beginning of August found them far to the east, approaching Ross's King William Land. This was found to be separated from the continent by a strait, three miles across at its narrows, Simpson Strait. Passing through this, they found on the right hand a low sandy cape, which men who had been with Back declared to be Point Ogle. This identification was confirmed when, circling into Chantrey Inlet, they touched at Montreal Island and obtained a distant view of Victoria Headland, recognized from 'Back's exquisite drawing'.

It was now mid-August, and they were many hundreds of miles from their base. Nonetheless, Simpson overrode the scruples of his easygoing superior, and sailed on to the northeast. He converted the Ripon Island of Back into Cape Britannia, and forty miles to the east reached his farthest on the Castor and Pollux

89

River at the base of Boothia Isthmus. Still unsatisfied, Simpson prolonged the voyage home by mapping the south shore of King William Land and building a cairn at Cape Herschel, according to his estimate, fifty-seven miles south of James Ross's pillar on Point Victory. Farther to the west, at Cape Colborne, he picked up the south shore of Victoria Island, and laid down 150 miles of its coast, including Cambridge Bay and Wellington Bay. Then the boats veered towards the mainland, and the continuity of Victoria Island with the Wollaston Land of Richardson remained unproved. They went up the Coppermine to Bloody Falls, overland to Fort Confidence, crossed Great Bear Lake in wild autumn weather, and reached Fort Simpson on the upper Mackenzie River in mid-October in a temperature of 14 degrees below zero. Simpson had accomplished the finest single-season voyage of discovery in the history of the American Arctic; the northern seaboard was now charted from Bering Strait to the isthmus of Boothia.

According to Simpson's observations off the Castor and Pollux River, that isthmus did not exist. The Rosses, he held, had been misinformed by the Eskimos, and one could complete the Northwest Passage by sailing direct from the mouth of Back's River to Ross's Felix Harbour. This error was apparently endorsed by John Barrow, who entered it upon the map of the second volume of his *Arctic Voyages* – whether because he believed it, or just to provoke John Ross, we have no means of deciding.

This opinion was harmless, especially as most authorities agreed with Ross in rejecting it. But Simpson made another mistake of much graver import. He concurred in James Ross's belief that to the north of the Castor and Pollux River a neck of land united Boothia with King William Land. James Ross had stretched a mythical barrier across the channel east of King William Land; Back, by loitering in the Fish River estuary, had missed the chance of correcting this mistake; now Simpson had helped to confirm it.

There remained one chance that the error might be exposed and the seas around King William Land correctly defined. Thomas Simpson was eager to prove his point by going down the Great Fish River and sailing through Ross's supposed isthmus to Fury and Hecla Strait. By attempting this impossible feat he would undoubtedly have anticipated Rae and found the channel dividing Boothia from King William Land. Unluckily, Dease was on extended leave, and George Simpson refused to send his nephew north without him. The London committee overruled him and granted Thomas authority to make the projected journey; but before advice of this reached him, the unhappy young man, over-wrought and possessed by a morbid fear that Dease would receive the credit for his magnificent exploit, elected to take leave in Europe also. He left the Red River with four half-breed com-panions on his way to New York and died by suicide or murder on the Minnesota prairie.

The death of Thomas Simpson is still shrouded in mystery. According to the sworn statement of one of his half-breed escorts, Simpson shot two of his companions in a fit of manic depression and then took his own life. His brother, Alexander, maintained that he must have killed the two men in self-defence before falling victim to a murderous assault, and this view, though based on conjecture only, found support among the devout Scottish fur traders, who were unwilling to believe that even madness could drive one of their number to crime. The doubt persists even today. It has been suggested that George Simpson, fearing that Thomas's explorations would open the Arctic to commerce and end the monopoly of the Hudson's Bay Company, deliberately procured his nephew's murder. A more improbable hypothesis has never been proposed. George Simpson had invited Thomas to undertake his Arctic survey, and the same George Simpson em-ployed Dr Rae to continue it after his death. Also, supposing him to be capable of such a crime, he was far too shrewd to employ as one of his accomplices the ignorant half-breed James Bird, who signed his sworn declaration with an *X*. Furthermore, it seems evident that Simpson's murder, if murder it was, was unpremeditated, and arose from a chance quarrel. Four men who have conspired to assassinate a fifth would not permit him to kill two of their number before they effected their purpose. An insulting word or gesture from one man to fix the victim's atten-tion, a blow from behind from another, and it would all be over. However it came about, the death of Thomas Simpson was a twofold misfortune. It ended, in his thirty-second year, the life of a man of most unusual gifts, and it left unsolved the geogra-phical intricacies of King William Land and Boothia.

From 1818 to 1839 public and private expeditions had, without intermission, been probing into the complexities of the North American archipelago. Several years of inactivity ensued, during which the impulse for a final grand effort was gathering force.

In the years 1839 to 1843, Captain James Ross, whose ambition it was to visit *both* Magnetic Poles, made three summer voyages of exploration in Antarctic waters, with the *Erebus* and the *Terror*. He was the first to produce an intelligible map of any considerable section of the southern continent; he gave the name of his first lieutenant to McMurdo Sound, a channel made famous early in this century by the journeys of Robert Falcon Scott and Ernest Henry Shackleton, and familiar today to hundreds of New Zealanders and Americans. His achievement, a considerable improvement on that of his immediate predecessors in those waters, the Frenchman Dumont D'Urville and the American Charles Wilkes, by a process natural, if illogical, revived hopes in the navigability of the Northwest Passage. The undertaking would be costly and offered no hope of commercial returns. But the pride of England, the world's greatest naval and commercial power, was again aroused. Simpson's great boat journey had narrowed the unexplored gap between sea and sea, and it seemed disgraceful to leave a task so nearly accomplished to the sailors of a foreign power. Sir John Barrow, now eighty years of age and on the point of retirement, was an ardent promoter of the scheme. The Prime Minister, the thrifty Sir Robert Peel, yielded. The *Erebus* and the *Terror* were chosen for the service, given a refit and equipped with auxiliary steam power. Sir James Ross (knighted for his Antarctic cruise) was offered the command. But Ross, forty-four years old and the holder of a record in polar travel that must be unequalled – for twenty-six years he had been almost continually employed in the one or the other of the frigid zones – declined, for he wished to marry. He used his influence to obtain the appointment for Sir John Franklin.

Barrow had intended the command for his gifted young friend James Fitzjames, who was as old and as experienced as Parry was in 1819, when he embarked on his great voyage to Melville Island. But in the last twenty years a corps of Arctic veterans, non-existent when Parry received his commission, had grown up, and it would have been unreasonable to pass them over in favour of a young man who had never been in the ice. Ross's recent second-in-command, Captain F. R. M. Crozier, much senior to

Fitzjames in rank, was also a candidate. Though otherwise well-fitted, Crozier was not too popular with his men; and this could be a serious disability on an Arctic voyage where almost the first requirement of a commander was the capacity to keep the men contented and happy in the prolonged idleness of winter quarters. Hence there was excellent reason for placing the elderly, but well-liked Franklin over them both. He was now fifty-eight, but despite his years he was passionately desirous of the appointment. In his recently completed term as governor of the colony of Tasmania he had promoted education and improved the lot of the convict settlers, but in other respects his administration had not been successful. The honest, simple-minded authoritarian had found himself out of place in the hustling frontier society, with its unscrupulous political climbers and crudely uninhibited press. Recalled by the Colonial Office with wanton discourtesy, the old sailor came home hurt and humiliated, and more than ready to restore his self-esteem by some notable exploit in his own field. 'If you don't let him go,' said Parry to the First Lord of the Admiralty, 'the man will die of disappointment.' So Franklin, Crozier, and Fitzjames were given charge of the expedition, and nothing remained but to draw up orders for their proper guidance.

In the Victorian Age, as in our own, the Establishment was an inviting target for irresponsible criticism, and in consequence the British Admiralty has suffered much censure for sending Franklin out on so dangerous a mission, and for its prolonged, costly, and fruitless endeavours to find him and bring him back. The censure is unjust or, at least, ought to be aimed at others than the top naval administrators. The planning and management of polar voyages had formed no part of their training and experience. They could, in response to popular demand, authorize such a voyage; they could provide ships and supplies and define the end purpose of the expedition; but for the method of fulfilling that purpose they were entirely dependent upon men with Arctic experience. Sir John Franklin drew up his own Orders with the help of Barrow, Parry, and Sir James Ross.

His task was much simplified by discoveries already made. He himself, with Richardson, Beechey, and Thomas Simpson, had laid bare almost the entire continental shore from Bering Strait to Boothia. But Boothia was rightly supposed to be part of the continent. There was no navigable passage by that route. From the east, Parry had thrust his way in through Lancaster Sound to Melville Island, overlapping by twenty degrees of longitude the eastward penetration of Simpson. Parry had been stopped by impenetrable ice, therefore there was little hope of a navigable route there. But his track lay only 300 miles north of the known continental shore. Cross that gap by sea and the passage was complete. Parry had observed no land to the south between Cape Walker and Banks Island, a distance of 300 miles. These considerations make the terms of the orders drawn up for Franklin easily understood. He was to pass through Lancaster Sound and steer west until he passed North Somerset, which was supposed to be joined to Boothia Peninsula; from Cape Walker he was to sail south or southwest for the continental shore. He was warned not to attempt Regent's Inlet, as being almost certainly a dead-end, and not to follow Parry's Melville Island route, as ice there was judged to be a permanent barrier. In brief, he was to make his southward jog between Cape Walker and Banks Land. If Dease and Simpson had proved the continuity of Victoria Land with Wollaston Land, this course would not have seemed so promising. In any case, in the event that the prescribed route was ice-choked, the expedition was given the option of going up Wellington Channel and attempting to pass north of Melville Island.

It is unlikely that Franklin and those who helped to draft his orders shared the cheerful confidence of the junior officers of the expedition. Those officers perceived that every expedition which had entered the archipelago had returned without major mishap and with fewer casualties than were usual on a tropical station. The sober old veterans who conferred with Franklin probably regarded these statistics as an example of luck. Parry's *Hecla* and *Fury* had been thrust violently on the shore – it was by mere luck that the *Hecla* had been refloated to bring both crews home. The survival of John Ross was to be ascribed to an almost miraculous combination of circumstances: friendly Eskimos and game on Boothia – by no means to be found everywhere in the Arctic – the wreck cache of the Fury, and the lucky encounter with a whaling ship in Lancaster Sound. The ice mass on which the *Terror* had been heaved up had tipped, plunging the ship into the water to her port rail. It might just as easily have rolled clean over, submerging ship and men without trace. Three near misses in seven voyages was an alarmingly high ratio. The proper course, as Franklin and his advisers knew, would have been to arrange for a relief ship to sail if the expedition was unreported after two years, with a rendezvous at Cape Walker, where the crews could retreat if the *Erebus* and the *Terror* became ice-bound. But the government, reluctant enough already, would have cancelled the whole enterprise rather than sanction this additional outlay. So Franklin sailed with no provision for his rescue if things went wrong. It was better, he and the others probably reasoned, to sail uninsured than not to sail at all.

It often happens, when officials suppress in the public interest some disturbing fact or condition, that some private person pops up to expose what they think it prudent to hide. It was so now. As early as 21 December 1844, Dr Richard King had written to Sir John Barrow urging that land-based expeditions working by boat were both much cheaper and more fruitful in geographical results:

'Had you advocated in favour of the Polar Land Journeys with a tithe of the zeal you have the Polar Sea Expeditions the Northwest Passage would long have ceased to be a problem, and, instead of a Baronetcy you would deserve a Peerage, for the country would have been saved at least two hundred thousand pounds.'

Like other controversialists, King provided fuel for debate and denunciation by wilfully misunderstanding the position of his adversary. Barrow had been *the* great promoter of both land-based and seagoing journeys, and deserved more courteous language from a polar enthusiast like King. Furthermore, as King well knew, the purpose of the expedition planned was not primarily to extend or add detail to the map; it was the specific feat of sending a *ship* through the Northwest Passage before any intruding foreigner did so. King, who could not help being insulting, went on:

'If you are really in earnest upon this subject, you have but one course to pursue; search for the truth, and value it when you find it. Another fruitless Polar Sea Expedition, and fruitless it will assuredly be, if not well digested, will be a lasting blot on the annals of our voyages of discovery.'

It is easy to imagine how such language from a young civilian would affect the fiery octogenarian Barrow, accustomed for forty years to the deference of learned scientists and grizzled post captains. In another letter to the Admiralty (20 February 1845) King made a very practical suggestion, this time in temperate language. By what must have been for him a great exercise of self-control, he admitted the validity of the Northwest Passage project, but urged that before it was attempted one boat party should descend the Great Fish River to unravel the complexities of the Boothia-King William Land area, and another, by way of Great Bear Lake and the Coppermine, to ascertain if Thomas Simpson had been correct in supposing Wollaston Land and Victoria Land to be separated by an arm of the sea. The latter proposal was eminently sensible in view of Franklin's intended course. Had it been carried out, it would have been ascertained that the 300-mile gap between Cape Walker and Banks Land was almost entirely taken up by the sprawling Victoria-Wollaston complex, now Victoria Island. It is a pity, perhaps, that King had not reversed the order of his letters, and made this practical suggestion *before* hurling defiance at Sir John Barrow. His suggestion was disregarded, and the *Erebus* and the *Terror* sailed from the Thames in May 1845. They were the best ships possible for the service and bore the finest crews and equipment their country could provide. The steam power with which they were furnished was thought to be a further assurance of success, though its use was restricted by a limited supply of coal. Sir John Ross predicted that they would never come back; King asserted that Franklin would have to try to drift through with the ice, and if he quotes himself correctly, added the ungenteel sneer that he would probably form 'the nucleus of an iceberg.' Despite these sinister prophecies, Franklin was to discover the Northwest Passage and almost sail through it. It is a droll reflection that, had Back heeded his surgeon when in the Fish River estuary and coasted up the west shore of Boothia, the Ross map would have been corrected, the *Erebus* and the *Terror* might have come through in triumph, and the credit would have been due to Richard King.

In the same year, 1845, Sir John Barrow retired. As true a friend as he was a good hater, he asked two favours in return for more than forty years' service to the State – a knighthood for Dr John Richardson and a post captaincy for Commander James Fitzjames. Both requests were granted. Richardson lived for twenty years to enjoy his honour; Fitzjames never knew of his.

Between the sailing of the *Erebus* and the *Terror* and the first move to bring them relief, a journey was made which introduced a new man and new methods to the sphere of Arctic travel. Sir George Simpson appointed a servant of the company, Dr John Rae, to survey the unknown coast extending from Boothia Isthmus to Fury and Hecla Strait. Rae's procedure was a modification of Back's intended method on his ill-fated *Terror* cruise. In the summer of 1846 he mustered at York Factory a party of thirteen – Orkney boatmen, half-breeds, Indians, and Eskimos – and travelled to the top of Repulse Bay, where he set up base at Fort Hope. He brought supplies for four months only, being resolved to live off the country, which he did with complete success by fishing and killing deer. In the spring of 1847 with six men and dog teams he crossed Rae Isthmus, laid down the west shore of Committee Bay and Pelly Bay, and arrived at a region which Sir James Ross from his description later identified as Lord Mayor Bay, where the *Victory* had been abandoned. After returning to his base he set out with a fresh party and went up the west side of Melville Peninsula to within ten miles of Fury and Hecla Strait. The entire continental shore was mapped except for the west side of Boothia Peninsula. Rae was to attempt that also seven years later with most unexpected results.

Rae's achievement was unique for his own age and made him the unacknowledged teacher of twentieth-century travellers such as Vilhjalmur Stefansson and the enigmatical Frederick Cook. Yet the irrepressible Dr King put the young man in his place as firmly as he had the patriarchal Barrow. While commending the economy of Rae's method, he censured him for travelling while the land was snow-covered – King himself had experienced on Point Ogle the impossibility of walking through the mud of the melting season – and for taking short cuts across capes and bays. These errors he charitably ascribed to Rae's inexperience. As King's own experience was confined to a voyage down and up an inland river under the tuition of a naval officer whom he heartily despised, his superiority of tone sounds somewhat ridiculous, but the doctor was one of those deerstalkers who fire at anything they see moving, man or beast. He was yet to snipe, unintentionally perhaps, at his Sovereign Lady, Queen Victoria.

D

4   Fruitless Search from East and West

Many months elapsed before any concern was felt or expressed for the safety of Franklin and his adventurous crews. It was well understood by the British public that the American Arctic was navigable for two summer months only. Consequently, Sir John Franklin, if he succeeded in making the passage, would emerge from Bering Strait in August or September; and dispatches left at a Russian post in Kamchatka would reach England late in the old year or early in the new. If none arrived at that season, hope must be deferred for almost twelve months. No concern was felt in early 1846 at the absence of news; there was no serious expectation that the cruise could be completed in one season. It was felt, however, by informed persons that unless Franklin was reported by the end of the year he must be in serious difficulty, and Sir John Ross, now in his seventieth year, wrote to inform the Admiralty that he had promised Franklin to head a relief expedition if he was still unreported in 1847. Their Lordships, after the deliberate manner of permanent officials, invited comment from Parry and others. When no dispatches arrived for the second season, no effective steps had been taken, but plans were formed for rescue operations in 1848. It was resolved to send two ships, well supplied, into Barrow Strait to trace the missing vessels to Cape Walker and beyond, and to station in Bering Strait the bark H.M.S. *Plover,* whose boats could search the Arctic shore of Alaska while a second boat expedition would traverse the coast from the Mackenzie to the Coppermine and, it was hoped, link up with the ships coming in from Bering Strait. It was a trim, if somewhat visionary plan of operations – if each

This is the Arctic as known when McClure came in from the west. It is identical with Franklin's chart on his last voyage except for the north and west shores of Somerset Island – just east of Cape Walker. These were surveyed by James Ross and McClintock in 1849.

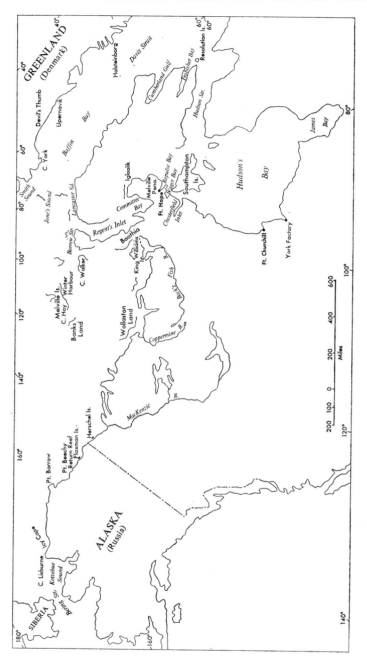

detachment fulfilled its assignment, Franklin's intended route would be covered all the way from Cape Walker to the North Pacific. But there was always the possibility that he had been deflected by ice from his prescribed course. Captain Beechey therefore recommended that a boat party be sent by way of the Great Fish River to Boothia and King William Land. Sir James Ross disagreed, firmly believing that the *Erebus* and the *Terror* had passed Cape Walker and become entangled in heavy ice drifting eastward from Melville Island. No hint of this danger is given in Franklin's orders, though no doubt Ross had privately communicated his fears to Franklin. But the Fish River hypothesis was not so easily dismissed, for by now Dr Richard King was alerted.

After his usage of Sir John Barrow, King was understandably shy of communicating directly with the Admiralty, but he stated his views at great length to Earl Grey, whom, as Secretary of State for the Colonies, he considered to be equally responsible for the safety of the missing crews. In a number of letters dated November and December 1847, he gives it as his belief that Franklin had come to grief to the west of North Somerset – the same theory, differently expressed, as that of Sir James Ross – and that proposed measures for his relief were inadequate. The ice was unpredictable, and the rescue ships might find Barrow Strait blocked and not even reach Cape Walker. In any case, vessels with sail only were not likely to penetrate as far as Franklin, who had the advantage of steam. Therefore King advised that the ships plant food depots at specified points in the Barrow Strait region, while he was to go down the Fish River by boat, proceed between King William Land and Victoria Land, find the ice-bound crews, and advise them where the depots were to be found. 'I have offered to Your Lordships to undertake the boldest journey which has ever been proposed. How, Your Lordship may inquire, is this Herculean task to be performed? Upon what grounds do I rest my hope of success? I would state in answer, that it is necessary the leader of such a journey should have an intimate knowledge of the country and the people through which he must pass – the health to stand the rigour of the climate and the strength to undergo the fatigue of body and mind to which he will be subjected. It is because I have these requisites, which I conscientiously believe are not to be found in another, that I hope to effect my purpose.'

If the noble and fastidious lord to whom these words were addressed winced a little at their vulgar boastfulness, he must have shuddered at the sequel. King let none of his correspondents forget that he had, as Thomas Simpson had proved, interpreted land features, seen at a distance from the Fish River estuary, more accurately than Back, and he perversely chose to believe that that officer who had served his country with distinction for thirty years, who had suffered wounds and captivity in war and near death on the tundra, had been knighted for mistaking Cape Britannia for Ripon Island! 'I am not, however,' King wrote, 'asking of your Lordship to recommend to Her Majesty the bestowing upon me a mark of approbation, as a reward for the soundess of my views, which has been bestowed upon those who contradicted them.' In other words, he wished the Queen to know that, though she had conferred a title on Back for being wrong, he was not insisting on a similar honour for being right. The luckless Dr King could never grasp the effect of the language he used. He intended merely a gibe at the detested Back, not perceiving that when he implied that a reward had been undeservedly bestowed, he was censuring not so much the recipient as the donor. It is not likely that Lord Grey acquainted his Royal Mistress with this awful piece of impertinence. If he did, we may be sure that Queen Victoria was 'not amused'.

Through the medium of a secretary Lord Grey wrote to inform King that the Franklin expedition was *not* a colonial matter, and referred him to the Admiralty. With misgivings, perhaps, but with unabated verve, King transferred his application to that body. The Admiralty transferred it to Sir James Ross.

Ross, believing like King that Franklin had sailed past Cape Walker and become ice-bound to the southwest, judged that his crews would either go forward to the Coppermine or back to Lancaster Sound, as the *Victory* party had done. 'I cannot conceive any position in which they could be placed from which they would make for the Great Fish River,' Ross opined and added that if King did go to their rescue with the limited transport he proposed he 'would more probably be in a condition to require than to afford relief.' King was to take a sumptuous revenge for this (perhaps deserved) sarcasm. The Admiralty, in reply to King's request for 'very early information' so that he might have time to dispose of his medical and scientific appointments, stated that they had 'no intention of altering their present arrange-ments, or of making any others that will require your assistance, or force you to make the sacrifices which you appear to contem-plate'.

Thus repelled with cold insolence by the authorities, King was inspired to antagonize the only private person who might have given him the polar command he so ardently coveted. Lady Franklin had offered a reward of £1,000 to any whaling ship that brought news of the missing expedition. King wrote to her with blunt discourtesy: 'Your offer is altogether out of the ques-tion.... You have been very ill-advised.' He suggested that the £1,000 would be better invested with himself. The lady's pride was deeply hurt. 'Of Dr King I wish to say nothing,' she wrote – perhaps, as her biographer wittily observes, 'because Dr King wished to say too much.' Lady Franklin's own idea was to send a ship by way of Regent's Inlet to the natives of Boothia. Her scheme was more justifiable than King's, and was just as likely to have succeeded. But neither was effectively applied.

In the autumn of 1854, when the truth about Franklin's crews was partially revealed, one newspaper affirmed that 'they died of official pig-headedness and Admiralty neglect'. Another asserted that 'his [Franklin's] blood and the blood of his brave com-panions' was on the head of the Admiralty. A third varied the metaphor by laying the blame at the door of Sir George Back. Earl Grey got away with milder rebuke. As Dr King's published collection of these press comments contains no reference to Sir James Ross, it is safe to assume that he escaped censure alto-gether.

These opinions are to some extent supported by Franklin's excellent modern biographer, G. F. Lamb. He believes that had King been furnished the means for his proposed journey, 'at least some survivors might have been rescued'. This is almost certainly an error. According to Eskimo report, the thirty or forty men who reached the mainland in the spring of 1848 died 'before the dis-ruption of the ice' – that is, when the Fish River was still un-navigable. To rescue them King would have had to come down the river in the summer of 1847, that is complete his voyage almost as soon as it was first proposed. The odds are that he would not have arrived before 1849. He would then, at least, have discovered the scene and nature of the disaster and spared the public several years of costly and fruitless endeavour.

King had no doubt as to where the blame for that lay. He compiled a list of those who sat on Admiralty boards during the years of the Franklin search, listing marginally their varying periods of service, so that the individual share in responsibility, 'the exact amount of guilt which lies at each man's door,' might be justly appraised. This is wholly unfair. Admiralty officials could not be expected to possess the specialized knowledge the crisis demanded. They took the proper course of consulting the 'Arctic Council,' a group of ten, including Parry, James Ross, Richardson, Beechey, Sabine, and Back. King objected to the inclusion of James Ross and Back because both had made 'very grave errors', and suggested himself and Sir John Ross as trustier councillors. The only guilt that can be attributed to the Admiralty was its rejection of this sage advice; for the rest, the Arctic Council must shoulder responsibility. In fairness to them, it must be remembered that the Fish River hypothesis was improbable as long as it was believed that Franklin had passed Cape Walker, and that this improbability was generally strengthened by the reports of officers returning from their unsuccessful search. It was also obvious that King was passionately insistent about the Fish River route because it was the only part of the Arctic of which he had first-hand knowledge. The Admiralty should have heeded Beechey's admonition that, whatever the probabilities, *no part* of the continental shore should be left unsearched, but James Ross and Back were incensed by King's attacks and rejected his ideas contemptuously. For the rest, the misdirection of rescue expeditions was due less to errors of judgment than to the same mysterious fatality which had led up to the disaster. Critics of the Admiralty and of the council forget that it was accident only which hindered Rae in 1851 and Collinson in 1853 from grasping the clue they sought.

In February 1848, the *Plover* sailed for her Alaskan station. An anonymous critic, the first of many, wrote to the press that she was slow sailing, and would not reach her destination that season. He was right in his prediction, but not perhaps in his implied censure. Such ships were chosen not for speed but for stowage capacity, and for a shape which rose to pressure. It is a fact seldom, if ever, noted that of all the naval vessels sent into the Arctic during this period, none was crushed by the ice until after abandonment by her crew. Richardson and Rae sailed for America on their way to the Mackenzie. With the coming of spring Sir James Ross in the *Enterprise* with Captain Bird in the *Investigator* set out for Lancaster Sound and Barrow Strait.

Ross's expedition was fated to the ill luck which King, with his usual inspired guesswork, had predicted. Yet the voyage was remarkable – if not for its achievement, for the ships and men who shared in it. The *Enterprise* and the *Investigator* were destined at a future date to make two of the most extraordinary voyages in the history of the north. And the first and second lieutenants of the *Enterprise*, Robert McClure and Leopold McClintock, Irishmen both, were to win reputations in the frozen seas second only to that of the great Franklin himself.

Ross was not long in getting a foretaste of the frustrations in store for him. He worked up the Greenland shore and was a little to the north of Upernavik, when he received warning from the whaler *Lord Gambier* that the 'close, compact and heavy' condition of the ice made passage through the Middle Ice out of the question that season. So he worked his way around by the North Water, and, ploughing through moderate ice with heavy pieces interspersed, made his way into Lancaster Sound and arrived off Cape York on north Baffin Island on 1 September, nearly a month later than Parry had been on his Melville Island voyage. McClintock was commended for taking a boat ashore and setting up a sign under difficult conditions. Ross pushed on for the west toward Cape Walker, where he hoped to find a record of the missing ships, but off Wellington Channel he was stopped, not by pack ice but by solid ice that lay unbroken by warmth and summer gales. Temperatures were unseasonably low, and with more than fifteen degrees of frost there was danger that the ships, like Back's *Terror*, would be frozen in the open sea. So they promptly put about and on 11 September worked their way into Port Leopold on the northeast angle of Somerset Island. A day later the harbour would have been blocked, and the ships left at the mercy of the drifting pack. The stubborn Ross tried to get the *Enterprise* out and steer again for Cape Walker but, perhaps luckily, was thwarted by the ice. Actually he was in a good position for examining various courses the *Erebus* and the *Terror* might have followed, being close to Barrow Strait, Regent's Inlet, Wellington Channel, and, though he did not know it, Peel

Sound. Cape Walker, Franklin's pivotal point, lay more than 100 miles to the west.

The two crews spent a miserable and depressing winter at Port Leopold. The abnormally severe ice conditions and the imprisonment of the ships on the very threshold of the field of search had a severe disappointment. No achievement had been registered to cheer the men and offset the long months of cold and discomfort. Parry's favourite officer James Ross was surprisingly aloof and neglectful of providing occupation and entertainment for the men; nor was Robert McClure the man to make up for his captain's deficiencies. Some employment and amusement were found in the trapping of Arctic foxes, which were turned loose again bearing metal collars with notes attached giving the location of the rescue ships and their intended course in the coming summer.

But the previous autumn had established the point, which the cold late spring of 1849 emphasized, that ships were not to be relied on for effective prosecution of the search. During the winter, carpenters constructed sledges, and as soon as weather permitted, Ross and McClintock, with twelve men hauling supplies on two sledges, set out along the north shore of Somerset Island in the direction of Cape Walker. They arrived at the Cape Bunny of Parry's chart and found the shoreline bending away to the south and a broad strait, Peel Sound, lying between them and Cape Walker. As they were confident of attaining Cape Walker on shipboard when the ice broke up, they followed the coast to the south and, after having charted in all 150 miles of new shoreline, ended their journey at Four River Point. Fifty miles farther to the south a massive headland, Cape Bird, was clearly seen. In the bright sunlight it was impossible to tell whether sea or snow-covered land lay beyond it. In fact it was sea, and the lost ships had sailed through it. One of the oddest circumstances of this prolonged manhunt was that although Ross and McClintock chanced upon the right lead at the outset, it was followed up only nine years later, after the scene of the disaster had been identified by other means.

The sledges used on this journey were clumsy and ill-designed; they had been made with no preliminary tests to determine the proper load per man, or what additional ration was required to support men performing heavy labour and give them resistance to the cold. As a result, Ross's sledge crews almost broke down.

D*

Two men were drawn home on a sledge; three others were barely able to walk. McClintock diligently took note of all defects in planning and equipment and pondered means of correcting them.

Three other sledge journeys had been made. Lieutenant Browne had crossed Regent's Inlet and gone some distance down its east shore; Lieutenant Robinson had gone down the west side of the inlet to Fury Beach and found that the depot there had not been touched. Captain Bird had sent Lieutenant Barnard across to the north side of Barrow Strait, but that officer had not reached Beechey Island at the entrance of Wellington Channel, where the *Erebus* and the *Terror* had found their first winter quarters. This was the climax of Sir James Ross's ill luck. Had he made that one concrete discovery, he might have been spared the censure a disappointed and anxious public was to inflict upon him for his purely negative findings. His sledge journeys had been laboured and feeble compared with those McClintock was soon to organize; but valuable lessons had been learned, and the man best fitted to apply them had been recognized. In an outbreak of scurvy which killed seven men, both Ross and McClure were disabled, and McClintock acted for a time as commanding officer of the *Enterprise*. His competence and resourcefulness in discharge of that duty, and in supervising the cutting of a canal out of the harbour, marked him as a fitting leader by land and sea for the journeys to come.

As commonly happened, the open sea broke up long before the ice moved out of Port Leopold, and the ships were not liberated until 28 August after a captivity lasting only two weeks short of a year. Ross set a course for Wellington Channel, but winter was again upon him. The loose ice through which the ships were ploughing was quickly welded together by young ice fifteen inches thick, and, in a solid ice field fifty miles in circumference, the crews were for the second time threatened with a winter in the pack. A westerly gale drove them along the south shore of Lancaster Sound towards a nest of icebergs, but this apparent peril was the means of their deliverance. Contact with the bergs shattered the ice field, and the ships warped their way into the clear. As there was little hope of recovering an Arctic harbour, even if the condition of his crews warranted exposure for another season, Ross determined to cut his losses and run for home.

The boat journey made by Richardson and Rae from the

106

Mackenzie to the Coppermine was even more fruitless. They found no trace of what they sought and had not, like Ross, the consolation of adding over 100 miles of coastline to the map. For once that gloomy but accurate prophet Dr King, who had declaimed against Richardson's unfitness, at the age of sixty, to make such a voyage, had missed his mark. Richardson had astonished Rae by his powers of endurance, while Rae, for his part, surprised Richardson at the ease with which he kept the party supplied with game. Richardson returned to England in 1849, while Rae temporarily resumed his post as an officer of the fur trade in the Mackenzie district. In that capacity he found himself during the winter of 1849-50 playing host to Lieutenant Pullen of the *Plover*.

The *Plover* had indeed failed to reach her Alaska anchorage in 1848, as the anonymous letter writer had predicted. She left England in February but, built more for capacity than speed, and deeply laden, she had made a slow passage, reaching Honolulu on 23 August. There Commander Moore had hoped to rendez-vous with Captain Kellett of the frigate *Herald*, who had been ordered to stop his survey work on the Lower California shore and aid in the search beyond Bering Strait. Kellet, it was found, had received his orders early, obeyed them promptly, and was by then far to the north. Moore's attempt to reach his Alaskan anchorage that season was defeated by the weather. On 13 October, when in sight of St Lawrence Island, he was caught in a gale and swept over to the Siberian side of Bering Strait. There he found a temporary anchorage and sent in a boat to make inquiries of the natives on the shore – Chukchee – or, as the historian of the voyage, Mate W. H. Hooper, prefers to call them, 'Tuski'.

At first there was some difficulty in communicating. All efforts to make the natives comprehend a meaning were met with a shake of the head and the emphatic negative, 'tam, tam'. With ponderous humour Hooper observes that 'our expressions of vexation at the ill-success of our efforts sounded, in many instances like their word of dissent'. The natives pointed out by signs a harbour where the ship might safely winter, and on 28 October she was berthed in Port Emma, opposite the little native village of Woorel. 'Lofty rugged mountains, majestic and snow-bewrapped, surrounded the ice-bound harbour,' wrote Hooper.

On 28 November, a gale almost drove her from her anchorage; after that she lay frozen-fast and secure. The men spent the winter in surveying the harbour, toting water, boiling oil from blubber, school, weekly masquerades, and an occasional play. It appears, too, that less reputable ways were found of passing the long winter months. A year later, Dr Rae, who, like other traders, was not well disposed to the Navy, and was addicted to ill-natured gossip, was informed by seamen of the *Plover* who were wintering on the Mackenzie that Commander Moore kept a native girl in his cabin and went driving with her after the manner of a Russian magnate, with one officer running before and one behind the reindeer-drawn cariole. It seems improbable that Moore, who was by no means a bad officer, was so forgetful of the respect due to the Service, as to impose this as a duty, and we may suppose that Rae or his informants misrepresented the casual outcome of a tipsy frolic as a practice.

Seldom can relations have been better between Europeans and a remote and primitive people than those between the Chukchee and the men of the *Plover*. They entertained one another on the ship and ashore without the least mistrust. Accustomed to some sort of subordination among themselves, the natives quickly recognized gradations in rank and granted each the deference due to it. They attended divine service with the utmost decorum. An orchestra was improvised for mutual entertainment. For this a sailor who, according to Hooper, 'had once itinerated with an organ and a tambourine girl,' and for some reason had exchanged that vocation for the Navy, made a tambourine and a tin flute. The natives shared freely in festivities, and soon taught the Europeans their language, although they themselves were slow in acquiring English.

Just after Christmas, when a granddaughter was born to the local chief, Akoull, Commander Moore observed the event by firing a royal salute of twenty-one guns. A week later, the same officer went with two or three others of his company to attend the infant's christening. The event was celebrated by setting off rockets. One of these failed to take flight and went sputtering along the ground. A native chased it but, luckily, did not over-take it.

Two kinds of people dwelt in the vicinity: the inland folk, who lived by pasturing reindeer, and the fishermen of the sea coast. Hooper preferred the herdsmen as being cleaner in their habits. Chief Akoull was jealous of the intimacy between the sailors and the people of the hinterland but could do little to prevent it. The more adventurous moved freely among them; Hooper ate with them, slept in their tents, drew lively pictures of their collective ways, and described their individual character- istics with as much ease and familiarity as if he were commenting on the guests in a London ballroom. 'Miyo, the charming *petite* sister of Mecco,' had 'a well-formed figure, with an easy dignified carriage'; Ka-oong-ah was 'a little girl, lithe of limb, prattling and rosy, and merry as a bird, a most ingenious little sempstress, and delighted to make all sorts of queer little bags and gloves and dolls for me whose especial favourite she was, and whom it delighted her to plague.' She was 'overflowing with fun,' he adds. The fun was not all on one side. Having heard of the fondness of northern people for grease, the officers mischievously offered a Chukchee woman a wax candle. To their astonishment she ate it with relish, finally drawing the wick out between her teeth to extract the last traces of the nourishing substance.

While charmed with the appearance of the younger natives, Hooper found the aged pitiful and repulsive. They suffered much from snow-blindness, and this often caused disfiguring oph- thalmia.

Numerous reports were obtained from the natives about ships recently seen, some of which might have referred to the vessels of Franklin. To check one of these rumours the commander appointed three officers, Moore (who bore the same name as his captain), Hooper, and Martin, to make a journey to East Cape, more than 100 miles to the north. They set out on 8 February 1849, with a dog sledge, supplies for twelve days – the estimated period of absence from the ship – a copper fiddle (the gift of the ship's armourer), and two natives, Moldoyah and his wife Yaneenga, as guides. In bad weather and poor visibility they strayed on to the sea ice; Moldoyah confessed himself lost, but with the aid of a compass they recovered the land and, almost frozen, sought food and shelter in a fishing village. Moore broke down and was carried back to the ship by the friendly natives, bearing a letter in which Hooper and Martin asked leave to com- plete their mission. The captain granted permission and sent them additional supplies. On the last lap of the journey the native escort gave up; Hooper and Martin, who would not be denied a a glimpse of one of the world's ends, pushed on alone and were rewarded with a view of East Cape (or Cape Dezhnev), a bold promontory with a village on its crest. They were back on the ship at the end of March.

With the advance of spring, work was begun with ice saws to speed up the release of the *Plover*. The breakup came earlier there than in the deep Arctic, and on 13 June she was free. She set sail for the Alaskan side of Bering Strait, where, in Kotzebue Sound, she found the *Herald* (returned after wintering in the south) and the private yacht *Nancy Dawson*, whose owner, Robert Sheddon, had offered his services and those of his ship to assist in the search. When the *Herald* had topped off the *Plover*'s supplies, the three ships steered north and east, following the Alaskan shore to Wainright Inlet, halfway between Icy Cape and Point Barrow.

There it was decided to launch the boat expedition, which was to follow through to the Mackenzie and thus, in conjunction with Richardson and Rae, ensure an examination of the shoreline all the way from Bering Strait to the Coppermine. Lieutenant W. J. S. Pullen was chosen for this service along with mates Hooper and Martin and twenty-two seamen. Four boats were assigned to them: the pinnaces of the *Herald* and the *Plover* (partially decked and providing some protection from the bitter winds that even in summer sweep over the ice-strewn seas) and two whaleboats, only twenty-five feet long and, Hooper ruefully observes, quite void of comfort. The larger ships now turned back, leaving the *Nancy Dawson* to escort the boats on the first lap of their long journey.

It is well known that the Franklin search not only unravelled by far the greater part of the Canadian archipelago, but also, under the auspices of Dr Kane, inaugurated the thrust that in half a century was to carry the Stars and Stripes to the North Pole. It is not so generally recognized that this search contributed to a very significant sequence in the Russian Arctic. After parting from Pullen, Kellett sailed north and west, made a landing on Herald Island in the Russian Arctic sector, and had a distant view of a larger body, later named Wrangel Island. It was these observations of Kellett that encouraged Lieutenant George Washington DeLong, U.S.N., to attempt penetration of the ice in that quarter, and years after it was the finding of relics of his *Jeannette* near Greenland that gave Dr Fridtjof Nansen the idea of putting his *Fram* in the ice for her famous polar drift.

In company with the *Nancy Dawson* the four boats sailed on to Point Barrow, which, as a well-known geographical feature, was a likely place for the lost crews to leave a record. None was found, however, and Shedden resolved to venture no farther along that shallow and dangerous coast. According to Rae, while Pullen was aboard the yacht bidding his generous friend farewell, Hooper and some of the seamen had escorted a number of Eskimo women out among the hummocks seaward, when 'an opportune disruption of the ice took place and caused a number of very ludicrous exposés'. Rae went on to remark: 'The circumstance I suspect Pullen is not aware of, as he is himself strictly guarded in his moral conduct.'

They had not gone far past Point Barrow when Pullen decided that the sea was too shallow for the pinnaces, so he sent them back in charge of Martin, and went on with Hooper, twelve men, and the two whaleboats and also an Eskimo baidar, bearing additional supplies.

Although in making the passage from Point Barrow to the Mackenzie in three weeks, they were a good deal luckier than their predecessors on that coast, Hooper has plenty to say about the trials and dangers met with on the way. Their comparative freedom from the ice that had so plagued Franklin and Simpson had its own drawback, for in open water the seas were heavy enough to wash into the boats and damage provisions. They discovered too that the wasted and honey-combed ice pieces of the late summer thrust out submerged projections, and watchfulness was needed to protect the bottoms of the boats. At Point Berens, a little to the west of Franklin's farthest point in 1826, they landed to plant a food cache for the possible use of the lost crews, and found nearby an encampment of thirteen tents and some hundred Eskimos. Means were found to divert their attention while the cache was being laid, but while the fatigue party was returning to the boats it was surrounded, and one Eskimo, dubbed 'Shovel Jack' by the sailors, seizing a shovel, stood on it and refused to budge. To tolerate open robbery was to invite worse outrage. The men thrust him off and got back to the boats with all their belongings. After expending much effort in the pursuit of a piece of ice, transformed by mirage into the likeness of a ship, they put in again at Point Beechey, and there found a threatening crowd of natives, among them Shovel Jack, who had followed them by land to continue the unfinished business of Point Berens. Following a common practice, Pullen drew a line in the sand which, by agreement, neither party was to cross. Individual Eskimos who came over were forcibly pushed back. But to bivouac there was plainly too dangerous. They made their getaway by menacing with firearms the throng which followed them to the beach. Pullen was reluctant to fire as, apart from the risk that his little party might be rushed and overrun with guns discharged, he feared to provoke possible reprisals against the lost crews, which – for all he knew – might be wandering in the vicinity. The harassed and weary voyagers pulled out to sea and made a landing on the windy and spray-swept Return Reef. There, too, the Eskimos followed them in their baidars, and, though a considerable sea was running, Pullen shoved off once more, but found wind and wave so strong against him that he gave the word to land, resolved to use force if again provoked. The Eskimos approached the encampment irresolutely and scampered back when the sentry charged them with fixed bayonet. Eluding the observation of their tormentors in the fog, the British took to the sea for the third time and coasted along the reef to its eastern end, where they cooked a hot meal and dried their clothes by a driftwood fire.

To the east they found the sea so shallow that not even the light-draught whaleboats could come within a half mile of the beach, and they sometimes ate and slept on the ice in preference to the labour and discomfort of wading ashore. They found a comfortable and apparently safe berth inside Herschel Island, but a change in the wind at night drove the boats ashore and damaged the remaining supplies. They were nearly home, however, and east of Herschel Island found the Eskimos friendly and accustomed to peaceful barter. As autumn was approaching a lively traffic was carried on in clothing. Back had commented on the readiness of the Eskimo women in 'disposing of their clothing, which they never hesitated to do'. Hooper more gravely relates: 'From one damsel I purchased the frock she wore . . . The loss of the garment did not seem at all inconvenient.' Perhaps because she modestly retained possession of the beads attached to it. Then with joy they came upon fresh water, yellow in colour, the mud-laden current of the Mackenzie flooding into the sea.

Pullen lost his way in the maze of shoal, water, and island that makes up the Mackenzie delta, and had gone up the Peel River to Fort McPherson before he discovered his error and turned back to the main stream. As the resources of no one fur post were equal to the maintenance of his party, he went upstream to Fort Simpson with three men, while Hooper, experiencing now – as King under Back had done – the burden which is apt to fall on a second-in-command, was sent with the larger party to pass the winter at old Fort Franklin on Great Bear Lake. Rae, who detested Hooper, alleges that he was unequal to the task of controlling idle men on so lonely a station, and so lacking in authority as to wash his own clothes and prepare his own meals. He busied himself collecting for his intended book tales of murder, starvation, and cannibalism among Indian and Eskimo, provoking Rae's comment: 'These self-sufficient donkies come into this country, see the Indians sometimes miserably clad and half-starved, the causes of which they never think of inquiring into but place it all to the credit of the Company....' Hooper's published work does not justify this censure. It was not malicious in intent, whatever its effect might have been; and he spoke kindly of Rae.

In the spring, in compliance with orders, the boat crews began the long journey by river with the fur brigade to Hudson Bay, whence a Company ship would bear them home. The first lap of the journey was barely finished when Pullen was met by a Company boat bearing dispatches from the Admiralty in which he was required to extend his search by way of Cape Bathurst to Banks Land, Parry's 'loom of land', 300 miles north of the cape.

It was left to Pullen's discretion to decide whether or not the voyage was 'practicable'. If not, it was to be attempted by Rae and Company boatmen. Rae would have required time to muster a reliable crew, while Pullen's was immediately available. It is to his credit and to the honour of his men that, after a trying voyage, the unfamiliar discomforts of a winter in the north, and the joyous relaxation of starting for home, they deferred that hope for a year to launch out on a second voyage of greater hazard than the first. Pullen (now promoted to commander) must have been of a buoyant disposition. He spoke hopefully not only of making Banks Land but even of passing on to the east, joining hands with Captain Austin in Barrow Strait, and winning the rank of post captain. Rae privately stated that he would do well enough if he came back alive. And this *was* all he accomplished. On emerging from the Mackenzie he encountered cold, rain, frozen rigging, and much ice, and on reaching Cape Bathurst concluded that the season was too far advanced to continue the voyage. On 15 August he put about for the Mackenzie. It must have been with bitterness that the crews later learned that, somewhere on their fogbound journey back, they passed Commander McClure, bent on the same mission as themselves in the comparative safety and comfort of the 500-ton *Investigator*. They wintered again on the Mackenzie and returned home. Pullen came back to command the *North Star* for three seasons in the eastern Arctic; Hooper, broken in health, died in 1854.

In 1850 orders had come too late for Rae to do anything in that season. For 1851 he was assigned the task of examining the shores of Wollaston and Victoria lands for traces of Franklin and determining whether or not these two lands were separated by an arm of the sea.

Few men could have been better fitted for the work. John Rae had been born in the Orkneys in 1813, and had spent his boyhood in a manner that moulded him for the career that lay ahead, by fishing, boating, and rock climbing. He studied medicine at Edinburgh, and on qualifying entered the service of the Hudson's Bay Company. He sailed for York Factory in the very year that Richard King, his future critic, set out with Back for the Great Fish River. For ten years he was posted at Moose Factory as clerk and physician, and spent his leisure trapping and shooting. He was reputed to be able to walk 100 miles in two days. He was, R. M. Ballantine says, 'muscular and active, full of animal spirits, and had a fine intellectual countenance' – *and* he was an excellent shot. He was a practical man with no trace of conceit, more inclined to expose the false pretensions of others than to advertise himself.

Rae spent the winter of 1850-1 at Fort Confidence, the jumping-off point for the Coppermine, and on 15 April with two men and two dog sledges set out down the Kendall and lower Coppermine rivers, and crossed the frozen sea to Wollaston Land. Travelling by night, when the glare of sun on snow was less intense, he went east from Douglas Island to Welbank Bay. As this was the western end of the survey of Dease and Simpson, he had proved that Wollaston and Victoria lands were one.

Turning back, he picked up a food depot and traced the coast in the opposite direction, northward up the west side of Wollaston Land. He entered Prince Albert Sound and ended his journey close to Cape Back. From a cliff 300 feet high he saw land forming the north shore of the sound. Lieutenant Haswell of the *Investigator,* as will be recorded, had reached a point almost directly opposite ten days before.

Rae's strenuous spring journey was only the prelude to a voyage less exhausting, but long and dangerous. He went back to the Kendall River, where two boats had been hauled across from Fort Confidence by their crew, and adroitly took advantage of the spring flood to get the laden craft downstream over rocks which might have made it impassable at normal level. After being much delayed by ice in the lower Coppermine, he reached the ocean and on 5 July set out eastward along the shore charted by Franklin on his first journey thirty years before. After a slow passage weaving through the loose ice of Coronation Gulf, he passed Point Turnagain, and reached Cape Alexander on 24 July.

Rae now found himself in the same situation as Back in the Fish River estuary. Open water was beckoning him eastward, along the continental shore to the region King had declared to hold the key to the mystery. Ice was blocking his way across Dease Strait to Victoria, whither his orders directed him. Like Back, Rae chose to go by the book, in this case with success. In three days the ice slackened enough to allow the two boats passage through the Finlayson Islands to the north shore just west of Cambridge Bay. It was at that point that Dease and Simpson, heading west, had begun their chart. To the east the shoreline was unknown.

Cambridge Bay had been barely observed by Thomas Simpson. Rae pushed into it and found a large and excellent harbour. He noted the abundance of fish, which two years after were to protect Collinson's crew against scurvy. On 1 August a violent gale dispersed the ice. Rae followed the shore to the east and laid down Anderson Bay and Parker Bay before rounding the southeast angle of Victoria Island. Beyond it he found that the ice lay so thick up to an offshore islet (named Taylor in honour of President

Zachary Taylor of the United States) that he was obliged to pass outside the island, where he observed floes so large as to ground in thirty feet of water. He was now entering the very strait (which he named Victoria) where the *Erebus* and the *Terror* had come to grief.

On 3 August, pestered by violent snow squalls, Rae sailed up a lane between land and ice until it broadened into an expanse of open water with an ugly choppy sea and contrary wind. The little boats were excellent sailors and plied bravely to windward until the strain on their seams proved too great, and obliged the stubborn explorer to put into a convenient cove. On the fifth, with the sea too rough for oars, the boats beat six miles to windward, and again had to put inshore with strained and leaking seams. Hampered continually by fog and ice, Rae fought his way up to Princess Royal Cape, but there, on the eleventh, the sight of 'large pieces of ice thrown up in great confusion,' convinced him that there was no passage for frail boats. With three men he went up the shore on foot. Jagged limestone debris tore away the soles of their moccasins, and they came to a final halt opposite Halkett Island at 70° 2' 36" N. and 101° 24' 47" W., a little to the north and some sixty miles to the west of the point where Franklin's ships had been abandoned three years before. The spectacle of heavy ice coming down from the northwest made Rae suspect the existence of a channel in that direction leading to Melville Island.

As progress to the north was blocked, Rae wished to cross Victoria Strait to King William Land, which lay eastward just visible some forty miles away, but high winds and ice again thwarted him. So he began to retrace his outward course, alert for any sign of a lane that would give him the desired opening. At Parker Bay he met a band of Eskimos, with whom he had no means of communicating. From the circumstance that he saw no articles of European manufacture in their possession it seems likely that they had not been across the strait and, unlike the people met later by Collinson, knew nothing of the ships. Following the Victoria shoreline westward, Rae picked up two pieces of wreckage. The first, measuring five feet nine inches, was apparently the butt end of a flagstaff with copper tacks marked with the broad arrow that identified government property. The other was an oak stanchion four feet long. These finds were made at

68° 52′ N., 103° 20′ W. – eighty miles from where the *Erebus* and the *Terror* had been deserted. Rae could not be certain of their origin; in any case, summer was ending and he had already exerted himself to the utmost. Stormy weather on the way home gave him cause to be thankful that he had tried his luck no farther.

Together, Richardson, Pullen, and Rae had traversed the continental shore from Icy Cape to Boothia, *except* for the shores near the Fish River, to which Dr King had expressly directed their search. But this was not mere perversity on the part of the Admiralty and its advisers. Had Franklin got past Cape Walker, a supposition which King did not attempt to dispute, he would have been no more likely to steer his ships towards the Fish River than a man making his way by guesswork from New York to San Francisco would be to find himself in the suburb of Boston. There remained an undeniable chance that Franklin had been diverted in the direction of King William Land by ice, and this chance was strengthened by Rae's discovery that Wollaston and Victoria lands were joined together to form a barrier in his intended course. The wreckage which he had picked up pointed to the same conclusion. Unluckily, both the public and the Admiralty assigned more importance to the findings made by Captain Penny that same summer in Wellington Channel. Nevertheless, Rae, as the Admiralty agent acting under its orders, had come very close to success. If he had gone straight east from Cape Alexander or found a way through the pack to King William Land, the search would have been over. It was bad luck as much as bad management that prolonged it.

5   The Search in Barrow Strait and Beyond, 1850-1851

Sir James Ross, with sickly crews and battered ships, came home early in November 1849. He fully expected to find that Franklin had freed himself by his own efforts and reached England before him. Consequently, the luckless captain had to endure both his own and the general frustration, and take blame which he had done little or nothing to deserve. Colonel Sabine, it is true, had warned Lady Franklin that Ross was not taking the voyage seriously enough. But blameless or not, he was sure to be blamed. Some felt that, in spite of the outbreak of scurvy, he should have stayed out a second winter. Dr King took abundant revenge for Ross's former sneer. 'His puny efforts,' he wrote to the Admiralty, '... are too contemptible for criticism.' Nonetheless, King *did* criticize them: 'I wish I could say a kind word for Sir James Ross. If ever one man sacrificed another, Sir James Ross sacrificed Sir John Franklin,' because, as King alleged, Ross had neglected the rescue of Franklin in favour of discovering the Northwest Passage. The accusation was false to the point of absurdity. Not being in Ross's confidence, King could judge of his intentions only by what he did. Ross had not got far enough with his ships to disclose any purpose; on his major land journey, down the west Somerset shore, he had been travelling in the very direction which King's theories prescribed. But the doctor knew his public. Ignorant people would accept the slander without question; pity and anxiety for lost and starving men would tempt others to countenance a falsehood that their sober judgment would have rejected. Lady Franklin's letters to Ross, says her biographer, never had the same friendly tone as before.

The expedition had now been missing for more than four seasons. Governments on both sides of the Atlantic took measures for its relief. Ross's two ships, the *Enterprise* and the *Investigator*, hurriedly refitted and remanned, were put under the command of Captain Richard Collinson and McClure, now promoted to commander, with orders to sail by Cape Horn to Bering Strait and carry on Pullen's work in the western Arctic. They were hustled off in January, 1850, in the hope, by no means certain of realization, that their unwieldy vessels would reach the field of search before the autumn freeze-up. The Admiralty purchased two brigs and put them under the command of Captain William Penny, a famous whaler of Aberdeen, Scotland, with orders to set out as early as the season permitted and search Jones Sound. A larger expedition was made ready to renew the effort in Barrow Strait. Lady Franklin equipped her own ship, the hermaphrodite brig *Prince Albert*, a cross between a brig and a schooner. By public subscription old Sir John Ross fitted out the yacht *Felix* to join in the search. A fifth expedition, directed to the same end, was being made ready in the shipyards of the United States.

Long before the ill-success of Richardson and Ross was known, Lady Franklin had addressed a letter to President Zachary Taylor soliciting American aid: 'I am not without hope that you will deem it not unworthy of a great and kindred nation to take up the cause of humanity which I plead, in a national spirit, and thus generously make it your own.' She went on in a manner that would have appalled the late Sir John Barrow to hint of the glory accruing to the United States if the rescue of her husband and the discovery of the Northwest Passage were achieved by American seamen. John M. Clayton, Secretary of State, replied on behalf of the President, promising all the help 'that the Executive Government of the United States in the exercise of its constitutional powers can afford'. This pledge was promptly and liberally honoured. With the aid of Congress, the New York merchant Henry Grinnell fitted out the brigs *Advance* and *Rescue*. Lieutenant Edwin J. De Haven took command of the expedition with Dr Elisha Kent Kane as his ship's surgeon. Samuel P. Griffin, captain of the *Rescue*, received a letter from Lady Franklin expressing her pleasure that she should be aided by one who bore her own maiden name.

The great search, now fairly under way, gave prominence to some personalities who might otherwise have been unknown to posterity. Not the least of these was the widow – for such she had been since 11 June 1847 – of Sir John Franklin. Jane Griffin,

born in 1792 of a prosperous mercantile family of French Hugue-
not origin, was in some respects what the novelist Jane Austen
might have been had she possessed wealth and a vigorous constitution. It was a period when the upper middle class prized
broad interests and cultivation of the intellect; Miss Griffin's
French blood and her mastery of the language, improved by
travel, gave her unusual breadth of view. Intellectual curiosity
made polar travellers particularly welcome guests in her home.
Miss Griffin met Captain John Ross and, quite in the manner
of Jane Austen, criticized his appearance but approved of his
manners and intelligence. At a larger assembly she censured the
appearance of Parry – he stooped in a way that no gentleman
should – found Captain Beechey, small, prim, and reserved, cast
a friendly glance at Lyon, and began to like Parry when he spoke
in praise of Franklin. Her criticism was governed by larger views
than that of her husband. Franklin, like others of his generation,
while most cordial in his attitude toward individual Americans,
was not prone to give them credit as a type. Jane was more
objective. It was once her fortune to sail the Mediterranean in
company with other English tourists as the guests of an American
man-of-war. When an artist belonging to her group became
panic-stricken in a gale, Captain Perry remarked indulgently to
his officers that such fears were pardonable in one who was unaccustomed to the sea; whereat Jane noted in her diary that 'an
American coward' would not have received such courteous
treatment on board a British cruiser.

Wealth, an independent spirit, and the cool analysis to which
she subjected her suitors kept Miss Griffin single until she was
thirty-five. Few wives have shown such untiring devotion.
Though the resources of two nations were employed in her husband's rescue, she sent out three expeditions of her own.

Harold Nicolson finds her a 'conceited prig' with a 'horrible
restless arrogance'. Such a judgment is impossible to justify and
difficult to comprehend.

Lady Franklin was shrewd but never malicious in her judgment
of man or woman; her only unwarrantable interference in her
husband's affairs was dictated by care for his reputation and peace
of mind. The generosity with which she offered the command
of one of her ships to Kane, who was neither a professional seaman nor a first-rate commander, shows her warmth of tempera-

ment. She addressed McClintock, to whom she was giving a chance of world-wide fame, in a motherly tone, without a trace of patronage. He, for his part, found her 'gentle and prepossessing'. When her life was nearly ended, the solemn and reserved Allen Young paid her a visit, sixteen years after he had ceased to be her officer in the *Fox*.

Private and foreign rescue expeditions were supplemented by the largest naval squadron yet sent into the Arctic. Two cargo vessels of the *Investigator* type, the *Resolute* and the *Assistance*, were commissioned, along with two screw steamers of 400 tons, the *Pioneer* and the *Intrepid*. Captain Horatio Austin, who had been Parry's first lieutenant in 1824-5, commissioned the *Resolute* as commodore. Captain Erasmus Ommaney took command of the *Assistance*. Lieutenants Bertie Cator and Sherard Osborn were appointed to the *Intrepid* and *Pioneer* respectively.

It was Sherard Osborn's destiny to add colour to the search both by making history and writing it. He was no orthodox officer. His portrait, preserved in a newspaper clipping in the Stefansson collection, is the nineteenth-century cartoonist's conception of the Irishman – sturdy in build with a square head, an aggressive nose, and upstanding hair – almost certainly red. He was born in the Far East, joined the Navy at the age of fifteen, and at sixteen was entrusted by his captain with the detached command of an auxiliary craft off the Burma coast. This appointment, which lasted for some months, was bound to foster independence of judgment and, on so small a boat, closer than normal relations with those under his command. From then on Sherard Osborn was an efficient officer, on the best of terms with those to whom he gave orders and mistrustful of those who gave orders to him. He was antipathetic to the Establishment, and it is to the Establishment's credit that his turbulence proved no bar to his promotion, and that he held the rank of rear-admiral when he died at the age of fifty-three. Another officer, who left his mark even more conspicuously on this and succeeding voyages, was the first lieutenant of the *Assistance*, F. L. McClintock.

McClintock, three years older than Osborn, was born in 1819 to a younger and impoverished branch of the Anglo-Irish aristocracy. As he was one of twelve children, his parents welcomed the opportunity of finding him a berth on board H.H.S. *Samarang*. The eleven-year-old cadet was conducted from Dundalk, Ireland, to the naval base of Plymouth by a servant, who, says Clements Markham, parted from him with these words: 'Good-bye, master Leopold, and never turn your back to the enemy while you've got a face to face him with.' Master Leopold must have heeded this advice, for twenty-six years after, when he took command of Lady Franklin's *Fox*, the same servant wrote urging him not to encounter danger needlessly.

The budding seaman was so small that when his cousin, Lieutenant Bunbury McClintock, came to look for him in the midshipmen's berth, he declared that it was like hunting a flea in a blanket. His introduction to the Navy was a kindly one. His captain swore that if 'Pat' had a sister with eyes like his he would marry her. (He subsequently *did*.) He modelled himself on his cousin, whom he greatly admired: 'Billy Bun doesn't drink or swear, neither will I.' He served on the American Pacific station with William Smyth, later to be Back's first officer in the *Terror*, was mate at the age of nineteen, and promoted to lieutenant in 1845 for services in the refloating of the British steamer *Gorgon*, driven hard aground in Montevideo harbour. He was with the *Frolic* at Hawaii, brought the ship home as her captain, and in the Strait of Magellan salvaged a quantity of specie from a sunken merchant ship. In Portsmouth in February 1848, as an unemployed lieutenant, he met his old shipmate Captain Smyth and was introduced by him to Sir James Ross, who took him to Barrow Strait as second lieutenant of the *Enterprise*. The experience of that ill-starred cruise gave him an important station among the officers of Captain Austin, who appointed him to organize sledging operations. It was an important trust because a ship with a cruising period of two months in the year, and liable to be handcuffed in a bad season as Ross's had been, was no instrument for a thorough and extended search. Its function was to serve as a base for small detachments radiating out on foot in every direction and making a minute survey for cairns and other traces of the lost ships. McClintock set himself to further this service by devising sledges and other equipment combining efficiency with the least possible weight.

While the squadrons were fitting out in the early months of 1850, Osborn at Woolwich kept up a lively correspondence with Penny at the Scottish port of Aberdeen. The subsequent quarrel between the naval and civilian branches of the search (in which

Osborn was to choose the side most injurious to himself) was already taking shape. For the present the fiery young lieutenant tried to act as peacemaker: 'You must not think ill of naval officers from the little disagreeable conversation you had with my leader [Captain Austin] – he is a hot-headed, but still a warm-hearted, sailor – blunt of speech perhaps but nevertheless, take my word, he will not be a bit more unwilling than I should be to claim you as a brother workman in a good and glorious cause ... I dine tomorrow night with Lady Franklin, and shall, of course, have a long conversation about you.'

Austin's four vessels left the Thames early in May, shortly after Penny had sailed from Aberdeen. They put in at Stromness in the Orkney Islands – where Osborn made the unusual complaint that whisky was too cheap – and then headed for Cape Farewell and Davis Strait. The captain of the *Pioneer,* who was attached to the commodore ship *Resolute,* while Bertie Cator in the *Intrepid* waited on the *Assistance,* complained bitterly of the structure of the vessels that the steamers were required to tow in calm weather. They exhausted his patience and broke his hawsers. Not exactly of clipper build in the first place, the *Resolute* and the *Assistance* had been so sheathed in extra planking that they were almost rectangular in shape and pushed the water ahead instead of passing through it. Osborn was very pleased with his *Pioneer,* a 400-ton steamer with schooner rig and a fine shaped bow shod with iron for boring ice. Her crew of thirty were tightly stowed, the men in a small compartment at the bow, the officers in a similar recess at the stern. The rest of the ship was packed with coal. For rations over a long term the steam tender was dependent upon the parent vessel.

On the way up Baffin Bay, Osborn's ship was caught in a narrowing ice lane and barely escaped being crushed: 'The poor *Pioneer* was in sad peril: the deck was arching with the pressure on her sides, the scupper-pieces were turning up out of the mortices, and a quiver of agony wrung my craft's frame from stem to taffrail ...

'The men – who, whaler-fashion, had, without orders, I afterwards learnt, brought their clothes on deck ready to save their little property – stood in knots waiting for direction from the officers, who, with anxious eye, watched the floe-cap as it ground past the side to see whether the strain was easing. Suddenly it did so and we were safe. But a deep dent in the *Pioneer's* side, extending for some forty feet, and the fact, as we afterwards learnt, of twenty-one timbers being broken upon one side, proved that her trial had been a severe one.'

The end of June found them far up Baffin Bay off the northernmost Danish settlement of Upernavik. Beyond that the high and rugged Greenland coast subsided, and the icecap, like an unsupported rug, sank down to sea level, forming the great ice reservoir of Melville Bay. There it was learned that the whaling fleet and Penny's two brigs were held up thirty miles ahead. The warm-hearted Osborn pitied the old whaling skipper, thus overhauled in spite of his efforts to keep ahead of the main squadron.

Arrived off the Devil's Thumb, a natural rock pillar that marked the southern limit of Melville Bay, Austin's ships were halted by the pack. While some men were released for recreation on the sunlit ice, each ship detailed a boat's crew to go inshore and shoot loons. Osborn's boat came back at 4 A.M. with ammunition all spent and nothing to show for it. More in bewilderment than anger the captain asked Abbott, the old sailor in charge, how he had contrived to spend one pound of powder and four pounds of birdshot and come back empty-handed.

' If you please, sir, we fired it all into a bear.'

' Shoot a bear with No. 4 shot! '

' Yes, sir, and if it hadn't been for two or three who were afeard of him, we would have brought him aboard.'

Old Abbott's story was this: Approaching the shore, they had found a polar bear on an offshore islet on the lookout for seal, and they began to deluge him with small shot. One man contrived to force a button and the blade of a knife down his muzzle-loader, and the discharge of this made the bear jump. Bleeding, the tormented creature swam off and climbed on to a piece of floating ice. Abbott and crew tugged after him, and Abbott was preparing to gaff his quarry with a boat hook when the more prudent members of his company backed oars and refused to go any nearer. Abbott always asserted that but for this mutinous conduct, he would have brought the bear aboard and trained him to draw a sledge. During the period of foot travel in the winter and ensuing spring, if he ever heard a younger man growling at the labour of sledge work, he would exclaim, ' Ah, if you had taken my advice, we'd have had that 'ere bear to do the work for us '.

It took forty days to traverse the 200 miles of Melville Bay ice. Penny was near at hand throughout. With a favourable wind, that adroit navigator weaved his way ahead through the narrow lanes; with wind adverse, the main squadron with the aid of steam would recover the lead. Early in August, Lady Franklin's *Prince Albert* came up with them, and the *Felix* of Sir John Ross with the 12-ton *Mary* in tow. At times the steamers would assist these also. On 13 August, Sherard Osborn had a clear view of Cape York, marking the northern boundary of Melville Bay.

Here occurred an incident which seemed insignificant and annoying at the time but was to touch off American scientific enterprise in a region formerly exclusively British, carry the United States flag to the top of the globe, and ignite a controversy which has lasted to this day.

Captain Penny was the first to near Cape York, and seeing Eskimos on the beach at its foot, he went ashore to question them. Along with his boat came one from the *Felix* bearing her captain, Commander Phillips, and Sir John Ross's interpreter, the Greenland native Adam Beck. Penny's interpreter, Carl Petersen, could get nothing out of the Eskimos relating to Franklin; so the boats put off. Phillips, finding himself cut off from the *Felix* by a shift in the ice, went aboard the *Prince Albert* along with Adam Beck. He was received in the captain's cabin by Commander Forsyth and his civilian officer, W. Parker Snow, the wielder of a very florid pen. Adam Beck in the meantime got into conversation with the steward John Smith, an old Hudson's Bay man, who had picked up a little of the Eskimo language at the northern trading posts. Soon Smith came aft with a dreadful tale. Adam Beck had learned from the Cape York natives that four years before (in 1846) two ships whose officers wore gold cap bands had put in at Omenak in Wolstenholme Sound, and there their enfeebled crews had been massacred by the natives. Adam Beck, though sharply interrogated, stuck to his story. Commander Forsyth hailed the *Assistance*, the nearest ship. Captain Ommaney came aboard and decided that the matter must be referred to Captain Austin. So he, Phillips, Forsyth, Snow, Smith, and Adam Beck took boat to the *Resolute*, where they were joined by Sir John Ross from the *Felix*. Unmoved by the evident scepticism of some of his questioners, the Eskimo vowed that he was telling the truth. A council of war was held.

John Ross, always a one-man minority, placed absolute confidence in his interpreter; the others were doubtful or hostile. 'Men of cultivated minds,' says the supercilious Mr Snow, 'are not easily caught.' It certainly seemed improbable that the Eskimos of Cape York should not have communicated to Penny through Petersen news that they had shared so readily with Adam Beck. Penny, whose brigs were lying in the ice to the west, was spoken to by signal, and it was arranged to return to Cape York and re-examine the natives. Snow could not get back to his ship so, he says, 'Captain Austin, with the courtesy which distinguishes that noble-hearted sailor, invited me to occupy an armchair in his own cabin '.

On the morning of the next day the parties concerned went aboard the *Pioneer* and steamed back to Cape York. There they were joined by Penny and Petersen, who again questioned the natives. The conclusion was that Adam Beck's story had no foundation other than the wintering of the *North Star* (a supply ship sent out the previous year to assist Sir James Ross) at Wolstenholme Sound and the death of one of her crew by tumbling down a precipice. Sherard Osborn thought that Petersen, whose long residence at Upernavik made him neighbour to the Cape York people, understood their dialect better than Adam Beck, who came from farther south. Osborn wrote of this incident: 'An Eskimo cross-breed – may he be branded for a liar – succeeded in detaining for two days the squadrons in search of Franklin.'

Being now fairly in the North Water, the ships were able to disperse on various missions. Captain Austin, deeming it prudent, if not for his own satisfaction, for that of the public at home, to recheck the story of Adam Beck, sent the *Assistance* and the *Intrepid* to visit Wolstenholme Sound, the scene of the supposed massacre, before crossing to search the north shore of Lancaster Sound. He himself with the *Resolute* and the *Pioneer* was to examine its southern side, the north shore of Baffin Island. The *Prince Albert* and the *Felix* set a similar course. Penny struck across the North Water to his appointed task in Jones Sound.

The cruise of the *Prince Albert* was short. Lady Franklin had directed Forsyth and Snow to go down Regent's Inlet to Boothia, not so much because she shared the theories of Dr King, as on the supposition that Franklin's shipwrecked crews might have visited Sir John Ross's friends around Felix Harbour. This was a most sensible plan, and had it been faithfully carried out might have ended the search then and there. The *Prince Albert* passed through Lancaster Sound, checked James Ross's wintering quarters at Port Leopold, and there found a record of the missing transport *North Star*. In compliance with his orders, Commander Forsyth headed down Regent's Inlet, and off Fury Beach encountered ice which both his ice-mates declared to be impenetrable. When they were returning past Port Leopold, Snow undertook an inshore reconnaissance by boat, lost his way in the floating ice pieces, and barely got back to the ship. Forsyth reported to Captain Austin on the north shore of the sound and returned home with the news that traces of Franklin had been found at Beechey Island. Both Forsyth and Snow incurred censure – Forsyth for giving up so easily instead of wintering over, Snow for scooping all other prospective authors who *did* winter over with a somewhat inflated and insincere but lively narrative of the labours and hardships of which, as the hard-bitten ones declared, he had barely had a taste. Posterity can forgive him, for an amateur chronicle giving details and colouring which the naval officer would either take for granted or suppress on professional grounds, is a welcome variant from the formal daily journal.

In the meantime, Penny, finding Jones Sound hopelessly ice-choked, had come down and mingled with the other ships straggling in by way of Lancaster Sound. Foremost among these were two new recruits to the rescue work, the American hermaphrodite brigs *Advance* and *Rescue*. On board the former was Passed Assistant Surgeon Elisha Kent Kane, U.S.N., as colourful as Snow in writing history and far more resolute in making it.

The Americans entered the Sound in a gale and fairly open sea. They met and spoke to Penny, 'staggering along under a heavy weight of canvas,' says Kane. The Americans laid to and lost sight of the skipper from Aberdeen. On the twenty-first, 'running down before the wind and shipping seas at every roll,' they overhauled a tiny topsail schooner, the *Felix*. Apparently Penny had got into trouble in the ice, for Phillips roared above the gale, 'You and I are ahead of them all'. Kane went aboard, introduced himself to Phillips, and was presented to Sir John Ross, who now came on deck. Like some others who are dour controversialists in print, Ross in person seems to have been pleasant-spoken, and he made a good impression on the young surgeon:

'He was a square-built man, apparently little stricken in years. [He had just completed his seventy-third year.] He has been wounded in four separate engagements – twice desperately – and is scarred from head to foot. He has conducted two Polar expeditions already and performed in one of them the unparalleled feat of wintering four years in the Arctic snows. And here he is again in a flimsy cockle-shell.'

Subsequently, in wind and ice the *Advance* became separated from her consort, and on 25 August she approached unaccompanied the entrance to Wellington Channel. Here at the southeast angle of Devon Island the lofty ragged masses of rock which compose it subside into the spit of Cape Riley, and just off it the tiny islet of Beechey crops out of the sea, separated from the mainland by water so narrow and shallow that Kane refused to call it an island at all. Observing two cairns on Cape Riley, De Haven put inshore to examine them. The larger cairn, which was quite fresh, contained a note dated two days earlier and signed by Captain Ommaney. It stated that there and on adjoining Beechey Island he had found traces of a European expedition. Parry, who had given the island its name, had not landed there; no other known expedition had gone so far.

Ommaney's note stated that in company with the *Intrepid* he had reached Cape Riley on the twenty-third. His attention was drawn by a cairn; he landed to examine it and found no written message, although scattered rubbish, rags, and broken bottles proved that the traces were those of Europeans. On Beechey Island another cairn was found as well as an abandoned tent site. Ommaney placed his own record and sailed on into Wellington Channel.

The pattern of the ice in Barrow Strait channelled all the incoming ships to Beechey Island; the news of the find, handed on by excited men to the newcomers, became garbled, and the record confused. Kane asserts that the *Rescue* was in company with Ommaney's *Assistance,* and that Mr Griffin shared in the discovery, and he censures Ommaney for not acknowledging American collaboration in his record. McClintock's version of what happened does not bear this out. In his *Fox* journal, under the date 15 August 1858, he writes, 'Twelve days later than this in 1850, when I belonged to Her Majesty's ship *Assistance,* with considerable difficulty we came within sight of Beechey Island, a cairn on its summit attracted notice; Captain Ommaney managed to land and discovered the first traces of the missing expedition. Next day the United States schooner *Rescue* arrived; the day after Captain Penny joined us, and subsequently Captain Austin, Sir John Ross, and Captain Forsyth – in all ten vessels were assembled here.' It will be noted that Kane and McClintock assign different dates for the first find.

Captain Ommaney suffered one piece of censure which he did not deserve. In an unpublished letter to his father, Kane tells how when Penny arrived and learned from the Americans of the traces discovered and the empty cairn, he broke into a rage, declaring that the cairn must have contained a notice of Franklin's intended course and Ommaney had suppressed it to keep the others searching in wrong directions while he followed up the clue and monopolized the glory of success and the reward of £20,000 for the rescue of the crews and £10,000 for the discovery of their fate if none had survived. The Americans could listen to this outburst without concern; they had no mercenary hopes, for in a noble gesture their officers and men had signed a pledge renouncing any share of the Admiralty reward to which they might become entitled. In this instance, Penny was soon appeased, for ice had brought Ommaney to a stop, and the exact truth about the cairn was quickly known. Austin's two vessels came in, steered by 'the irresistible guidance of the ice'; the *Pioneer* grounded on a limestone reef and canted over with the ebbing tide. Penny drew alongside and took off a quantity of her stores, permitting her to float off at the flood. As any advance to the west or to the north was blocked, Penny and the Americans began an intensive search of the neighbouring land: it was at first supposed that the scanty relics found by Ommaney were those of a party travelling east on foot. This opinion was soon altered when Penny found on Beechey Island what had evidently been winter quarters – the site of armourer's and carpenter's shops, a garden, a pair of gloves lying on the ground and weighted down with a stone, and the graves of three men, two of the *Erebus* and one of the *Terror.* These, dated January and April 1846, afforded conclusive proof that there Franklin had spent the first winter of his cruise. Sledge tracks were traced for some distance

E

on Devon Island, but a relentless search there and on Beechey Island uncovered no record or any indication of Franklin's intended route in the summer of 1846.

This omission not only remains unexplained to this day, but seems incapable of satisfactory explanation. The binding duty of every discovery captain to plant, whenever opportunity offered, information of what he had done and of what he planned to do, of the health of his crews, and the period for which they were supplied was well known to the veteran explorer Franklin. And if he had forgotten, there were others to remind him of his duty, not merely as a part of routine, but as a means to their own preservation in event of mishap to the ships.

It is difficult to believe that some record was not left in a conspicuous place. But, if so, what became of it? Eskimos were prone to rob cairns, but there were no native settlements within hundreds of miles. Polar bears, McClintock thought, mistrusting anything vertical, were in the habit of knocking down upright poles, but they could hardly so demolish a cairn as to make it unrecognizable. The stone pile in which Hobson did find the expedition's one substantial record was crumbling but still conspicuous enough *It* had stood for eleven years instead of four. It is possible that Franklin had deferred the planting of a notice until his course for the summer was finally resolved upon, and that a sudden gale drove the solid ice out of the harbour and the ice-bound ships with it. McClintock, who was to experience such an accident at Dealy Island, thought that the form of the Beechey Island anchorage excluded this possibility. In any case, even with his future course undecided, Franklin might have been expected to deposit beforehand a record of the striking voyage he had made in the summer of 1845.

This important but inconclusive discovery was all that the amalgamated squadrons could achieve in their first season. With ice blocking Wellington Channel to the north and Barrow Strait to the west, they did not much improve upon the effort of Sir James Ross. During the consequent inactivity, Dr Kane went aboard the *Resolute,* where he met Lieutenant Willy Browne, the sailor-artist whom he had known previously in the Philippines. He also conferred with Sir John Ross, whose opinion it was that Franklin, finding other courses blocked, had sailed west to the forbidden region of Melville Island. Thither the rescue ships tried to shape a course, with little success. The Americans took the lead, causing some agitation among the British crews, who clamoured that the Yankees – one wonders whether the Southern gentlemen who sailed with De Haven knew that they were being so described? – must not be permitted to carry off the prize. They need not have worried. On 11 September all were icebound near Griffiths Island, barely thirty miles beyond Wellington Channel. Penny was observed, says Kane, 'like an indefatigable old trump, as he is, pushing, working, groping in the fog'; the rest, 'five black masses, their cordage defined by ice and snow,' lay resignedly moored to the shore ice. A gale arose and the cable of the *Rescue* parted. She faded away into the fog amid churning ice. She found refuge in the lee of Griffiths Island, and there lay unmanageable with her rudder split. A breakup permitted the *Advance* to come to her assistance and take her in tow. Here ended the Americans' participation in the search. De Haven's orders were to return before the onset of winter, for which he was manifestly ill-prepared. On his visit to the *Resolute,* Kane had been disturbed to note the abundance of clothing and heating facilities there provided. 'If these are necessary,' he thought, 'we are utterly unfitted for the winter.' De Haven offered to turn over some of his supplies to Austin. Fortunately, as it proved, the latter declined, and the Americans set an easterly course for the exit by Lancaster Sound. Austin's four vessels became solidly fixed near Griffiths Island, seaward from the modern post of Resolute Bay. The luckier Penny and Ross were able to work their small vessels into a snug anchorage in Assistance Harbour.

It would have been well for De Haven if the ice had hardened sooner and compelled him to pass the winter at Griffiths Island in company with the well-equipped and hospitable Austin. For off Wellington Channel he was beset in heavy ice pieces, quickly welded by frost into a solid mass. Southerly winds began to work on the sea ice, driving it and the two ships into and far up Wellington Channel. In fog and the shrinking hours of daylight – for the Arctic night was almost upon them – the Americans could still note land features and measure their daily rate of advance. Twenty miles above Cape Bowden, Parry's northernmost observation, the high bluffs of Barlow Inlet on the west side of the channel faded from view; new features were taking shape ahead and on either side. Kane recalled the torments which Back's *Terror* had undergone when similarly trapped, but he reasoned hopefully and, in this instance, correctly that at so high a latitude the ice would freeze too solidly to be so violently convulsed. On 22 September they were sixty miles north of Cape Hotham on the western side of the channel entrance, and frozen in so firmly that furious gales from the north did not budge them. Early in October the upward thrust relaxed and the two ships drifted slowly back to Barrow Strait and there remained for a month eddying around with the ice which gripped them, and hoping to be fixed there within reach of the British squadron thirty miles to the west.

The British were totally ignorant of the nearness of the Americans, though Penny feared that they would become ice-bound before getting out of Lancaster Sound. This situation was to give rise to some international unpleasantness. Owing to fog and departing daylight, De Haven's sixty-mile penetration of Wellington had not been too rewarding geographically. But he had identified and named a number of features, including a range of hills seen at a distance north and east and named after the expedition's patron, Henry Grinnell. In the following spring, Penny was to make a much deeper penetration of the channel by sledge and boat, assigning his own names to various features, which he duly reported for insertion in Admiralty charts. This slight, deliberate or not, was vehemently resented in the American press. The Baltimore *Sun* denounced the 'astounding impudence of the English Government . . . On their Admiralty 'maps of Arctic discoveries' they have actually stolen the American discovery of Grinnell Land.' William Scoresby, a former whaling captain and an Arctic authority, wrote a letter of protest to the London *Morning Post*. American names were restored – if not to the same, then to similar features. The name Grinnell Land is now attached to the northwesterly peninsula of Devon Island, which probably lay beyond De Haven's vision but, as a prominent feature, fittingly commemorates the generous merchant of New York.

De Haven's crews fairly earned that recognition, for they passed one of the grimmest winters that any ship's company has lived to report. For most of November they lay welded in their ice cake, keeping the same relative position and slowly circling in relation to the land. On the twenty-ninth, it became evident that fears long present had become fact; they had swung far enough out into Barrow Strait to be caught in the eastward drift and were being carried through Lancaster Sound toward Baffin Bay in ice drifting steadily and liable to sudden fracture. On 2 December alarming convulsions occurred around the ships; bags of pork, sugar, and bread were packed and placed on deck. Such alarms recurred frequently; Griffin, who, with De Haven disabled by sickness, was in virtual command, made systematic provision for abandoning ship at a moment's notice. So they passed out of Lancaster Sound into Baffin Bay, and were carried southward with the drift. The officers, judging that in the broader waters of the bay there was not much danger of the ships parting company by the breakup of the floe, decided on a temporary desertion of the *Rescue,* and for the sake of company, morale, and the conservation of fuel, they huddled all hands on the *Advance.* They were soon far out at sea, with nothing visible in the Arctic twilight except smooth ice, varied by hummocks draped in snow. Kane found this irksome: 'To look at the completely unbroken area which shows itself from our masthead, motion would be the last idea suggested. In Lancaster Sound the changing phases of the coast gave us a feeling of motion, progress, drift. ... But here, within this circle of impenetrable passive solidity, everywhere around us, it is hard to believe that we move. ... Yet we have thus travelled upward of three hundred miles.'

Scurvy was prevalent, and the officers were too depressed to do much to provide entertainment, but the men, like the British Investigators, when suffering a like neglect, organized their own shows. Washington's birthday was celebrated on a stage where the temperature was thirty degrees colder than Parry's coldest, and the actors moved about in the fog of their own congealing breath. 'Any extra vehemence of delivery was accompanied by volumes of smoke,' reported Kane.

Insufficient clothing, defective diet, and the seeds of scurvy had not robbed the brave fellows of their spirit. In the bitter cold of late February they hacked and dug the ice away from the waterline of the *Rescue* to repair damage to her hull. Two more months elapsed before she was remanned on 22 April, and six weeks more before she was again afloat. On 5 June she was manageable under sail. 'A beautiful sight it was to see once more in this labyrinth of rubbish, a moving, sail-spread ship,' says Kane. On the eighth the *Advance* was freed from the crumbling floe. She had been imprisoned for almost nine months.

The way home was open, but neither De Haven nor his crews were ready to admit defeat. They worked their way over to the Greenland shores and there met two Scottish whalers, fresh from their home port. 'They left us newspapers, potatoes, turnips, eggs and fresh beef enough to eat out every taint of scurvy,' Kane noted.

Moving north, they fell in with a number of British whalers held up by the ice of Melville Bay. Quail, master of the New England *McLellan*, 'made us pay freely' for supplies furnished, Kane recorded, but the British, in gratitude for American aid, would accept neither payment nor receipt – 'Their malt and brandy and vegetables and quarters of fresh beef covered our decks.' (In *Moby Dick*, Herman Melville, who was not generally friendly to the British Mercantile Marine, also praised the lavish hospitality of their whaling vessels.) With a healthy diet thus assured, the Americans pushed into the Melville Bay ice, and there in July they were overtaken by the *Prince Albert*, coming up a second time with Captain William Kennedy and Enseigne de Vaisseau J. R. Bellot in charge.

The rescue ships in Barrow Strait had in the meantime passed the winter in reasonable comfort. Penny and Ross had a secure anchorage in Assistance Harbour. Austin's four ships were in the frozen sea to the west, a dangerous situation when the ice broke up in summer, and also a handicap for spring sledge journeys. While Penny could use all his men for travel except half a dozen caretakers, Austin would be obliged to leave working crews with his vessels for fear that an early breakup might carry them away.

McClintock spent the interval between the freeze-up and the final disappearance of the sun from that latitude in trying to plant food depots westward for the use of spring travelling parties. He found the sea ice still thin and liable to be shattered by gales and tidal action, and could make his farthest cache only forty miles ahead of the ships. Observations convinced him that only a narrow belt of heavy ice caused their detention at Griffiths Island, but for which they might have matched Parry's voyage to Melville Island.

As soon as winter quarters were fairly established, Penny and Austin held a conference at which it was decided that Penny with his two crews would search to the northward along the shores of Wellington Channel, while Austin's detachments would call at Cape Walker (where they still hoped to find a Franklin record), search the north shore of Barrow Strait, and visit Melville Island, 300 miles to the west. Franklin's orders had warned him away from that region, but such a prohibition was not expected to be binding, if, as now appeared all too probable, he had found other avenues blocked.

It was not for nothing that Austin had served under Parry on a winter station. He exerted himself for the maintenance of health and morale, and all officers zealously co-operated. Dramatics provided occupation for many and entertainment for all; the artistic among the crews made snow sculptures; school was set up for the seamen, with lectures by those officers who were gifted that way. Also tedium was relieved by pursuit of the Arctic fox and the polar bear.

During the winter spent at Port Leopold, Sir James Ross had created the 'Arctic Postman' by trapping foxes and freeing them with metal collars attached, giving notice of where the rescue expedition was wintering and where food depots had been placed. In imitation of this practice, Captain Austin issued stringent orders that no fox caught alive in a trap was to be killed – after which 'they were all unaccountably dead, unless it were some unfortunate wight whose coat and brush were worthless,' Osborn records. The sailors valued pelts more than they did postmen. Sherard Osborn, who seems to have known more about the pranks of petty officers and seamen than was quite fitting for one of his rank, justifies this illicit traffic in furs by observing that no fox which had once fed at the ships' garbage dump would wander away in any case. The polar bear was also coveted as game – with little success. Only one was killed in the course of the winter. Spring guns were planted, 'from which,' says Osborn, 'the proprietor daily expected a dead bear, and I a dead shipmate'. (Captain Austin must have been ignorant of this dangerous practice.) Cruder methods, as appears from a story told by Osborn, were equally unsuccessful. 'My captain of the forecastle, whose sporting propensities I have elsewhere noted [he was the man who had assailed a bear with birdshot] nigh cured me of a momentary mania for trophies of the chase. A large bear and her cub, after coming towards the *Pioneer*, for some time halted, and were fired at by three officers with guns. Of the three barrels only one went off, wounding the cub, which, with its mother, made for Griffiths Island. I chased, followed by some of the men, the foremost of whom was my ancient mariner, who kept close to my heels urging me on by declaring that we were catching the brutes. . . . By the time we reached the island both bears were within shot, climbing with cat-like agility the steep face of the cliffs: again and again I failed to get my gun off.' And as the mother bear had paused with a menacing aspect, 'I looked round at my supporters, who were vehemently exclaiming that "we should have her in a minute." They consisted of old Abbott, armed with a snow-knife, and some men who had followed because they saw others doing so.' The captain ordered a prompt retreat and on the way back to the ship asked a seaman if Abbott's knife was sharp. 'I was figuratively told, "The owner, John Abbott, could have ridden to the devil upon it without injury to his person."' With the return of sunlight these casual occupations were given up, and all concentrated on the preparation of sledges, rations, and clothing for the forthcoming spring journeys.

The performance of the ships in the previous autumn had been disappointing. The penetration to Griffiths Island had not exceeded that of Sir James Ross by more than sixty miles. Hence, a heavy burden was imposed upon the foot travellers, if an extensive search was to be made. Crews dragging food, fuel, and tenting supplies on sledges could not hope to travel more than 100 miles before a shortage of rations would compel a return to base. On this and the succeeding voyage, McClintock vastly increased their range by two means. One was to advance food depots beforehand along intended routes. A cache fifty miles from the ship would permit an outward-bound crew to top off its supplies and leave a reserve for the last lap of the homeward journey. Such a cache must be placed on land because the sea ice was always liable to rupture and displacement. If not well secured, it might be torn down and its contents destroyed by bears. There was in addition the risk of plunder by a roving band of Eskimos. A more reliable aid was the system of supporting sledges, later adopted by Robert E. Peary on his journey to the Pole. One or more laden crews would accompany the main party, feeding themselves and it, and thus enabling it to cover a great distance with its own supplies undiminished. The supporting sledge would then return to the ship and, if there was need, would go out again to plant supplies for the main party on its return journey. It was characteristic of McClintock that, while he took pains to keep the weights down, he reversed the harsh rule of Sir James Ross, and included a quantity of tobacco in every sledge cargo.

The months of April, May, and June were the season for sledging. The sun had returned and temperatures were moderating, while the snow remained to provide easy sledging on land; and the sea, frozen by then to a thickness of six feet, was safe, except for the occasional rupture by gale, tide, or current.

Storm and cold delayed the departure of the travelling parties after everything was made ready. The perverse Osborn, who in the course of the winter had fallen out with Captain Austin, whose ill report might have ruined him, took the opportunity of running over to Assistance Harbour to pay his respects to Penny and to Sir John Ross, an irascible old eccentric, who could do him neither good nor harm. They were three strenuous individualists, with much in common.

On 15 April 1851, the principal detachments set forth, with McClintock commanding the western and Ommaney the southern party. The latter, with Osborn, Mecham, and Browne, headed for Cape Walker on the opposite side of Barrow Strait. The cold was severe and the north wind blew strong. Making the best of a bad job, the sailors rigged sails on the sledges, thereby greatly reducing their labour. Nonetheless, the journey was hard for inexperienced men. Crews were shuffled and a number of frost-bitten men sent back with the first supporting sledge. In a week they crossed the strait and made land at the base of Cape Walker, a tremendous sandstone conglomerate, towering up to a height of 1,000 feet and sloping away to the southwest. Mecham and Browne searched this way and that for cairn and record, but to no purpose; not a trace appeared to show that the *Erebus* and the *Terror* had, as orders required, passed that way.

Cape Walker proved to be part of a detached islet (Russell Island) backed by a larger mass of land, unknown to Parry, and now named Prince of Wales Island. To its left lay Peel Sound, the channel whose eastern shore had been traced two years before by James Ross and McClintock. Ommaney directed Lieutenant

E*

Browne to examine this strait on its west side, while he and Osborn followed Franklin's intended course southwest from Cape Walker, along the shore of Prince of Wales Island. At first they avoided the winding beach and set a direct course over the frozen sea. But the ice was found to be too rough for this to be practicable – 'up steep acclivities and through pigmy ravines in which the loose snow caused them to sink deeply,' says Osborn – and so they turned landward and followed the beach or smooth ice along the shore.

Despite the absence of a record at Cape Walker, the sailors trudged along full of cheer and hope, and, says Osborn, regularly expected to find what they sought on the other side of the next cape. The hardship of the daily journey was offset by cheer and good fellowship in the evening tent. There were three officers in the party – Ommaney, Osborn, and Webb – a sturdy young mate, who, rather than forgo the journey, had volunteered as a sledge-hauler. Distinctions of rank were laid aside as the officers exchanged yarns with the men, or listened while a crusty marine lectured a young seaman ambitious of promotion: 'There's captains and admirals paid to look after you, and why should you wish to alter your station?' Arrived at Ommaney Bay, the captain sent Osborn across, while he completed his outward journey by circling its shore. On reaching land, Osborn traced the coast southward to two peculiarly shaped conical hills and tried to cross the sea to the west, but was foiled by rugged ice, fog, and wind. He may have wondered how Collinson and McClure were faring in their voyage in by Bering Strait, but did not suspect that when he ended his journey, Mr Wyniatt of the *Investigator* was on the shore of an unknown land some hundred miles to the west. They started back none too soon, for with sun, wind, and tide the ice was beginning to rupture. Osborn got back to his ship safely; Ommaney barely got his sledge over a rift in the ice on a bridge of boarding pikes. Back too came Willy Browne from his journey down Peel Sound, the channel which had led the lost ships to destruction. He and his crew had been tormented by continual wind and blizzard. He reported no tidemark past Cape Walker, and probably no tide in that wind-vexed channel. In his opinion, it froze to the bottom and was 'rarely, if ever, open to navigation'. Ommaney and Osborn were equally sure that no ship could have navigated the dense and heavy pack to the west of

Prince of Wales Island. If these opinions were correct – and the Admiralty had nothing else to guide them – the lost ships would not be found to the south of Barrow Strait.

The westward search had been no more encouraging. McClintock had set out in that direction with Lieutenant Bob Aldrich, Dr Bradford, and supporting sledges. Morale was high and the men as keen as the officers. When the time came for supporting crews to go back, men would conceal their frost-bitten feet in their determination to share the honour of the 'extended journey'. Bob Aldrich was detached to go up the west side of Bathurst Island, and Dr Bradford to search the Melville Island east shore. The doctor, popular and a keen sportsman – he had been a great friend of Fitzjames – sprained his ankle shortly after parting from McClintock; his men refused to go back, and planting him on the sledge along with rations and tents, carried out the task assigned. McClintock kept on steadily to the west, passed seaward of Winter Harbour and reached Parry's farthest advance at Cape Dundas. There, he judged the condition of the ice to be such that no ship could have passed *that way*. He went up Liddon Gulf to the old encampment where Parry's land transport had broken down. He brought away fragments of a broken cart wheel, and noted bones of ptarmigan, on which Parry and Sabine had fed thirty-one years before, still brittle and untouched by decay in that cold dry air. From there he went overland to Winter Harbour and on the top of Parry's 'monument' placed a metal cylinder containing a record of his journey and the position of Austin's ships (McClure of the *Investigator* was to find it the following spring). The return journey was cheered by summer weather, the appearance of sandpipers, brant geese, and gulls, with the less agreeable accompaniment of pools of water and spongy, yielding snow. McClintock reached the ships on 4 July. He had been away eighty days, forty-four out and thirty-six home, and had travelled a total of 770 miles to a distance of 300 miles from the ships, setting a pattern of polar travel that only the advent of aircraft would make obsolete.

While Austin's ships lay at Griffiths Island, awaiting the gale that would shatter the rotting ice and give them release, that faithful comrade Sherard Osborn kept his glass trained across the ice on Assistance Harbour, where lay Penny's brigs, the *Lady Franklin* and the *Sophia*. Of all the travelling parties, Penny's alone was still absent, somewhere up Wellington Channel, braving fog and wind-driven ice in an open boat.

The previous summer, Parker Snow had described the sturdy whaler as ' daring, pushing, ardent, enthusiastic . . . bronze-faced, fur-capped, jacketed, with a spy glass slung around him, ready for any emergency that might suddenly meet him '. This flattering picture, confirmed by Kane, had been more than justified by the vigour, flexibility, and promptitude shown by Penny in his survey of Wellington Channel. As noted, he had the advantage of a sheltered harbour and ships securely anchored. Hence only four men on board. An early and impetuous start by the rest was foiled by gales and low temperatures. All parties came back to the ships, the better, perhaps, for the experience gained on their involuntary trial run. Early in May they were off again, rounded Cape Hotham into Wellington Channel, and divided. Captain Stewart and the ship's surgeon, Dr Peter Sutherland, took their sledges across the channel to trace its eastern shore as far as supplies permitted. Surgeon Goodsir, brother of Fitzjames's 'canny Scot,' with Mr Marshall went up the western side. He found no record of the lost ships, but in a shallow cove did pick up a piece of charred wood, which, as we now know, probably belonged to them. His progress was halted by open water washing a shoreline impassable to sledges.

Stewart and Sutherland in the meantime took their sledges up the channel's eastern shore until, at Prince Alfred Bay, they found it bending away to the west. At this point (220 miles from their base), Sutherland was detached to follow in detail the shore of the bay and then return to the ships. Stewart went on to the west and reached Cape Becher with Sir Robert Inglis Bay on its farther side. He, too, was stopped by water.

On his way back to the ship, Sutherland met Penny with a party dragging a whaleboat mounted on a sledge. After getting his sledge parties off, the skipper had gone up the frozen channel with Petersen and his dogs – the only such team used on the expedition – and the seaman Alexander Thompson. Around Baillie Hamilton Island, situated at the kink in the channel, they came upon decayed ice, broken by a powerful tide into water lanes, and saw walrus, eiders, and burgomaster gulls – all signs of approaching summer. Though more than 100 miles from his base, the enterprising skipper hurried back and borrowed Sir John Ross's two carpenters to aid his own in building a sledge on which a boat could be hauled to the water's edge. He was able to muster a crew from supporting parties that had come back, and set out on 10 June. Meeting Sutherland, he found the surgeon's men so far from being used up that some begged to be added to the boat crew. Shortage of rations compelled a refusal. As Penny moved north, he found open water extending south to meet him. Afloat on the seventeenth, he entered Maury Channel between Baillie Hamilton Island and the Cornwallis shore.

Penny had hoped to travel 1,000 miles on his boat excursion, but the success which his resourcefulness and energy so richly deserved was not to be had. Contrary gales – on one occasion a 'perfect gale with heavy squalls' – bringing down fresh ice from the north, hindered him from getting around to the north of Baillie Hamilton Island. Finally, he passed it to the south on a side wind only to find progress to the west blocked, and was forced to put in at Stewart's farthest by land, Cape Becher. From its summit to the northwest the frustrated explorer saw water in the distance and beyond it a watery sky, marking the final northward bend of the strait, now rightly called Penny Channel. He concluded incorrectly that Cornwallis Island was linked by an isthmus to Bathurst Island to the west. Not until 1859 was it known that there was a channel there, and that the *Erebus* and the *Terror* had sailed through it.

Though saved from a dire fuel shortage by the killing of a walrus whose blubber was used for cooking, Penny could wait no longer for the ice to disperse. He headed south down Wellington Channel to find that the north winds that had so cruelly disappointed him were still working against him. The lower reach of the channel was so jammed with broken ice that the last 100 miles was covered on foot. Splendid men and splendid leadership brought them over jagged rock, through ice-cold water and sludge, back to the ships on 25 July.

Though inadvertently altering the place names of De Haven, Penny was not forgetful of his allies. He placed on his chart the names of Grinnell, De Haven, Kane, and Griffin, as well as that of the great American oceanographer Maury. Echoing the British practice of adorning the map with the names and titles of royalty, he named a President's Bay in honour of the chief magistrate of the Union.

A charming entry in Penny's journal shows that his courage and vigour were matched by his Christian piety. In the crisis of his boat journey, he still took care to observe the Sabbath with all possible strictness, and notes for Sunday 22 June, 'After morning Service, the people went out with their guns, this being considered a work of necessity.' When they came back empty-handed, Penny felt pangs of conscience. 'A small still voice whispered to me: "Is it a work of necessity?" I feared it was not.'

Penny had picked up a piece of English elm at Maury Channel, which, like Goodsir's pinewood, had probably belonged to the lost ships. The unfortunate results of these finds was to lessen the significance of the wreckage Rae found later in the summer off Victoria Island. It did not seem possible that relics placed so far apart could have the same source. Rescue expeditions had been so fearfully obstructed by ice that no one then imagined that Franklin could have ascended to the top of Wellington Channel and then swooped down to within 100 miles of the continental shore. In the official opinion it was *either, or;* and in view of the open condition of Wellington Channel early in the 1851 season, the decision to make a further search there, though mistaken, is hardly surprising.

That costly error might, however, have been avoided if Penny had had his way. Back at Assistance Harbour he engaged in vehement debate with Austin. Judging Wellington Channel quite navigable to a powered vessel, he wished to borrow one of the naval steamers and extend the promising search he had already made. Austin refused. It was his intention to circle eastward and reach the waters above Devon and Cornwallis islands by way of Jones Sound. With nothing else to do, Penny sailed for home.

Subsequently, Austin must have regretted rejecting Wellington Channel, virtually a 'bird in the hand', for the uncertainties of Jones Sound. He found it ice-blocked and got nowhere. In addition, he nearly lost a ship and crew. The *Intrepid* was nipped between an iceberg and a moving floe, pushed up the side of the berg, and only by a miracle of luck slid back upright and undamaged. Kane's *Advance* was to suffer the same mishap, but her escape was less remarkable, as she had not one-third of the British ship's tonnage.

Baffled at all points, Austin sailed back to a disappointed and resentful homeland.

6 Kennedy and Bellot in Regent's Inlet

In the spring of 1851 when the detached parties of Austin and Penny (and of McClure) were weaving their way around hummock and rock in every direction except the right one, the *Prince Albert* for the second time set forth for Regent's Inlet and the Boothia Isthmus. Franklin's undaunted widow had sidelined Forsyth and Snow and put in command William Kennedy, a Canadian fur trader of Scottish Orkney descent. The crew, too, was largely made up of Orkney men, either fur traders or fishermen in their native waters, some experienced travellers in the sub-Arctic, and all good boatmen. The sailing master was an old Greenland whaler named Leask. As second-in-command Lady Franklin appointed one of the two volunteers whose achievements, and the journals in which they relate them, so enrich the story of the search for Franklin.

Joseph Réné Bellot was born in Paris in 1826 to a family that would have been described in the patronizing language of the time as the 'deserving poor'. When five years old, he moved with his family to Rochefort, where his father worked as blacksmith and farrier. Bellot was one of many children, and his family's means were small. Young Joseph Réné, however, so distinguished himself in elementary school and was so highly recommended by his schoolmaster that the municipality at the suggestion of the Mayor awarded him a scholarship to the College of Rochefort. From there, at the age of fifteen, he qualified to enter the naval school. By extreme self-denial his parents supplemented help from other sources and enabled him to complete training as a naval officer. Bellot was almost morbidly conscious of his indebtedness to his family and his obligation to make the most of opportunities which had been provided at such cost. His Latin temperament saved him from developing into a self-righteous drudge. 'His character was sad and thoughtful, his spirit gay,' said a relative.

With all his earnestness he was a good fellow and accepted modes of thought alien to his own with a readiness too spontaneous to be called tact. At the age of eighteen, as *élève de marine* (midshipman), he sailed for Africa, took part in operations along with the British against the natives of Madagascar, and was awarded the Cross of the Legion of Honour. As an *enseigne de vaisseau* (sub-lieutenant) he served in South American waters. Back in France in 1850 and with no immediate prospect of another seagoing commission, he obtained a leave of absence to take part in the Franklin search. He wrote to Lady Franklin, and on her invitation went to England, where he was closely quizzed by that prudent lady, who feared bad publicity if a foreign officer, whose offer of service was widely known, failed to make good. Completely satisfied, she appointed him to serve with Kennedy on the *Prince Albert*.

On the 90-ton schooner he made the voyage as far as Stromness, where the ship was held up for several days by contrary winds. Bellot spent the time in social activities and in studying Scottish character. 'Decidedly these people are civilized – highly civilized,' was his conclusion. Rather than be thought irreligious, and for the honour of France, he endured a Scottish sermon, which he found 'dull and stupefying', while with characteristic objectivity he was pleased to hear a special petition offered for the crew of the *Prince Albert,* and the prayers of the faithful invoked for their safety. More to his taste was a visit to a Scottish home where 'the young people [by what means he does not say] got rid of papa whose religious views do not accord with dancing'. His wit did not spare his own captain. Learning that the austerely religious Kennedy would allow no intoxicants on board, he observed ruefully, 'no doubt this precaution will give an unprecedented lustre to our expedition'. And he commends the foresight of Lady Franklin and Miss Sophia Cracroft (Sir John's niece) for interlarding Kennedy's sailing orders with prayers and pious thoughts – it was the only way to make sure that Kennedy would read them!

Lady Franklin had come up to Stromness to see her ship off. She exhorted Bellot to restrain the impetuosity of Captain Kennedy, who had already lost a jib boom by carrying too much sail. She examined his wardrobe and equipment and observed that he still needed a mother. In his diary the enthusiastic Frenchman declared that he accepted the relationship and would 'seek my father with the inexhaustible devotion of a son '. He noted with approval that the extravagant propensity of the Scot to favour those of his own race has its limits. Mr Leask, on being admonished that instead of taking his own ship out of Stromness harbour – which he was perfectly capable of doing – it would be becoming to hire a pilot and secure the guinea fee for a countryman, replied drily, 'it would *not* be becoming, when the guinea came from Lady Franklin's resources '.

On 3 June 1851 they were at last away. They passed the pinnacle, the Old Man of Hoy, and the red-faced, wind-beaten cliffs, to find themselves in their tiny craft alone on the open sea.

Accustomed to larger ships, Bellot was very ill at ease on the light schooner. 'She rolls most frightfully . . . I try to walk on deck, but am flung violently against the bulwarks. Alas! I try in vain to hide it – I am seasick. O shame, O despair! I look around furtively to see who are the witnesses of my dishonour; happily I have only accomplices. Messrs Leask and Hepburn, who alone are spared by this fatal disease, are not on deck. . . . An odour of whisky proves to me that not all my companions are incommoded merely by the motion of the ship; some of them have been bidding a last farewell to the pleasures of this world before becoming real teetotallers.

Bellot with ready good humour adjusted himself to the society of men so different from himself in background and tastes. Kennedy's deep and earnest religion he treated with amused tolerance, a trace of boredom, but with understanding and respect. 'Mr Kennedy was educated by a minister to which circumstances without doubt he owes his excessive piety,' he says, and notes with a sort of grimace that one Sunday, when sickness confined him to his bed, the captain came down to read prayers with him in his cabin. Yet Bellot was too intelligent not to feel the genuineness of Kennedy's religion, and too sensitive not to be impressed by it. 'If the piety of our men is not very enlightened, at least it appears sincere, and if it were only a matter of habit, the influence of that habit on their way of life is genuinely wholesome . . . I know of no spectacle which inspires one more to serious thought than the sight of a few men singing praises to God in the vast ocean solitudes. . . .' Bellot occasionally conducted religious services in the place of the captain.

With Mr Leask, Bellot seems to have remained on terms of

formal courtesy. It is not unlikely that that veteran officer resented the elevation of Lady Franklin's young Lafayette to a rank above his own. On the other hand, Bellot became much attached to the supercargo, 'the good Mr Hepburn'. A crew of eighteen hardly required such an officer in addition to a clerk-in-charge, but Hepburn was sixty-one, and Lady Franklin may well have enlisted him more because she did not have the heart to refuse than for any essential service he could render. Bellot, who greatly admired Franklin's *Narrative* describing the earlier voyage, was delighted to find in Hepburn a shipmate who had shared in that perilous journey. He was never weary of listening to yarns of ice pack and tundra, and of the period – to him legendary – of Napoleon's wars, during which Hepburn had been a prisoner of war of both French and American navies.

By the beginning of July, the *Prince Albert* was across the Arctic Circle in Davis Strait. Keeping watch for the first time in the ice-strewn seas, Bellot exclaimed at the exhausting task of navigating among ice pieces, several times as large as the ship, stifled all the while by 'a thick envelope of fog'. 'Heavy detonations' like cannon shots warned him that he had crept within two cables' length of a towering berg, rotting in the heat of summer and capable at any moment of crumbling or overturning.

By the middle of the month they were at the lower angle of Melville Bay. There they met no fewer than ten whaling ships, held up and tacking back and forth in a relatively open space to escape besetment in the denser ice which lay around. The tiny *Prince Albert* proved her manoeuvrability in this exercise, though Bellot, lying in his berth, found the ceaseless grinding of the ice disturbing, and thought gloomily of Leask's prediction that they would not get by Melville Bay that season. He pitied Franklin's men, starving somewhere in the icy wilderness to the west, and Lady Franklin's distress on learning that her second venture had failed more completely than the first.

Exertions to avoid entanglement in the moving pack ice were not so great as to hinder friendly exchanges with the whalers. From these they learned the details of the Beechey Island find, but could gather nothing of Austin's movements that spring and summer, or of his present whereabouts. The *Advance* and the *Rescue*, they were told, after a winter of hardship in the ice, had made a fresh attempt, and were at that moment beset not more than twenty miles to the north. Bellot remarked that their misfortunes would teach people to think more kindly of Sir James Ross.

The Americans were even then working their way southward, and on the sixteenth the *Advance* was sighted from the masthead. Soon Dr Kane and Mr Murdaugh came aboard and introduced themselves. Bellot noted with amusement that before the Americans had been aboard five minutes they were as relaxed and intimate with their new acquaintances as if they had been friends from infancy.

For nearly a month the two ships exchanged almost daily visits. Bellot's new friends taught him how to stalk a seal by crawling over the ice on his elbows as if on flippers, raising his head from time to time like a seal on the watch for a prowling bear. Bellot does not inform us whether he ever deceived a seal by this subtle approach; he did impose on a fellow hunter, who luckily was beyond gunshot at the time. On one occasion, Kane tried to chase a polar bear around an iceberg into an ambush laid by Kennedy and Bellot, but the wily creature scampered off to lose itself amid the surrounding hummocks. Both Kennedy and Bellot fired at him and Kane thought that the bear *heard* the shots. When the American officers attended divine service on the *Prince Albert,* Bellot was impressed by the sincerity and fervour with which Kennedy prayed for their safety: 'Is not this one of the good sides of their religion, that every man of character can officiate without having taken Holy Orders?'

Leask was openly advocating giving up the Melville Bay route and attempting the Middle Passage. Kennedy disagreed, and kept the men busy warping the ship northward whenever a lane opened in that quarter. Bellot suggested using cylinders of blasting powder. Kennedy, he says tartly, denied the value of this agent because he did not know how to use it. Charges exploded under Bellot's direction yielded only a small gain in northing. So they gave up, bade farewell to the Americans at latitude 74° 30', dropped down south to latitude 72 degrees, and wheeled into the Middle Pack. Ultimately, De Haven gave up and returned home.

On 18 August, the *Prince Albert* was well into the Middle Ice in fog, snow, and rain. On the twenty-first, for the first time in weeks, they felt a slight swell. They had got across to the west side of Baffin Bay. On the twenty-sixth they were in Lancaster Sound off the north Baffin shore.

They were six weeks out of Upernavik, victims of the bad luck which haunted all of Lady Franklin's expeditions, not excepting the last. But for the time lost on the fringe of Melville Bay, they might have penetrated Regent's Inlet as far as John Ross's old anchorage, Felix Harbour; and from there, by efforts rightly directed Bellot might have achieved the honour he coveted – discovering what remained to be discovered of the lost men and ships. 'I will write books that shall be [a characteristic expression of self-forgetfulness] marriage-portions for my sisters.' Despite all his visions he remained alive to immediate practical requirements. He was well read in Arctic journals, and on their authority he advised his captain that so late in the season he should at once secure a safe winter harbour. Mr Kennedy had the more ambitious idea of sailing direct down Regent's Inlet before the freeze-up.

Above all it was urgent to learn what Austin and Penny had accomplished. For aught they knew, the lost crews might have been discovered that summer. So they approached the west side of Regent's Inlet, a repulsive shoreline of upheaved rock and snow-filled gorges, and brought to off Port Leopold. There was a likely place to find a record, but the harbour was ice-choked, and Leask declared that neither ship nor boat could get in. So the impetuous Kennedy pushed on, and at Fury Beach, where the *Fury* had been wrecked and John Ross's *Victory* had almost come to grief, he was caught between a shallow coastline and an advancing pack. He wriggled out and over to the east side of the inlet. On 8 September came the crisis. Kennedy still insisted on going south; Bellot, with the naval officer's instinct for securing men and material, insisted on the need of berthing the ship at once. He spoke sharply, and the cross-grained but essentially humble Kennedy apologized.

Now chance took a hand and put an end to uncertainty. Both agreed that they should recover the west side of Regent's Inlet, where at least no sea would separate them from their field of search in Boothia. On 9 September they were again off Port Leopold.

Here Kennedy, observing that, though the harbour was full of ice, the approaches were open, determined to go in with a boat crew of four, check James Ross's depot, and search for a record by Austin. He rashly set out with nothing in the boat except rockets and lanterns. He had not been long gone when a change in the wind drove ice in to block the harbour entrance, while the seaward pack was threatening to move in and crush the ship on the shore ice. Bellot had no choice but to make sail and leave his comrades to their fate. He could only hope that they had made land before the ice moved in. Rejecting the idea of crossing to Port Bowen and so putting the sea between them, he felt his way down the east shore of Somerset Island and found a safe anchorage in Batty Bay, thirty miles south of Port Leopold.

With winter so close upon him, Bellot dared not put out to sea again for fear of never getting back. On the other hand, it was urgent to give notice of their whereabouts to Kennedy, who, in the darkness, could not have known of the course taken by the ship and might, Bellot feared, attempt to cross the inlet to Port Bowen. So, as soon as the ship was secured, he took three men and set out for Port Leopold by land. When they camped for the night after a difficult journey against wind and snow, the men insisted that it was impossible to go farther without snowshoes. Inexperienced in Arctic travel though he was, Bellot was most unwilling to abandon his comrades. But when John Smith, whose brother was with the boat crew, assured him that the men were right, Bellot was forced to agree. The next day, plunging through new-fallen snow, they made their way back to the ship. In grimly practical terms, there was no longer the same need for haste in attempting a rescue. If Kennedy and the boat crew had been cut off from the harbour, they must have perished from famine and exposure. If they had reached land, Ross's depot at Leopold would provide food, fuel, and the means of shelter. As travel by land over icy rocks and through snow-filled ravines was neither safe nor easy, it was decided to wait until the rapidly advancing winter made a road along the shore ice. In the meantime, the Canadians in the crew busied themselves preparing snowshoes.

During the captain's absence, Bellot, who knew the importance of maintaining routine in the idle months of winter, kept up the practice of regular religious worship, exhorting the less godly of the crew that if Kennedy came back alive the conducting of service would prove that they had not forgotten his 'wholesome counsels'; if he were dead, the maintenance of prayers was due 'as a homage to his memory'. Few things are quainter or more entirely praiseworthy than the spectacle of a young French Catholic, not too precise, as he confesses, in the observances of his own creed, thus exerting himself to keep alive the zeal of Scottish Calvinists.

On 13 October Bellot was off again with the doctor and two men along the frozen margin of the sea. It was too early in the season for such a road to be safe. John Smith, scouting ahead, broke through thin ice. The sledge and supplies were partially immersed, necessitating a second return to the ship. Bellot hurriedly organized a third attempt – for the Arctic night was almost upon them – and this time reached Port Leopold to find the missing men safe and well. They had rigged themselves quarters in a boat roofed over with canvas. Bellot good-humouredly observed that the worst privation Mr. Kennedy had suffered was that of his Bible which he had carelessly omitted to take with him into the boat. With all men safely back on the ship, Bellot took a party out to recover equipment left behind on former journeys, and camped for the night in a heavy snowstorm. Yielding to the remonstrances of the dog driver, he turned his favourite dog out of the tent to pass the night with his comrades in the storm outside. In the course of the night, Bellot peered out to see how the animals were faring, and 'what was my surprise on seeing my favourite dog, aroused by the sound of my voice, emerge from a drift more than two feet deep. Barely perceptible undulations in his neighbourhood showed me that the rest of our pack were reposing in the same fashion without appearing in the least perturbed by the world of snow in which they were buried'. The Orkneymen told him that in their native Islands sheep left out in winter were sometimes buried under fifteen or twenty feet of snow. Yet, there they could still 'with the warmth of their respiration open a passage for the renewal of vital air'. The young Frenchman nearly had a chance of testing the possibility of survival under such conditions. He had camped in a storm and set up the tent with its entrance to the lee side and with a snow wall to protect the other sides from the drift. In the course of the night the wind veered, almost buried the tent, and sifted snow through the doorway in an advancing dune. On digging themselves out, the occupants found the hills behind which they had sheltered 'effaced' by a smoothly sloping ramp of snow.

Fully alive to the danger of idleness, Kennedy took advantage of a full moon to make a journey at the beginning of January. Its purpose was to harden the men for the forthcoming spring journey and to discover the condition of Parry's wreck cache at Fury Beach, which was to be the jumping-off point for their travels farther south. John Smith, the most experienced man in sledge work, as well as the only builder of snow houses, tried to make trouble by asserting that the equipment was inadequate for the depth of winter. Kennedy did not trouble to argue, but added a tent to the sledge load 'in order not to be at the mercy of the caprices of Mr John'. Bellot, for his part, gave the captain enthusiastic support, 'delighted to show them once again that a French officer will not hang back, but on the contrary thinks always of taking the lead'. The journey, a round trip of seventy miles, was made in ten days.

In the ensuing weeks, when weather permitted, supplies were advanced stage by stage to Fury Beach. For as long as a chance remained of Franklin's men being alive and in want, the depot there would be touched only under extreme necessity. Bellot furnishes a lively picture of the danger of these outings, especially when weather signs were not heeded. 'We are just back from an outing which all but cost us dear. Yesterday A.M. Mr Kennedy and myself with Mr Anderson, the carpenter and Mr Andrew Irvine, set out to advance another portion of our provisions. The weather did not look at all good, but precisely for that reason, rather than hang back, I joined myself to the party of which Mr Kennedy took personal charge. [This sounds as though the men objected to starting in such weather, but Bellot, though sympathizing with their scruples, joined to set an example of obedience.] The snow, very soft beyond the margin of the bay, made our journey trying all the way to the small depot which I had planted the preceding week; but as the ice was firm and good we added to our load the provisions which it contained and carried two miles further five cases of pemmican [450 pounds], six gallons of *esprit-de-vin* [fuel alcohol?] – in a word, all that the dogs could haul. Darkening skies and thickening snowdrift had been warning us for some time that the homeward journey would not be accomplished with ease.

'Scarcely had we turned our faces to the wind when we were all violently frost-bitten; happily the breeze moderated, and continually rubbing our faces with snow, we went staggering over the trail back to Batty Bay. It was quite dark by the time we reached the southern point of the bay. Having had nothing since morning except a morsel of biscuit without water – in order not to waste time – we were all very feeble, and turn about would lie on the sledge. Doubting the possibility of going much further, we debated whether to cover ourselves with the buffalo robe [one robe for five men] and to rest as best we could under the snow, or to return to our provision cache. It was decided that the best course was to go on as before.

' By the time we quitted the south side of the bay the darkness had become so absolute that the opposite side, though only a mile distant, had disappeared; and the wind changing direction every instant no longer served as a guide. In consequence we were wandering by guesswork until through a gap in the overcast the polar star showed us the direction to take. This circumstance permitted us to reach the north shore of the bay, but there we knew not whether we were to the east or the west of the ship. The hills which lined the beach, drifted under or obscured by whirling snow, were unrecognizable; and after having followed for what seemed a long time the direction which appeared the right one, we had to turn back for we found ourselves outside the bay on the open sea.

' The wind was still beating against us with violence; our dogs, spent with fatigue, stopped dead, and even though we cast them off from the sledge, lay down and refused to guide us. Perhaps the poor creatures were as frightened and bewildered as ourselves. The men who composed our troop were somewhat angry and dis-heartened. Altogether our outlook was far from pleasant. Every five minutes we must stop to rub our faces and to melt the snow which clung like glue to our eyelashes. The pebbles of the beach – which we dared not quit for fear of losing our way entirely – were painful to our feet. Poor Mr Anderson was every instant staggering from one stone to the next – we were obliged to guide him by the hand. Happily those of our dogs who had been released from the sledge came upon their former tracks and accompanied by those still harnessed to the sledge set off at a gallop, showing us that we were in the right direction – in good time to revive our drooping spirits. Following the windings of the bay, we arrived at our powder-magazine, and even this we would have missed, though only a few metres away, but for an oar whose colour, standing out against the snow, caught our eye.

' The ship, only two hundred yards away, was quite invisible.

So, forming a line parallel to the beach and in sight of one another, we marched seaward, and so came on board where we were warmly received and overwhelmed with the congratulations of our comrades, who had been very uneasy on our account. It was then 10 P.M., and as we had arrived at the opposite side of the bay at five, we had spent five hours turning and twisting in the neighbourhood of the ship. The men had been even more alarmed as two of the dogs let go had reached the ship about nine o'clock, and they had searched them in vain for some note or hint that might reveal our position.

'. . . . At present we cannot help laughing at our faces, puffed and scarred as if by blows of the fist. For a while the doctor feared that the nose of Mr Kennedy was frozen solid. As for me, *Dieu merci!* I find myself the least disfigured of our party, thanks to my unremitting attention to parts exposed, not hesitating to take off my mittens, if the need arose; they proclaim me an experienced traveller. A little intelligence and resolution have, I think, given me that experience in a short time, and fill me with hope for our coming journeys. True, we are in the hands of Him who watches over all his creatures, but one must help one's self *a little.*'

The day after this lucky escape, Kennedy informed his lieutenant that in his view it would be impossible from their remote winter quarters to carry out in full the orders received from Lady Franklin. Therefore, instead of tracing the entire west shore of Boothia, he would go only as far as the North Magnetic Pole. Bellot thought this 'a reasonable modification'. Winter journeys had given both him and his captain an insight into the logistics of sledge travel and the degree of exertion to be expected from the men. Privately, Bellot had decided that when the spring journey was over, he would take the boats at Port Leopold, round the north of Somerset Island to the west, and extend Sir James Ross's explorations in Peel Sound down to the continental shore 'east of the Coppermine'. On his way back he hoped to cross Boothia and visit Ports Felix and Victoria, in case any of the unfortunate wanderers might be found with the Eskimo friends of Sir John Ross. That is, he proposed to use Port Leopold as a base for the very search which Dr King had advocated by way of the Great Fish River.

When the time came, this voyage was ruled out by the outbreak of scurvy among the crew of the *Prince Albert*. Another entry in Bellot's journal shows that, given his own way, he might have brought the search to a successful end in a simpler manner. While he had accepted the shortening of the spring journey, he did not approve of its direction to the Magnetic Pole. He would have preferred to go down the east shore of Boothia straight to Ross's Eskimos. Franklin had admittedly met disaster to the west of Boothia, as his orders required him to by-pass Regent's Inlet and make for Cape Walker. But as news would travel fast among the Eskimos, especially news so sensational as the marooning of over a hundred Europeans among the islands, Bellot believed that Kennedy's first duty was to find and question them. 'For my part I attach great importance to this enquiry,' he wrote, and he was right. It was Eskimos, not deliberately sought out as they should have been, but accidentally met by Rae, who were to furnish the clue ardently sought for seven years. Bellot had scruples about pressing his views too urgently. 'As for my plans and my objections which I enter in my journal without reserve, I have only been able to express them timidly to Mr Kennedy, who, without doubt, knows better than I, the best course to pursue, but above all because I see that he takes offence easily. . . . He alone is responsible, and I will obey with the utmost promptitude orders clean contrary to what I myself think best.' Bellot would not disagree openly with his captain because he felt the need to set an example of unhesitating obedience. The winter journeys, which had given the enthusiastic Frenchman confidence, had bred only discouragement in some of the men. 'A number of our men are sick, or say that they are,' he wrote at Fury Beach. 'One has an incurable cough; another suffers from rheumatism or other pains which keep him nailed to his couch.' Kennedy told them that 'nothing would alter his determination, and that, if the rest hung back, he and Mr Bellot alone would march forth to the accomplishment of our enterprise. . . . I was not a witness to the delivery of this downright ultimatum, but I was delighted by Mr Kennedy's confidence that I would support him with good will and all the strength I could muster.' Either unjustly suspected or 'recalled by shame to a sense of duty,' the men protested their willingness to follow their captain wherever he led.

They set out from Fury Beach on 29 March, directing their course across Cresswell Bay down into Brentford Bay. Here,

Kennedy proposed to cross Boothia Peninsula in order to go down its western side. The supporting party was ordered to return to the ship. The two officers and four men remained to make up the travelling party.

At the outset, without realizing it, they made an important geographical discovery. Probing into the innermost part of Brentford Bay, they found, walled in on both sides by towering cliffs, a channel leading westward, which they mistakenly supposed to be a mere extension of the bay. Actually, this was Bellot Strait, which divides the peninsula of Boothia from Somerset Island.

On arriving at the larger waters at the west end of Bellot Strait, where Peel Sound merges into Franklin Strait, neither of the officers was clear as to their precise position or the pattern of land and water around them. The weather was hazy, and the conscientious but narrow Kennedy, taking literally Lady Franklin's reminder that he was not in the Arctic for geographical and scientific discovery but to rescue her husband, would not allow his lieutenant time for the observations necessary to determine the direction and distance they had travelled. Looking north up Peel Sound, Kennedy saw what he supposed to be ' a continuous barrier of land extending from North Somerset to an extensive land which we could distinguish on the other side of the channel' – Prince of Wales Island, already discovered by Ommaney and Osborn. At least, Kennedy asserted, there was no navigable channel in that quarter, thereby lessening the responsibility of Lieutenant Willy Browne, who had made the same damaging error the year before. Bellot agreed with him. This mistaken impression led Kennedy to a deviation from his orders. He should have followed the land south to the Magnetic Pole. But seeing what he supposed to be land lying across Peel Sound to the north, he concluded that Franklin could not have come down that way and that his proper course was to push on west until he found the open sea that could have afforded passage to the *Erebus* and the *Terror*. This was to mistake his duty. Lady Franklin had not asked him to trace the course of the missing ships, a duty already undertaken by Penny and Austin, but to find out where they were, without troubling himself about how they got there. Though Bellot fully understood this, he seems, perhaps from a sense of discipline, not to have resisted the change of plan. On

8 and 9 April 1852, they made the crossing of Peel Sound and landed on Prince of Wales Island.

Here Bellot's journal affords an amusing illustration of the difficulty of distinguishing the polar sea from land when both are covered with snow. In one entry he expresses surprise that Sir James Ross should have reported high land at a point where it is so low as easily to be mistaken for the frozen sea. In the same paragraph he says, 'In any case it is evident that the sea to the west of Somerset Land is closed to the north of Cape Bird' – which it is not. Possibly both observers were deceived by mirage. So they journeyed across Prince of Wales Island, seeking the western channel which actually they were leaving behind them. Kennedy grew discouraged and spoke of returning to Fury Beach and going south into Boothia, as Lady Franklin had wished. Bellot rightly answered that it was now too late. They reached the sea at Ommaney Bay, recrossed the island to Browne Bay, and followed the shore north to Cape Walker, seeking in vain for a record of Franklin. The name Bellot Cliff commemorates this visit. They then made haste to cross the north end of Peel Sound, as they were dangerously short of rations. They obtained supplies at the Port Leopold depot and reached the ship at the end of May to find that their comrades, like themselves, were suffering from scurvy.

A few days later, Kennedy informed Bellot that on reviewing the discoveries of the journey west from Brentford Bay, he had concluded that they had passed through a strait linking Brentford Bay to the western sea, making North Somerset an island and the south shore of the strait the northernmost part of the North American mainland (a distinction which has been wrongly claimed for Point Barrow, Alaska). Bellot made the tart response that he would not presume to refute Mr Kennedy's views, as he had been hindered from making the observations on which alone a sound opinion could be based. But he would not agree to amend their map by second thoughts conceived, as he supposed, two months after the event. He and Kennedy disagreed as to the precise course they had steered when crossing the sea west of Bellot Strait. Although as a scientific navigator, the Frenchman was correct in insisting that observations, however partial and suspect, should be recorded as they appeared at the time, in this instance the untutored instinct of the skipper was right. The strait in which Bellot did not believe now bears his name.

When the ice broke up, Kennedy took his ship across to Beechey Island, where he spoke to Commander Pullen of H.M.S. *North Star*, berthed there as depot ship to a new naval expedition under Sir Edward Belcher. He then returned home.

During the next winter Bellot, now promoted lieutenant in the French Navy, was invited by Lady Franklin to take command of her little steamboat *Isabel* on a rescue voyage by way of Bering Strait. Kennedy had volunteered his services as second-in-command. Reflecting, perhaps, that that excellent man would be as trying a subordinate as he had been as a superior officer, Bellot declined the appointment. It was a wise but fatal decision. In 1853 he joined Commander Inglefield in H.M.S. *Phoenix*, carrying supplies to the Belcher expedition. On reporting to the *North Star* at Beechey Island, Bellot volunteered to carry dispatches to Sir Edward Belcher, who was somewhere up Wellington Channel. He set out with four men (one an old Navy man, William Harvey – later chief quartermaster of the *Fox*), a sledge, and a rubber boat. On the evening of 14 August, judging the ice over which they were travelling unsafe, Bellot resolved to camp on land. Harvey and one seaman had carried a rope over a lead when the ice broke, carrying Bellot and the other two men away into the darkening sea. As they were sitting disconsolately in their tent at daybreak, one of the men observed that the Americans had been carried away in the same manner and had come to no harm. Bellot replied, 'If God protects us, not a hair of our heads will fall to the ground.' He then tied up his books and said that he would go out to observe the course of their drift. When he had been absent for four minutes, the men, growing alarmed, went out of the tent; their officer was nowhere to be seen. After searching all around the tiny floe, they caught sight of his stick floating on the other side of a thirty-foot lead. Apparently, while emerging from the tent, stooping and off balance, Bellot had been caught by a gust of wind and swept into the water, too tightly buttoned to swim.

By his death, Bellot did make the provision for his sisters, which had always been his earnest desire. The Royal Geographical Society raised a fund for a monument to him, with the balance, if any to be used for the relief of his family. Over £2,000 were contributed, and the trustees, with a reversal of priorities which the affectionate brother would certainly have approved, gave handsome dowries to each of his five sisters before setting up his monument at Greenwich Hospital, on the south bank of the Thames.

7 Cruise of the *Investigator* – Northwest Passage Discovered

In the early months of 1851, Rae on Wollaston Land, Osborn on the west shore of Prince of Wales Island, and McClintock at Winter Harbour were all in fairly close proximity to travelling parties of the *Investigator*. It is time to trace the course of that vessel and ascertain how those near contacts came about.

When Sir James Ross returned unsuccessful from Barrow Strait in late 1849, his ships, the *Enterprise* and the *Investigator,* were promptly refitted and remanned. Captain Richard Collinson was appointed to the *Enterprise,* with Robert McClure promoted to commander under his orders in the *Investigator.* Collinson was directed to proceed by way of Cape Horn to Bering Strait and to search for Franklin in the unexplored seas north of Alaska and the Mackenzie River. In prosecution of these orders, the ships left the port of London on 10 January 1850, and sailed down the English Channel. Rough weather compelled them to put in at Plymouth, where further supplies were taken aboard, and a most original character enrolled in the expedition.

For nearly a century the evangelical Moravian Brotherhood had maintained stations on the coast of Labrador, where their missionaries had mastered the Eskimo language and way of life, and had done much for the spiritual and material welfare of their native flock. The Admiralty therefore requested the head of that order in London to furnish Collinson with a man who had served in this field, in the hope that the dialect spoken in Labrador might be intelligible to the natives of the western Arctic shore. The request was agreed to readily because Sir John Franklin had been a great friend of the society, and a young German, Johann August Miertsching, was appointed to the expedition.

Miertsching, thirty-two years of age, had just returned to Europe from Labrador, and was spending his furlough in Saxony with his mother and his sister, Johane. Orders arrived too late for him to join the ship at London, so he was hurried by train to Plymouth, where he reported to Collinson on 18 January. Taken to the *Enterprise* by boat through pouring rain, the young missionary had the dazed sensation of the country lad plunged into the turmoil of a great city. Coals and other supplies were being taken aboard. The deck was encumbered with rope, casks, and crates. Many men were drunk, and one offender was seated in irons near the wheel. Collinson greeted him kindly and gave him a bed in his own cabin. The next day the captain took him ashore, presented him to Admiral Gage, purchased him a seaman's outfit and then left the poor missionary, who did not speak a word of English, to haunt the town and waterfront until he concluded his own business and took him back to the ship. There, Collinson took a step which he was to regret to his dying day. There was no cabin for Miertsching on the *Enterprise,* nor leisure to prepare one, so he transferred the interpreter to the *Investigator* with a promise that when the ships reached Valparaiso he would be given a berth where he belonged, on the commodore's vessel. Commander McClure received his guest courteously and said many polite things, which Miertsching did not understand. He found the *Investigator* in a state of disorder and discomfort – once in his cabin he could scarcely get out of it through the litter of unstowed cargo.

At 6 A.M., 20 January, the ships got under way. 'The anchor hoisted, the sails spread, and out we go to sea.' The quiet pietist, torn from all that was familiar to him and flung into a noisy and intimidating environment, felt uneasy forebodings: 'Shall we see England and Europe again? and when? . . . The future is wrapped in obscurity.' Dinner in the officers' wardroom brought him little comfort. He was treated with personal courtesy, but could not understand what was said, and found the tone in the mess noisy and quarrelsome.

Besides McClure as commander, the officers of the *Investigator* were William H. Haswell, first lieutenant; Samuel Gurney Cresswell, a gifted watercolour artist, second lieutenant; Robert J. Wyniatt and Hubert Sainsbury, mates (sub-lieutenants); Stephen Court, sailing master; and the ice master, Newton. The surgeon Alexander Armstrong, who came of the same Anglo-Irish stock as McClure and McClintock, was a man of about Miertsching's age. He had already earned a distinction in his profession which

Captain Sir John
Franklin, R.N.
(from a drawing by
Negelin)

Lady Franklin
(Jane Griffin,
aged 24)

H.M.S. *Erebus* and *Terror* in the Antarctic pack ice, January 1842

Captain Sir Robert McClure, R.N.

Johann August
Miertsching

S. G. Cresswell and
J. A. Miertsching sledging
from Banks to Melville
Island (from a water-
colour by Lieutenant
S. G. Cresswell)

H.M.S. *Investigator* in danger at Ballast Beach, Banks Island, 29 August 1851 (from a watercolour by Lieutenant S. G. Cresswell)

Above left: Admiral Sir Leopold McClintock, R.N.
Above right: Dr Elisha K. Kane, U.S.N.

Opposite: The Franklin record. Discovered by Lieutenant W. R. Hobson of the *Fox* at Point Victory, King William Island

The *Fox* at Beechey Island (from a drawing by Captain W. W. May)

H. M. S. *ships Erebus and Terror*
{ Wintered in the Ice in

28 of May 1847 } Lat. 70°5' N Long. 98°23' W

Having wintered in 1846—7 at Beechey Island
in Lat 74° 43' 28" N. Long 91° 39' 15" W after having
ascended Wellington Channel to Lat 77° — and returned
by the West side of Cornwallis Island

Sir John Franklin commanding the Expedition. Commander.

all well

WHOEVER finds this paper is requested to forward it to the Secretary of
the Admiralty, London, *with a note of the time and place at which it was
found*: or, if more convenient, to deliver it for that purpose to the British
Consul at the nearest Port.

QUINCONQUE trouvera ce papier est prié d'y marquer le tems et lieu ou
il l'aura trouvé, et de le faire parvenir au plutot au Secretaire de l'Amirauté
Britannique à Londres.

CUALQUIERA que hallare este Papel, se le suplica de enviarlo al Secretario
del Almirantazgo, en Londrés, con una nota del tiempo y del lugar en
donde se halló.

EEN ieder die dit Papier mogt vinden, wordt hiermede verzogt, om het
zelve, ten spoedigste, te willen zenden aan den Heer Minister van de
Marine der Nederlanden in 's Gravenhage, of wel aan den Secretaris der
Britsche Admiraliteit, te London, en daar by te voegen eene Nota,
inhoudende de tyd en de plaats alwaar dit Papier is gevonden geworden

FINDEREN af dette Papiir ombedes, naar Leilighed gives, at sende
samme til Admiralitets Secretairen i London, eller nærmeste Embedsmand
i Danmark, Norge, eller Sverrig. Tiden og Stædit hvor dette er fundet
önskes venskabeligt paategnet.

WER diesen Zettel findet, wird hier-durch ersucht denselben an den
Secretair des Admiralitets in London einzusenden, mit gefälliger angabe
an welchen ort und zu welcher zeit er gefandet worden ist.

Party consisting of 2 Officers and 6 Men
left the Ships on Monday 24th May 1847

Gm Gore Lieut
Chas F Des Vœux Mate

London John Murray, Albemarle Street 1845

William Gibson surveys the remains of some of Franklin's men, which he discovered on Todd Islet, King William Island, in 1931

The Arctic Council, 1848-9; *l* to *r*; Sir George Back, Sir Edward Parry, Capt. Edward Bird, Sir James Ross, Sir Francis Beaufort (seated), John Barrow, Jr., Lt-Col Sabine, Capt. Baillie Hamilton, Sir John Richardson, Capt. F. W. Beechey (seated).

could have secured him a more dignified appointment, but he had presumably volunteered for the service on account of the opportunities it offered for original scientific work. Miertsching's enrolment along with these men was a piece of singular good fortune both for them and for posterity. As full of kindness as he was of missionary zeal, he was to do much to keep up the morale of his shipmates in the dreadful trials ahead, and, as a landsman and a foreigner, he entered in his journal many circumstances which an Englishman bred to the sea would have taken for granted.

Four days out from Plymouth, they encountered head winds rising to a gale. The *Investigator* carried away her foretopmast and lay rolling with the sea breaking over her in cataracts, and water washing back and forth in the cabins. A bitter quarrel broke out between captain and officers – on what ground Miertsching could not understand. It was a week before the cabins were dried out.

On the thirty-first, Captain Collinson spoke to his consort by signal. In storm and mist, they were losing much time trying to sail in company. Orders were stringent that they should keep together in the ice, but until then he judged it best that each ship should make all the speed she could independently, as there was a serious risk that they might lose an entire season by not reaching the Arctic before autumn freeze-up. So he set a rendezvous on the Alaskan shore and left the *Investigator* to make her own way. On 2 February the ships finally parted.

As they neared the tropics, they met with fairer winds and warmer weather. McClure, aloof and reserved with his officers found leisure to entertain the young German, whose status was more that of a guest. He invited him daily to luncheon, permitted him to keep his books and guitar in the captain's cabin, which was better protected against water, and, as Miertsching's command of English improved, listened with good nature and respect to his religious admonitions.

On 5 March they crossed the equator. McClure gave permission to the crew to observe that event with the customary rites, which required every man entering the Southern Hemisphere for the first time to be stripped and have his body smeared with tar, which was then scraped off 'with a razor fashioned from the rusty hoop of an old keg.' The surgeon Armstrong, one of the initiates, dismisses this ceremony with curt expression of aristo-

F

cratic distaste. The emotional German was less restrained: 'It is truly more than any Christian man can comprehend that such men as our sailors should exist! ... I have met insolent and godless men, yet were they angels compared to these brazen sinners: I feel as if my lot had been cast among half a hundred devils.'

He also grumbled at the warm, stale water, which was all they had to slake their thirst. Armstrong, though better used to the ways of the sea, echoes this complaint, and describes how, in sudden tropical showers, officers and men dashed on deck with any utensil available to catch what they could of the falling rain.

On 31 March muddy water showed that they were near the mouth of the Río de la Plata. Here the ship was struck by a violent storm, driven off course, and lost sixty miles of southing. There was apprehension aboard that the better-sailing *Enterprise* would get so far ahead that Collinson would tire of waiting at the rendezvous and enter the ice without them, perhaps taking the *Plover*, stationed at the Bering Strait as consort and leaving to the *Investigator* that vessel's lookout duties in Kotzebue Sound. Impatience and the fear of being robbed of the adventurous and honourable service they had anticipated heightened the ill temper of the ship's officers.

About this time, Miertsching witnessed the first flogging – 'A horrible punishment so to flay the back of a fellow creature, but with a rabble like our crew some such punishment there must be.'

Miertsching's strictures on his shipmates must be taken more as an expression of the cold purity of his own previous environment than of the viciousness of character among those with whom he sailed. McClure thought highly of the zeal and alacrity of his men, and Armstrong, who made up for a supercilious attitude towards his brother officers by a warm sympathy for the men of the lower deck, confirms his captain's estimate. There was among the crew a Negro name Anderson, who called himself a Canadian – a fugitive slave, no doubt – and since emancipation had served as a cook on German emigrant ships and had learned a little of their language. Miertsching early tried to converse with him but shrank from him as one 'wholly forgotten of God'. Armstrong speaks highly of the Negro's character, and his is the more practical judgment. The severity McClure thought necessary for the maintenance of discipline was unusual in the Arctic service. In a cruise lasting five and a half years Collinson flogged two men only, and that was for a peculiarly flagrant case of theft. McClure's harshness, perhaps unavoidable under the circumstances, was probably due to a deficiency in his own personality and to a poor understanding with his officers. Their lack of harmony was certain to be reflected in the conduct of the men.

Early in April sea bottom was found with the lead, and soundings grew steadily shallower as they neared the east end of the Strait of Magellan. On the fifteenth, almost three months out from Plymouth, Cape Virgins was sighted. McClure hove to for the night. On the sixteenth, approaching the entrance to the strait, he sighted the Royal Navy steam vessel *Gorgon* (under Commander Paynter), lying at anchor. Dispatched from Valparaiso to help Collinson's ships through the crooked and tide-vexed strait, she had towed the *Enterprise* halfway through, when Collinson, who was most unjustly suspected of wishing to leave his consort behind, sent her back to wait for the *Investigator*. In the *Gorgon*'s tow, the *Investigator* crept slowly past the forest-clad heights of Tierra del Fuego. At the convict station of Sandy Bay, they were welcomed by the commander of the post, an Irishman named Dunn. A little later they were passed by the American steamer *New World*, bound from New York to San Francisco. The fastidious Dr Armstrong was repelled by the appearance and manners of her passengers and crew – perhaps with reason. They were foot-loose adventurers on their way to the gold fields of California.

Late on the seventeenth the *Gorgon* and the *Investigator* sought refuge from a storm in Fortescue Bay, and there found the *Enterprise*, the *New World*, and other ships already at anchor. While his own ship was taking on water, Miertsching paid a visit to fellow countrymen on board the *New World*, and then, in response to an invitation from Collinson, dined on board the *Enterprise* with the three British captains.

That evening in the captain's cabin of the *Enterprise* a decision was taken of fateful import to both Miertsching and Collinson. The latter suggested that, as the ships had accidentally met, the interpreter should pack up his belongings and transfer immediately to the cabin prepared for him on the commodore ship. Miertsching exclaimed that in the wind and rain his books and all his effects would be drenched; and McClure civilly supported his request that the change should be postponed until they docked at Honolulu, which had been substituted for Valparaiso as their port of call on the way to Alaska. Collinson good-naturedly consented. This decision made near the bottom of the globe was to alter history at its top.

As they approached the western outlet of the Strait of Magellan, they found the country growing rocky and bare. Armstrong and Miertsching noted with pity the wretched condition of the Tierra del Fuegans who paddled out in their skin canoes to beg gifts of the passing strangers. On the twentieth, emerging from the strait, they encountered a northwesterly gale and tremendous seas. Commander Paynter did his best to keep the two ships in tow until they had a safe offing, first by tugging them together and then separately. But as no hawsers were strong enough to haul such deadweights against labouring seas, he gave up and set a course north for Valparaiso, leaving the discovery ships to struggle northwest in the teeth of the gale. On the twenty-first, the *Investigator* lost sight of her consort for the last time.

The next three weeks were a period of the sorest trial. The ship could not carry enough sail to make her manoeuvrable; there were fears that she might be driven back on to the rocks of the Patagonian shore. Actually, she was carried south, in squalls of rain or snow, to the latitude of Cape Horn before she was brought under control and headed to the north. A strong east wind, Miertsching noted, on 1 May, but a heavy swell from the northwest. The rolling of the ship was intolerable; water was surging back and forth in the cabins and several officers were seasick. Tempers, otherwise sorely tried, were further inflamed by the fear that this delay might cost them the honour they coveted. On 14 May the ship was without steering way in a dead calm, but so buffeted by the swell that she was rolling her yard ends under water. The calm was broken by a squall, which almost capsized her. The sight of wreckage heaving in the sea nearby aroused fears for Collinson. Another fearful squall, striking when Haswell, officer of the watch, had left his post to go below for a few minutes, carried away all three topmasts. The mild Miertsching was appalled at the captain's fury. The damage was repaired while the ship lay wallowing, with the ocean surge breaking in cataracts over all.

As soon as new spars had been improvised, an inquiry was held into the cause of the disaster; Haswell was suspended from his duties and confined to his cabin under arrest. He was permitted to walk the deck two hours daily under a guard of marines, but could speak to no one. McClure declared his intention of replacing him at Honolulu, and Miertsching, vexed by the 'devil of discord' which seemed to possess his shipmates, wished that he too could bid the *Investigator* farewell. With fair weather and favouring winds, they began to make rapid headway, and on 29 June they raised the first of the Sandwich (Hawaiian) Islands.

On the morning of 1 July as they were running into the port of Honolulu, all eyes scanned the harbour for the familiar rig of the *Enterprise*. It was nowhere to be seen. When the pilot came aboard, he stated that Collinson, after a stay of four days, had sailed barely twenty-four hours before. 'This caused our captain no small alarm,' noted Miertsching.

The Royal Navy brig *Swift* lay in the harbour, and her crew volunteered to look after the lading of the *Investigator*, setting her crew free for uninterrupted shore leave. Miertsching, with the assistant surgeon, Mr Piers, visited missionaries and studied their work with a friendly but by no means uncritical eye. He found 'many baptised persons who are not true Christians,' and was a little staggered by the rule which barred from the Christian Communion all who took any form of intoxicant. The child of a German merchant named Altin remained unbaptized because his parent took one glass of wine daily. This is confirmed by Armstrong, who tells of an American awaiting the arrival of a warship with a chaplain who could perform for his child the baptismal rite that the local clergy refused.

On 3 July, the Royal Navy corvette *Cockatrice* arrived, bringing mail from Great Britain *via* Panama. Her officers and those of the *Swift* intervened to procure the reinstatement of the unfortunate Haswell. Armstrong and Sherard Osborn (who was to compile a history of the voyage from McClure's journal) make no mention of this affair; from Miertsching's account it appears that McClure consented only after much persuasion. If the other captains refused to give him a substitute for Haswell he had little choice, as he mistrusted his other officers – Wyniatt was energetic but irresponsible, and Sainsbury was in poor health. It was a lucky escape for the first lieutenant: his neglect had all but wrecked the ship and the plea of sickness would hardly have saved him before a court-martial.

McClure's act of forgiveness may have been inspired by his haste to get under way again. He saw a chance of stealing a march on Collinson and achieving single-handed a great exploit. Between Hawaii and the Bering Strait lay the partially submerged mountain chain of the Aleutian Islands – uncharted and treacherous in the finest weather, and usually blanketed in fog. It had been Collinson's intention to round this obstacle by running down the trade winds northwest to longtiude 174° East, and there pick up westerly winds to carry him northeast to his rendezvous in the Bering Strait. Though roundabout, this was the prescribed route, and any officer departing from it did so at his own risk. Yet a chance meeting between Armstrong and other officers with an old Yankee trading skipper confirmed McClure in a purpose which perhaps he had already formed. This man assured Armstrong that the direct course through the Aleutians was navigable, if followed with caution. This hint was all that McClure required. He left Honolulu on the evening of 4 July and steered straight north. Armstrong regrets that he had forgotten the name of that 'fine intelligent old sailor' – he had made Arctic history.

The men of the *Investigator* in the meantime had made the most of their brief shore leave. Armstrong and Osborn, with the dishonesty which Victorian standards of propriety made almost mandatory, not only conceal but deny the excesses they committed. Miertsching, with his usual straightforwardness, informs us that a number of men, whose release from jail McClure had obtained by paying their fines, were brought on board by a guard of marines; that two weeks after departure five men were still on the sick-list, regretting the frightful excesses they had committed at Honolulu; and that not until 16 August, when the ship was deep in the polar ice, were the last of these waterfront casualties released from the doctor's care.

They sailed from Honolulu on the evening of 4 July 1850. Miertsching had by now acquired a working knowledge of English and was using it for the regeneration of his shipmates. Though inhibited by his rank as an officer from pressing the gospel on those who expressed no desire to receive it, he gave counsel freely to men who sought it. Furthermore, by chance or through the tact and courtesy of McClure, he had been assigned as servant Corporal Farquharson of the Royal Marines, who was as fervent an evangelist as himself and who readily undertook the distribution of religious literature. A few of the men would withdraw themselves from the dancing and uproar – intensely distasteful to Miertsching – which was the sailors' evening entertainment, and gather in the interpreter's cabin for prayer and meditation. McClure regarded all this with indulgent scepticism. He told Miertsching that the gospel of meekness might do on land, but 'at sea a man must have spirit and not hang his head.' The young German, as manly as he was pious, replied: 'I would gladly call myself and really *be* a Christian, and yet I held my head every whit as high as he.' The two men frequently discussed serious topics. The captain of a man-of-war is a lonely figure, and McClure availed himself of the interpreter's unusual situation to treat him as a friend rather than a subordinate. When the conversation grew too earnest, he would ask the young German to play some sacred music on his guitar.

The relations among the officers and between them and the captain had grown pleasanter. This was due perhaps to McClure's clemency to Haswell and to relaxation from former anxieties; for, barring shipwreck, they were certain to reach the Alaska shore as soon as Collinson. With favourable winds they made rapid progress, and two weeks out of Honolulu they were near the Aleutians and in fog so dense that from time to time a dull thump would be heard aloft as some sea fowl flew blindly into sail or rigging. They had no accurate charts, nor was the visibility such that charts would have been of much use. Soundings were taken frequently, and a man was sent aloft, where, removed from the noises of the deck, he might *listen* for the sound of surf breaking on a reef. On 20 July the fog lifted opportunely to reveal through the haze Amlie Island on the port bow; a little later Tschunan appeared ahead and a little to starboard. Accurate navigation had brought them to a break in the chain of shoal and island, the Seguam Pass. They passed through this into the Bering Sea and continued their northward course towards the shallow and island-studded Bering Strait.

On 26 July, they passed St Lawrence Island in fog, with neither sun, moon nor stars visible, and reckoning confused by violent and variable currents. All officers and a double watch were kept on deck. The passage between the Diomede Islands which now separates the territories of the United States from those of the Soviet Union, was the most dangerous of all. Visibility was less than a quarter of a mile, and the ship was being swept under imperfect control through narrows where the tide runs like a millrace. 'The noise was so great that you could not hear what was said without great vocal exertion; the sea was breaking into the channels, and the deep sea lead showed that the ship was sweeping over twenty-two fathoms of water only,' wrote Miertsching.

Soundings began to grow deeper. The tidal cataract diminished to a ripple and then died away. McClure's gamble had won – his ship was safe and sound in Arctic waters, three weeks ahead of the speedier *Enterprise*.

On 29 July they were off Kotzebue Sound, firing guns in the fog as a signal to the *Plover*. They sighted a dead whale and met two whaling ships. In the afternoon the *Plover* herself loomed up through the mist and, after an exchange of signals, conducted the guest ship to an anchorage in Kotzebue Sound.

Though McClure had been expressly placed under Collinson's orders for the period of the expedition, his bold dash through the Aleutians had given him temporary freedom of action, for the written orders which he bore from Collinson made no provision for what neither officer had thought possible – the arrival of the *Investigator* in the Arctic ahead of the commodore vessel. McClure hoped to conduct his own independent mission. But, being aware of the Admiralty's wish that the ships should enter the ice together, it was his cue to pretend that the *Enterprise* was still ahead of him and that he must do his utmost to overtake her. Commander Moore of the *Plover* had seen nothing of the *Enterprise* and refused to countenance this supposition.

While the two officers were discussing this question, Miertsching was studying the Eskimo settlement gathered on the shore, and regretting that there was no missionary there to evangelise them. He rightly judged that the officers and men of the *Plover* were unsuited for this work of piety. Moore had selected a young Eskimo woman as his interpreter and brought her to his cabin; on shore, an 'Anglo-Eskimo colony' was taking shape. It was not the first time that the mariners of England had transgressed the moral conventions in that region. Captain Cook's assistant surgeon, that philandering humorist Dr David Samwell, tells us not without relish that in October 1778, when Cook's vessels were berthed for three weeks at Unalaska, the Russian traders of those parts were shocked at the moral laxity which permitted European seamen to associate with Eskimo women who were *not Christian*. This must be the drollest plea ever urged by a moralist against extra-marital relations.

Having turned over to the *Plover* letters and dispatches for transmission to Europe, the resolute McClure weighed anchor and proceeded upshore to the final rendezvous appointed by Collinson, Cape Lisburne. He had already raised that bold headland at a distance of twenty miles when the *Herald* came in sight, and sailed on in company. Post-Captain Kellett, a grade above McClure in rank, came aboard and did his best to dissuade his junior from going forward without his consort. It was now 31 July: Collinson was only thirty days out of Honolulu; the *Herald*, a trim, fast-sailing warship, had spent no less than fifty days in rounding the Aleutians from Hawaii to Cape Lisburne; the *Enterprise* must be far behind. McClure argued that Collinson might at the last moment have resolved upon the same short cut as himself and have passed the straits in fog unobserved by either *Plover* or *Herald*. That Collinson would have done so without leaving dispatches with the *Plover* was unlikely, but Kellett was unwilling to restrain the *Investigator* by a positive order. McClure had seen Collinson's orders and knew the Admiralty's wishes better himself. So the *Investigator* was permitted to proceed, while her officers and crew, bursting with eagerness for an independent expedition, noted with uneasiness that the *Herald* continued to shadow them from a distance. Toward evening she made sail and, rapidly overhauling the sluggish cargo vessel, hoisted the signal: HAD YOU NOT BETTER WAIT FORTY-EIGHT HOURS? McClure replied: IMPORTANT DUTY, CANNOT UPON MY OWN RESPONSIBILITY. Kellett indicated dissatisfaction by asking that the signal be repeated. McClure defiantly repeated it, thus challenging his senior officer to give a positive order or refrain from interfering. Kellett preferred the latter alternative. Unhindered, the *Investigator* went on to encounter the triumph and agony which lay in store for her.

McClure's reputation has suffered from this escapade at Cape Lisburne. A fair verdict would be that he employed improper means to a justifiable end. Had his mission been one of mere survey and exploration his neglect of Admiralty orders by going

F*

169

alone into the pack would have been without excuse. But he was on an errand of life and death which admitted of no delay. The loss of a few days, as he and Kellett well knew, might mean the waste of a whole season – Collinson, arriving three weeks later, was held up by the unpredictable pack. McClure's fault was that he achieved his end by subterfuge which deceived no one, not even the officers of his own ship. He had, it is true, a second and less worthy motive for his haste. Parry, coming in from *the east*, had sighted a distant shore to which he gave the name of Banks Land. This lay barely 300 miles from the continental shore east of the Mackenzie. A ship reaching that coast from *the west* would have a fair chance of reaching Banks Land and completing the long-sought-for Passage. But the accusation that in his eagerness to steal this honour from Collinson, McClure neglected the search for Franklin, is quite unjust. As will be seen, he submitted to repeated delays in order to question the Eskimos for news of the lost ships.

They parted from the *Herald* on July 31. On 2 August, heavy ice was encountered off Cook's Icy Cape. Finding his efforts to penetrate it and set a direct course for Banks Land thwarted, McClure began to grope his way eastward with the land on one side and ever-present ice on the other. Generally, the land was low and the sea shallow. Ice with seven-eighths of its bulk submerged grounded far from the shore, leaving the ship a channel of progress, broad, but infested with reef and sandbank. On 5 August they were beset in five fathoms – less than twice the draft of the ship. On the seventh, five boats and forty men towed the *Investigator* around Point Barrow – frightfully exhausting work. On the twelfth a number of Eskimos paddled out in umiaks and were received aboard. They were friendly but extremely thievish and expert in what one would have thought to be the civilized art of picking pockets. An Eskimo woman tried to conceal a stolen crank by sitting on it, Miertsching observed, 'as Rachel formerly had done [Genesis xxxi, 34 – 35]'. When Miertsching scolded her and called her 'thief', she replied indignantly that *she* was no thief – it was her husband who had taken it into the boat. On the fourteenth, close to Franklin's Return Reef, the ship took the ground in a nest of shoals, and as the tide receded, the ice pushed her over on her side. Supplies were taken off into the boats, and the lightened ship eventually refloated, but two tons of salt beef were lost when one of the boats capsized. The impatient McClure quitted the shore and plunged a second time into the seaward ice. 'The wind was strong and fair; the lanes between the ice-masses were so narrow that on both sides of the ship not only the copper plating in which she was sheathed but also splinters of wood were torn from her sides and remained hanging from the ice-blocks. The wind drove us at seven to eight English miles an hour. The shocks sustained were frightful,' wrote Miertsching. Eventually the ship was beset in floating ice which rose from twelve to fifteen feet above the level of the sea. 'Many [pieces] are so broad that one could plant a city thereon.' With difficulty the ship was extricated and towed shoreward by her boats. The over-worked crew was sullen and almost mutinous: 'To the captain dared no man speak.' On the twenty-second, they were off the mouth of the Mackenzie.

During his progress along the Alaska shore, McClure had omitted no opportunity of communicating with Eskimo settlements; and Miertsching found his Labrador dialect well understood by the natives of the Arctic shore. No intelligence, however, was obtained of the lost ships of Franklin.

East of the Mackenzie they found the same conditions, a channel between land and ice, with winds often contrary. Miertsching wrote: 'Today, in the teeth of a strong headwind, the ship is beating to windward in a channel seven English miles broad ... Two English miles from the land and sea is only three fathoms [18 feet] deep. ... Every time we tacked towards the land we saw Eskimos and tents ... By continuous beating to windward we make a little headway; in the last two days only fifty miles ' – a mile an hour! On 24 August they were off the settlement of Tuktoyaktuk, and McClure, impatient as he was to reach Banks Land that season, went ashore with Dr Armstrong, Miertsching, and six seamen. The Eskimos, unlike the natives of Alaska, strangers to Europeans, would receive no overtures and menaced the newcomers with knives, spears, and drawn bows. But after Miertsching came forward in Eskimo dress and prevailed on them to lay down their arms, 'the captain and the rest came forward, also without weapons, and at last we were good friends '. The old chief, Kairoluak, was courteous and communicative. On learning that Armstrong was a medicine man, the chief conducted him to a tent where his son lay with a leg broken a little above the ankle. Armstrong examined the fracture, which was infected, but declared that he could do nothing unless permitted to take the patient aboard the ship. To this the natives would not consent. 'Probably in a few weeks this fine young Eskimo will no longer be alive. If the Eskimos see no prospect of the speedy cure of an invalid, they quickly give up hope altogether, and when the family moves to another region they leave the sick one in a lonely place where no Eskimo dogs come, set a little food by him, and thenceforth think of him no more.'

The curiosity of the Europeans was aroused by a grave marked with a peculiar wooden monument. In response to Miertsching's inquiry, the natives told of strangers who had arrived in a boat, attempted to live by hunting, and had one by one died of starvation. This story stirred interest when reported at home, but lost significance when Franklin's actual fate became known. No doubt it was, as Miertsching supposed, a garbled tradition of some Indian incursion.

Continuing her eastward course, the *Investigator* neared Cape Bathurst, where another native encampment was observed. Again, McClure, Armstrong, and Miertsching went ashore – with considerable difficulty, for they found themselves in shallows of eighteen inches half an hour's pull from the land. Again they met with a hostile reception, but so prevailed over the fears of the natives that they 'laid their little ones in our arms that we might observe them more closely.' Miertsching was quite charmed with the chief, Kenualik, with whom he entered into a discussion of the Creator and his works. Kenualik tried hard to persuade the kind missionary to remain with him, offering his daughter, sixteen years old and 'of very lovely appearance', as an inducement. Miertsching, pleading that he must 'seek his friends who were lost in the ice', bade him a loving farewell.

That night the ship rounded Cape Bathurst and was becalmed on its eastern side. A number of kayaks and larger boats came off to the ship, where their occupants were given a good reception, though alertness was necessary to restrain their practice of thieving. A woman told Miertsching 'that recently she had been collecting mussels, and sea-grass along the shore; her only child was playing with pebbles a short distance away; she heard him scream and ran to him and – what horror! – a polar bear was dragging the child off in his jaws, gripping him pitilessly with his fangs; he swam off to a piece of ice, and the poor bereaved mother saw how the savage beast tore and devoured her beloved and only child. She wept bitterly as she told me this story. I told her that a Great Spirit dwells above the stars, that he sees all that we do, and created the first men; and from his lofty dwelling-place watches what every man does, and knows all our thoughts. I told her how she should live, what she should do and not do, and comforted her with the assurance that, if she followed these words, she would see her child again and dwell with him in a heavenly land where there is no sorrow or weeping.'*

East of Cape Bathurst lay the broad, deep inlet of Franklin Bay. An unbroken ice field forced the impatient navigators to keep inshore and follow the line of the bay, noting how the flat and monotonous shoreline was beginning to swell up into a massive wall of cliffs. Towards evening on 4 September, a great column of smoke rising on land caused them much perplexity. As darkness came on (the Arctic summer was almost over), rockets were discharged, but no answering signal was observed. On the morning of the fifth they were within eight miles of this phenomenon, but were held off by a contrary wind. Mr Newton, the ice master, declared that by telescope he had seen men and tents on land. Miertsching observed that no Eskimo would place his camp where there were high cliffs and no beach. Lieutenant Cresswell was detailed to take Armstrong and Miertsching with him in the whaleboat to seek a solution of the mystery. They had not gone far on their course when a man exclaimed, 'The ship is on fire!' and turning their heads, they saw a thick column of smoke rising from the *Investigator*. Without signal of recall they dared not turn back and so rested on their oars with feelings which may be imagined. If the ship blew up, as well she might with all the powder she carried, they themselves, with no food, no extra clothing, and no tools, would be helpless, doomed to perish with scarcely a struggle for life. To their relief, they saw the pillar of smoke break off and fade away to leeward. With renewed cheer they pulled for the smoking cliff.

The smoke proved to be a sulphurous exhalation rising from

*Readers interested in Miertsching's kindly and sympathetic sketches of the Eskimos met on this cruise are referred to the translation of his *Reisebeschreibung, Frozen Ships* (Toronto, 1967).

the rubble of a landslide fifty feet above sea level. The ground was doughy, and when an oar was thrust into it, the smell of sulphur was intensified. The officers collected specimens of the clay – and burned handkerchiefs and the linings of their pockets by doing so. McClure, who claimed samples on their return to the ship, arranged them on the mahogany table in his cabin, and so covered it with pock marks as if acid had been spilled on it. That night they rounded Cape Parry, a headland rising almost a quarter of a mile above the sea, and reached another crisis in the voyage.

During his cruise of five weeks from Cape Lisburne, McClure had repeatedly tried to haul off from the coast and bore through the ice directly to Banks Land. He had now ceased to entertain any such ambition. The season was closing in, and, with vivid memories of his cruise in Back's *Terror*, he sought nothing more than the snug winter harbour which the continental shore was most likely to afford. But just when he had given up his original plan he was forced to adopt it. To the east of Cape Parry the shore was seen to be heavily ice-infested, while to the north only scattered pieces were visible. So he turned away from the land and began a northerly zig-zag through a heavy but broken pack. About noon on 6 September the lookout reported land ahead; late in the evening a high mountain was plainly seen rising abruptly from the sea. On the morning of the seventh the ship anchored under a headland, perpendicular and 800 feet in height – Nelson's Head. A party landed to hoist the flag and found an abundance of Arctic flora (the land faced to the south), a variety of wild fowl, and traces of larger game. The game was welcome as the new land was certain to be their wintering place. McClure named his discovery Baring's Land, after the First Lord of the Admiralty. He may have guessed, but could not know, that it was the south side of the very Banks Land that he had been aiming for.

Deep water along the south shore and ice dashing violently upon the rocks obliged McClure to turn the other way and set a course to the east of north, with Baring's Land on his left hand. Fog and snow came on, but despite them, on the morning of the ninth, the lookout made out little Ramsay Island on the starboard bow backed by an extensive coast named Prince Albert Land. Inclining to the north, McClure steered into the supposed bay formed by the new lands to the right and left.

As they sailed on, the opposing shores drew closer together. With mountain barriers on either side and the eternal mist overhead, one might have imagined, says Armstrong, that they were on a pleasure cruise on a Scottish loch, except for the masses of grounded ice which lined the shores. On 10 September, a projecting cape, interrupting the forward view, aroused fears that they had come to a dead end. But on rounding the cape they found the channel again broadening, with two islets, the Princess Royal Islands, in the centre. They were now barely 100 miles to the southwest of Parry's farthest on Melville Island. The *Investigator* was destined never to clear that last hurdle. On the eleventh heavy ice came streaming down from the north; the ship was beset and badly battered in the currents eddying around the Princess Royal Islands. During the next few days, still a prisoner, she was carried northward and on the seventeenth reached her farthest for that season, only eighty miles from Melville Island. On the strength of tidal observations, sailing master Court asserted that they were in no bay, but in a strait which must open out into Parry's Viscount Melville Sound.

McClure now found himself in the same dilemma as Dr Kane three years later in his North Greenland backwater. Should he retreat and seek a safe anchorage to the south, or should he cling at all costs to the ground he had won, with the prospect – if he survived – of making a monumental discovery? Like Kane, he chose the bolder course. He unshipped his damaged rudder and awaited developments. The sailors, quite undisturbed by the perils that surrounded them, spent the evening of Saturday, the twenty-first, in the 'uproarious noise and recreation' that Miertsching found so distasteful. 'It seems,' he observed, 'as if the men must work themselves into a state of absolute exhaustion on Saturday night in order to observe Sunday with the strict repose which English custom enjoins.'

On Monday, wind began to blow down the strait driving the ice back towards the Princess Royal Islands. McClure was thus thwarted in his purpose of planting a supply cache on land as insurance against shipwreck. He moored the ship with hawsers to a large floe and went south with the pack. The fury of the gale increased and drove the ship to the point where the islets and the cape retarded the southward drift and caused a frightful turmoil in the moving pack. Now on her broadside, says Armstrong, now heaved up out of the water, the ship was driven clean around the Princess Royal Islands by current and backwash. At one time a rocky cliff was seen close at hand looming through the fog. McClure records the remark of a seaman, 'The old craft will double up like a basket when she gets alongside them rocks.' The depth of the floe, much greater than the ship's, saved her. But for seventeen hours all hands, assigned to boats, stood on deck holding bundles of food and clothing, their pockets sagging with powder and shot, while the ship rocked back and forth in the churning ice. In the pressure she groaned like an animal in torment; her planks sprang apart and oakum dangled from the gaping seams. Cabin doors would neither open nor close; casks packed tightly in the hold were cracked. 'Some sailors, with neither hope nor the fear of God before their eyes, burst open the chamber where the spirits were stored, made themselves and others completely drunk, and stupefied their senses, so that in this condition they might escape the agonies of death. Our helplessness and danger had reached its highest point – the ship was flung over on her broadside and a towering ice-heap was threatening to cover her with rubble . . .; then spoke the mercy of God: "Thus far shalt thou go, but no further"; the commotion in the ice died away. . . . The ship was lying on her side and we stood rigid, expecting a fresh outbreak of this frightful volcanic upheaval; but the good Lord held the ice in His mighty hand; it lay quiet and motionless.'

As was natural at that season, the storm was followed by severe cold, which bound the shattered ice fields into a solid sheet. No violent shocks were felt after the first ten days of October. The ship was worked back into an almost horizontal position, and her interior dried out. With comfort and comparative security restored, McClure turned his attention to discovery on foot.

The large masses of ice blown down the strait, which had so nearly wrecked the ship, had obviously not been formed in the inner recesses of a bay. They had drifted in from Viscount Melville Sound, not many miles to the north. A sledge journey to confirm this and detail it on the chart could not be safely undertaken until the sea was frozen to a greater depth. In the meantime, McClure resolved to climb a mountain on nearby Prince Albert Land (the western end of Victoria Island) which might afford him a view of his intended course.

On 10 October the captain, with Cresswell, Armstrong, Miertsching, and a number of seamen, set out for the western shore of the strait. After a walk of two hours they reached it, and leaving the sailors to build a cairn on the beach, they climbed a hill 1,200 feet high to gain a partial view of the last link of the Northwest Passage. The opposite side of the channel, Prince of Wales Strait, could be traced stretching away northeast, apparently merging with Viscount Melville Sound, whose frozen surface was distinguishable on the northern horizon, swelling up over the hilltops. On their way back to the ship, they encountered a difficulty which sailors might have foreseen. The tide crack, the line of cleavage between the landfast ice and the frozen sea, which rose and sank with the tide, had opened into a rift many feet wide. There was enough breeze to drown cries and gunshots, so the luckless travellers paced up and down the margin of the canal, observing the rockets which Lieutenant Haswell aboard the ship was setting off for their guidance. They were stranded until midnight, when Mr Court and party came to the rescue and ferried them to safety with a Halkett rubber boat.

Determined to prove his exploit before the Arctic night set in, McClure left the ship on 21 October with Mr Court and a sledge crew to travel up the strait. Sledging proved difficult in the early winter season. Broken ice and water oozing up on to the surface of the frozen sea made very sticky hauling, and the men suffered much from thirst. On the twenty-sixth, by following the shore of Baring, or what now appeared to be Banks Land, they reached Point Russell, where the northeasterly trend of the coast broke sharply away to the northwest, and before them lay a broad sea which must be Viscount Melville Sound. From ocean to ocean the Northwest Passage was complete.

McClure was not long to enjoy the luxury of this great exploit. As was later proved, Franklin's crews had found an alternative passage at least two years before.

On the ship, normal preparations for winter had already been made. The upper masts had been sent down and a great canvas housing set up over the upper deck to permit the men to walk about in a sheltered spot when the winds were too fierce for exercise in the open air. A snow wall was built around the ship to shield it from the gales that came roaring down the funnel of the strait. Internal provision for warmth and dryness (which included red-hot cannon balls hanging in the cabins) satisfied Armstrong, who was ever ready to censure his captain. But the surgeon complains with reason at McClure's neglect of systematic recreation. The only dramatics were what the men provided for themselves. School was conducted by the very junior Mr Paine, clerk-in-charge, assisted by Stephen Court. It does not appear that the commissioned officers concerned themselves with the schooling, lectures, and dramatics in which Parry and all of his officers had so heartily participated. The order and cohesion preserved on board through several years of fearful hardship may be credited to Court perhaps, and certainly to Armstrong. The surgeon's *Narrative* does not reveal a good-natured personality; he was aloof and superior in his treatment of his equals; we have it on Miertsching's authority that he was, or later became, on the worst of terms with the captain and the wardroom officers, but he was friendly and sympathetic to the men. When the voyage was over he received a handsome token of their gratitude.

In mid-December a most peculiar incident varied the winter routine. William Newton, ice master, approached the captain and asked why nothing had been done about the fragment of planking and topmast which he had discovered and reported to the first lieutenant as being perhaps wreckage of the *Erebus* or the *Terror*. Haswell, on being summoned, denied all knowledge of the discovery. So did the three men who had been with Newton when he was supposed to have made his find. Thereupon, McClure sent the first lieutenant and the ice master to settle their dispute at the place indicated, with the three men accompanying them as arbiters. It was strange conduct for McClure to permit a man of Newton's rank openly to challenge a senior officer, and to appoint three seamen to determine which was telling the truth. He might have had the matter quietly investigated by Court. The five men searched for hours in vain; and Haswell compelled Newton to drag to the ship the piece of driftwood he had imagined to be a plank. Some indulgence is due to the justly provoked first lieutenant, but it was the act of a bully.

With the approach of spring, preparations were made for an extensive search of the neighbouring coasts. Haswell was assigned the duty of following the shore of Prince Albert Land – the east side of Prince of Wales Strait – to the southwest. Wyniatt was to follow the same coast to the northeast and, on emerging from the strait, to travel east to Cape Walker. Cresswell was to trace McClure's route to Point Russell and follow the northwest trend of the Banks Land shore to discover whether it was linked to Melville Island. The men assigned to sledge duty, so Miertsching tells us, showed none of the keenness that marked the crews of McClintock and Osborn in that same spring. They may have lacked confidence in their officers, but more probably were alarmed by the position of the ship. She lay not in a secure harbour, but in an open channel, liable, as they well knew, to violent convulsions which might wreck her or drive her far away before the travelling parties came back. A boat and supplies were laid up on the shore of Prince Albert Land as a means of escape for a sledge party in case of such an accident. And a large cache on one of the Princess Royal Islands was to serve the entire crew should the ship be wrecked in the spring break-up. Armstrong censures the captain for not sending a party across Viscount Melville Sound to leave word of their ship's whereabouts at Winter Harbour. Such a notice, planted before the end of May, would have been found by McClintock in June, assuring the crew of the *Investigator* of the rescue which, in fact, came about only by a lucky accident.

The sledge parties set out on 18 April. When they had been out almost three weeks, Wyniatt's party was sighted in the distance crawling over the ice back to the ship. When more than a week out, Wyniatt in a fall from a hummock had broken his chronometer, and had come back for a new one. McClure, who had supposed his early return to be due to the finding of a Franklin record, was wild with disappointment and rage. He 'reprimanded him so bitterly that he went back covered with shame.' Twelve hours' rest only was permitted to his crew, and they were sent back without a chronometer and with the reminder that Spanish and Portuguese navigators had crossed great oceans before that instrument was invented. Wyniatt's action was certainly odd. His mission was one of rescue, not of precise survey, and he could not lose his way as long as he kept to the shoreline. His return may have been partly due to his men's fears, which he had been unable to control.

It was now the season of perpetual daylight, though several weeks must elapse before the spring thaw. Small parties were sent

179

with tents and supplies to hunt on Banks and Prince Albert lands. In the previous autumn five musk oxen had been killed. Now there was nothing larger to be had than hare and ptarmigan.

One by one the travelling parties came back with charts extended, but no news of Franklin. Cresswell returned to the ship on 22 May. After emerging from the strait, he had followed the northwesterly trend of the Banks Land shore for eighty miles. His men had suffered much from wind and cold. Two sustained severe frostbites, which threatened to become gangrenous, so he cut his journey short and came back hauling the disabled men on the sledge. The connection between Banks Land and Melville Island, if any, remained undisclosed.

Cresswell had been out thirty-four days, less than a week short of the prescribed forty. He had exercised a proper discretion in shortening that period – the disabled men were found to require minor amputations, and a few more days' outing might have been fatal to them. Yet, with what seems a harsh expression of displeasure, McClure promptly detailed Cresswell and the six members of his crew who were still fit to make an exact chart of the Banks Land shore south to Nelson's Head. The lieutenant was probably a necessary choice as the only surveyor available, but it was tyrannical to subject his crew to a second period of toil and exposure when numerous shipmates were free to hunt rabbits and wild fowl.

Haswell came back on 29 May, having travelled 720 miles in 41 days. He had failed to prove the continuity of Prince Albert with Wollaston Land, ending his journey on the north shore of Prince Albert Sound, across the water from Rae's farthest in the same season on the opposite shore. Armstrong praises the care which he took of his men: in this he was aided by finding game and plenty of drift-wood. Wyniatt came back on 7 June after a second outing of thirty-one days. His farthest was on the north shore of Victoria Island, perhaps not more than sixty miles west of Osborn's turning point on the west shore of Prince of Wales Island. His journey had been curtailed, Miertsching tells us, because foxes had made away with some of his provisions. McClure had some excuse for dissatisfaction with his officers.

In the meantime, McClure and Miertsching had made a rapid journey to the south. Haswell reported meeting an encampment of Eskimos sixty miles south on the Prince Albert Land shore,

with whom, having no interpreter, he had been unable to communicate. McClure, though over forty and frail in health, was no
shirker. He resolved to take Miertsching with him and inquire of
the natives for the lost crews and get what information he could
on the geography of the region. He set out on the day of Haswell's return, and after a strenuous journey of three days (or
rather nights, for the glare of sun was less trying when it was
low in the north), hampered at times by wind and fog, he arrived
at the Eskimo tenting place. The suspicion of the natives was
quickly set at rest by Miertsching's native clothing and Eskimo
speech, which they understood perfectly. They knew nothing of
Franklin, but on being presented with a large sheet of paper, they
traced a considerable stretch of the southwest and south coast of
Victoria Island. Miertsching found time to learn the religious
beliefs of his new friends and to tell them something of his own.
The stay was shortened by the condition of one of the seamen,
Hewlett. His canvas shoes had shrunk in the wet, cutting off cir-
culation in his feet and causing frostbite so severe that he could
no longer walk and was in great pain. A hurried departure was
enlivened by a charming incident. As the sledge was getting under
way, McClure, evidently a man of warm and impulsive nature,
snatched a red shawl from his neck and wrapped it around a
young Eskimo woman who stood near with a baby on her back.
She was much embarrassed, for by the Eskimo code every gift
must be acknowledged by an equivalent, which she was unable
to produce. Finally she drew the child from her hood and, 'still
covering it with kisses', offered it to the captain. With some
trouble, Miertsching made her understand that the shawl was
hers – unconditionally. 'She looked at the captain in a friendly
manner, and laughed, delighted that she could keep her child.'
She wished to know from what animals' skin the shawl was
made, but Miertsching had no time to explain the source of
fabrics.

To speed return, they left the coast and steered a direct course
across a bay – possibly Dean Dundas Bay – urged on by a
following wind with rain and moist snow. Summer was near at
hand and the ice beginning to rupture. They worked the sledge
across a four-foot cleft and kept on steering by the wind, which
was rising to gale force. At midnight they came to an eleven-
foot canal, impassable without a boat, and having no idea where

the land lay, they set up tent and refreshed themselves with grog and biscuit. Sleep was out of the question, as the tent would have been blown away if not held down by its inmates. When the weather cleared they made land, ate a hot meal, and slept. And so back to the ship, drenched and often wading knee-deep in water or sludge. Three men were placed under the doctor's care. Armstrong unfairly blames the captain for disabling them by his excessive haste, but apart from the need for getting medical care for Hewlett, the melt might have made travel impossible had they loitered on the way.

The next five weeks were a period of comparative warmth, eternal daylight, and wearisome inactivity. They were cut off from the land as the ice was rifted, and all sorts of devices, including the sailing of model yachts on the open pools, were used to pass the time. On 14 July the spring tides began to disperse the broken ice. The ship moved slowly northwards until a northeaster drove her back to near shipwreck on the Princess Royal Islands. By the beginning of August she was at the northern outlet of Prince of Wales Strait, but all efforts to break out and set an easterly course for Barrow Strait were thwarted by 'frightful ice coming down from the polar sea' – that same ice stream which had baffled Parry thirty-one years before on the opposite side of Viscount Melville Sound. Autumn was coming on; young ice was forming; further delay would mean the intolerable fate of a second winter in the same spot. On the sixteenth McClure put about; with a favouring wind he went down the strait, past the Princess Royal Islands, which he had hoped never to see again, and in late evening was off his first discovery, Nelson's Head. Far to the south the white edge of the ice pack was faintly visible; elsewhere lay open sea.

McClure had achieved all that the authorities could have reasonably expected of him. He had sought Franklin along hundreds of miles of coast, and he had made a sensational geographical discovery. Cape Parry and the shoreline of North America lay less than 100 miles to the south. A prudent captain would have steered for it and returned by the way he had come. Nevertheless, McClure resolved to circumnavigate Banks Land and enter Viscount Melville Sound from the west. It was late in the season; Banks Land was of unknown extent and separated from Melville Island by an ice-choked strait which had baffled Parry and which

Franklin had expressly been ordered to avoid. Yet McClure was obsessed with the thought of carrying his ship home through the Northwest Passage, and his choice was approved – at least, it was not condemned – by that dourest of critics, Dr Armstrong. The prospect of the voyage out by way of Alaska, down the Pacific, and home by Cape Horn or the Cape of Good Hope seemed intolerably long and tedious to homesick seamen who hoped, irrationally but naturally, that a lucky chance would give them passage between Banks and Melville Islands and bring them home in a matter of weeks. Nor was the hope too unreasonable. They came within an ace of realizing it.

So McClure steered west along the south Banks Land shore, with the ship for the first time in many months pitching in heavy rollers which washed over the deck back to the fore hatch. Several men became seasick. At the southwest angle of Banks Land a harbour – Stefansson's Sachs Harbour – was examined and a notice left which Collinson found three weeks later. Around Cape Kellett the coast fell away to the northeast, pointing to Viscount Melville Sound and Winter Harbour.

The coast was lined by cliffs, 40 to 100 feet high; the sea, as off Alaska, was shallow and held off at a distance of six miles the polar pack, which had reappeared menacingly to the west. Beyond the islets of Norway and Robillard – where Stefansson was to land after his journey over the Beaufort Sea – the coast grew bolder; and the water suddenly deepened from seven to 60 fathoms, 400 yards from the shore. The monstrous polar pack lay so close to Cape Prince Alfred that they dared not round it for fear of what might lie on the other side. McClure reconnoitred by boat and found room for the ship. As the channel was too narrow for controlling her under sail, she was towed around the cape by her boats. A few miles more – along a canal walled by the cliffs on one side and on the other by ice which towered above the main deck – and the ship was brought to a standstill. 'Here,' wrote Miertsching, 'is the true polar ice. This seemed to be the end of water and the beginning of eternal ice.' The average height of the floating pack was estimated at 10 feet, giving a submerged depth of 70 to 80 feet. They moored the ship inside a stranded berg – there was no going back, for she had no room to 'round to' – and waited for an offshore gale to remove the obstruction.

As the distance from the land could be measured in feet the crew was able to roam ashore at will. Up a ravine, 300 feet above the sea, they found petrified tree trunks. Caribou bones and the remains of Eskimo dwellings were discovered, but little animal life except hare and ptarmigan. What game there was they hunted assiduously: by mishandling his gun the boatswain, Mr Kennedy, scorched his stomach with exploding powder, and was carried aboard by his sorrowing shipmates, who believed him a dead man, thereby provoking Armstrong to almost the only joke in his lengthy *Narrative*.

As supplies were consumed, the ship was growing lighter, and the men set to work gathering stones for ballast, hence the scene of their enforced stay was named Ballast Beach. And a beach it was, unprotected by cape or sandbank if the wind should blow inshore. On 29 August a westerly gale set the pack in motion. A floe jammed against the berg to which the ship was moored and tipped it until it overhung the deck and threatened to drive the ship up the sea bottom and crush her against the cliffs. At the critical moment, the floe split and the rebounding berg dragged the ship into deeper water 'in the midst of ice in the wildest commotion'. She was gripped afresh and thrown over on her side. McClure ordered her cables cut in the hope that, instead of being crushed, she might be pushed ashore, where her hulk could still afford shelter to her crew. Before the order could be carried out, the wind subsided, and the sea, under the weight of millions of tons of ice, grew calm instantly. 'The appalling evidence of pressure in the huge masses that were piled together and forced up along the shore' testified to their miraculous escape.

In the calmer weather which followed, heavy snow fell and the young ice grew to a thickness of four inches. All hope of release for that season was given up. McClure, while refraining as yet from striking his upper masts and setting up the housing, ordered a road to be levelled to the beach for winter use and established the harbour watch of only one officer and two men. A southwesterly wind began to blow along the shore and set the ice in motion, but no relief was expected for the ship, heaved up as she was on the shore ice.

Deliverance came when they had ceased to hope for it. At 1 A.M. on 11 September a petty officer, coming to read the tide pole, was astonished to see it apparently floating away. The ice in which the ship was docked had been lifted by the spring tide and was drifting out to sea.

All hands were aroused, and the ship, disengaged by blasting from her ice cradle, was again seaborne. As her rudder had been unshipped, she was manoeuvred by sail to an anchorage fifteen miles beyond Ballast Beach and once more made ready for sea. After a careful reconnaissance she worked her way around Cape Wrottesley, whence the shore trended southeast to Viscount Melville Sound. The *Investigator* had arrived at the entrance of what is now known as McClure Strait, the source of that stream of heavy ice which terminates 400 miles southeast on the shore of King William Island. For the next few days the ship was worked between landfast ice and the floating pack down a channel so narrow that when she rolled her yard ends would strike on the ice wall she was so closely skirting. 'There was nothing,' wrote Armstrong, 'deserving the name of bay or harbour along any part of this coast, not any protection or shelter for the ships; and exposed as it is to all the fury and violence of westerly and north-westerly winds, it stands without parallel for the dangers of its navigation in any part of the world.' The crew, kept on deck with little intermission and exhausted by warping, towing and ice-cutting, were kept going by an extra ration of grog. As the nights were growing longer, and navigation in these conditions was most dangerous in darkness, McClure made it a practice, when possible, to anchor inshore behind a large piece of grounded ice and wait for daylight. There remained the danger that the inner edge of a moving floe would catch on the shore ice or sea bottom and pivot landwards to drive the ship up the beach.

'Through the long, dark night, the sullen grinding of the moving pack, and the loud report made by some huge mass of ice which burst under the pressure, boomed through the solitude, and as the starlight glimmered over the wild scene to seaward, the men could just detect the pack rearing up and rolling over, by the alternate reflected lights and shadows,' wrote Osborn.

Armstrong complains that in these last days of that fantastic cruise the captain's nerve, hitherto equal to the most appalling crisis, failed him. He wasted much time by his reluctance to leave an anchorage and commit the ship again to the pack.

The story of 23 September, the last day of that extraordinary voyage, reads in the pages of Miertsching's journal more like the fantasy of an ancient bard than the sober record of modern days. The night had been passed at anchor in a deep pool only fifteen paces from the beach. At 3 A.M. the boats towed the ship into the clear, and at four she was under sail before a rising wind. The steersman had no prescribed course, but guided the ship by instructions relayed from the crow's nest through the officer of the watch. Fog kept visibility down to half a mile, a snowstorm in the forenoon reduced it still further. All that could be seen ahead was a dark, narrow pool whose farther end kept receding with the advance of the ship. Suddenly there was a roar from the crow's-nest – 'Heavy ice ahead!' All hands sprang to take in sail when, by some convulsion, the ice sprang apart and opened a channel, passable, but so narrow that yard ends were knocking and scraping on the wall of ice as it wheeled by. Miertsching thought of the Children of Israel passing through the Red Sea, and overheard a bearded old sailor observing to his comrades, 'My mother used to read a great book and tell us marvellous tales of times gone by, of men changed into stone, of ramparts falling at the sound of the trumpet. They had no ships in those days. Thousands of people crossed the English Channel on foot, the waters having parted to give them passage. It was then that England was peopled. My poor mother said that since the time of Richard the Lionheart such miracles have not occurred and will never occur again. What is she going to say when I tell her what I have seen with my own eyes?'

On emerging into broader waters, McClure stationed four men in the bow with orders to take a sounding every two minutes and, crowding on sail, went forward at six knots. He was nearing the stretch of coast traced by Cresswell that spring and only 200 miles from Winter Harbour. As twilight began to fall, they were still sailing through fog and snow on a phantom pool which, still opening up ahead, seemed to move with the ship. This ghostly navigation was telling on the nerves of others besides the captain. 'The ice-pilot, quitting his post aloft without leave, apologized to the officer of the watch, and said that he could not longer endure to be aloft: all was ice ahead and not a spoonful of water to be seen, and yet the ship was speeding on without hindrance, as could be plainly observed from the land features which we were leaving behind us,' wrote Miertsching. In the thickening darkness, McClure gave orders that at the first convenient floe the ship was to heave to and anchor for the night. Before this could be done, and just after a sounding had been taken in fifteen fathoms, the *Investigator* struck a sandbank with such violence that she remained hard and fast with her bows thrown up several feet. If the pack, dimly visible to port, moved down with a change of the wind, the ship's destruction was certain. She was lightened, anchors were laid astern, and all hands strained at the capstan bars – in vain. She had struck hard and was solidly embedded in the sand. The captain bade the dripping and exhausted men to give up, and called Miertsching to his cabin.

'He met me as I entered with an open book in his hand, crying, "See how Holy Writ mocks me; in this crisis and extremity, with all our lives trembling in the balance, I opened the Bible to find words of comfort, and thus it answers me in Psalm 34, verses 3 and 4 – in flat contradiction to our present situation".' Miertsching read the two verses aloud:

'O magnify the Lord with me and let us exalt His name together.'

'I sought the Lord and He heard me and delivered me from all my fears.' McClure added, 'I thank God that my mind and understanding are unclouded, and I well know what our situation is.' The good evangelist was administering comfort with all the confidence which the situation allowed, when the ship trembled throughout her frame from a staggering blow. 'More prompt than lightning,' McClure was on deck. Miertsching, clambering after him, felt the ship roll under his feet. Drifting ice had caught her on the broadside toward the stern and in a moment pried her clear of the mudbank. She was anchored in six fathoms, and the crew busied themselves in recovering and restowing the casks and boxes which had been stacked on grounded ice. In darkness and among shoals they dared not again weigh anchor. Yet there was no sleep that night. 'As midnight came,' writes Armstrong, 'the night wore as wild and tempestuous an aspect as any of us had, perhaps, ever seen at sea. The wind had increased to a gale from the westward, which, while it brought some heavy loose ice about us, kept the pack off shore; the snowy whiteness of the former presenting a strange feature in the scene, looming ominously in the darkness; while the cold raw atmosphere, the howling of the wind, the darkness of the night, and the chance there existed of the pack setting down on us, assisted to form a picture of Arctic cruising which I cannot fully describe, but can never cease to remember.'

Towards dawn the wind subsided and the sky cleared. Daybreak revealed that the sandbar on which they had so nearly made shipwreck was the submerged end of a cape, which sheltered an ice-free bay running back far into the land. The far side of the bay entrance was marked by another sandy cape, Point Back, seven miles away. In the space between, according to Armstrong, lay nothing but loose ' sailing ice '. For once, McClure elected to be cautious. Mr Court was ordered into the whaleboat, and, carefully sounding, he piloted the ship around the sandspit into the sheltered waters beyond. There, three miles up, the gallant *Investigator* cast anchor for the last time.

Armstrong was very bitter at this decision. Beyond Point Back, he states, the sea lay open, affording a passage through the usually compact ice stream to Winter Harbour and possibly to Baffin Bay and the Atlantic. A few days later, when Mr Court took a sledge party to connect the Bay of Mercy with the farthest of Cresswell's spring journey a little to the east, he found open sea beyond Point Back, a rift in the ice stream such as might not soon occur again. By then, it was too late for repentance, for the tranquil waters of Mercy Bay were frozen several inches thick.

By hindsight, the surgeon's judgment, in which he says several officers concurred, seemed justified. It is probable that McClure's unaccustomed prudence robbed him of the opportunity of navigating the Northwest Passage in a sailing ship, and brought himself and his crew to the verge of starvation and death. But he could not have foreseen that Mercy Bay would remain unbroken for several summers; his officers and men, without sleep for thirty hours, were in a state of physical and nervous exhaustion; so, taking into account the lateness of the season, he could hardly have done otherwise than snatch at the first secure berth which offered.

The ship was anchored near the entrance of what McClure gratefully named the Bay of Mercy, an inlet nine miles in depth and backed by mountains and broad valleys. The valleys were the haunt of caribou, but for which the near tragedy of the *Investigator* might have been tragedy complete. Hunters were out whenever weather and light permitted, but their successes were offset by the discovery on board of a quantity of tainted meat. In consequence, the daily ration was reduced to two-thirds immediately, and progressively to one-half.

With hunting suspended during the season of darkness, privation and hunger were made more intolerable by passive brooding. Candles were in short supply, and a large proportion of waking hours were passed in idleness except by those who had had the forethought to learn to knit or crochet.

Hunting was resumed towards the end of January (1852), but with caution, as the period of light was short. On one occasion the Negro Anderson parted from his comrades in pursuit of a deer and lost his way in darkness and fog. Sergeant Woon of the Royal Marines found him lying exhausted on the snow and persuaded him to get up; he fell again, convulsed and bleeding at the nose. Careful, even in that extremity, of government property, the sergeant slung both guns over his shoulder, dragged the hapless seaman for miles, tumbled him down a precipice to arouse him from the deadly drowsiness which had possessed him, and delivered him still alive to a searching party. Both men were badly frostbitten, and Anderson lost several toes and part of his nose.

For 18 February, Miertsching records, 'A snowstorm, of which no one in our country could form any conception, has lasted without a break for a week, and has so buried the ship that only the masts are visible at the top of an enormous white mass. We groan at being restrained from hunting; for the chase is doubly precious to our appetites, which are always craving and never satisfied. Yesterday's hunger simply seems to add itself to the hunger of today.'

Under the pressure of these irritations, animosities long-suppressed broke forth. There was a violent quarrel between the captain and Armstrong. Miertsching, who of all his shipmates seems to have disliked no one but the surgeon, charges him with lying. He was probably merely echoing what McClure had said, and such language rather proves the serious nature of the dispute than marks the real offender. If the difference has a rational ground it was no doubt the reduced ration, which Armstrong asserted was too small for the preservation of health.

Towards spring, the school was closed owing to poor attendance. The sailor who has tramped all day through the snow in pursuit of hares, tired, his stomach empty, has no desire to learn. 'Far rather would he, in a circle of intimate friends, share and discuss the hunting events of the day with a pipe of tobacco in his mouth. So, for instance, one man reports that he had shot three legs off a hare, but after a pursuit lasting two hours the hare made its escape. Another with a well-aimed charge of small shot took the fur off one side of a hare, but it got away and is now travelling around half naked; such interesting narratives do much to shorten the long evenings.'

McClure had berthed his ship in the Bay of Mercy, the more readily because he was confident that Austin's expedition had reached Winter Harbour from the east, and that if Austin was not anchored there himself, he would have left a substantial depot of supplies. To confirm this hope he took Stephen Court with a sledge party and set out on 11 April across the ice of Viscount Melville Sound. They reached Parry's old anchorage – about 150 miles distant – to find neither Austin nor the supplies they so urgently required. On top of Parry's sandstone 'monument' they discovered a metal cylinder containing the record planted by McClintock in the previous June. From this, McClure learned that Austin's squadron had been held up at Griffiths Island for the winter of 1850–1851. As McClintock's foot journey to Melville Island had revealed no traces of Franklin, Austin would have no motive for bringing his ships farther west in the summer of 1851, and McClure concluded that he had either gone home or was making search in some other quarter. So depressed was he at this disappointment that he 'wept like a little child'. Whether or not Mercy Bay broke open in the coming summer, the *Investigator* was fenced in by the massive polar pack. To attempt a return by the hideous route around Banks Land was unthinkable, nor was there any guarantee that an attempted exit along the coast explored by Cresswell would be easier or safer.

The summer brought some, but not much, relief to the half-starved and disheartened crew. Even that season was plagued by fog and sudden squalls of snow. The clay of the valleys brought forth an abundance of vegetation, which delighted the industrious botanists Miertsching and Armstrong. The former discovered a sorrel, which did much to check the symptoms of scurvy, now all too evident. But the caribou migrated inland for the summer, and the permafrost, which hindered the drainage of melted snow, left the valley bottoms a sea of mud, impassable to weak and undernourished hunters.

The sea responded much more slowly than the land to the warmth of summer. On 10 August the ice was seen to be in motion beyond the cape, and around the shore of the bay a margin of water appeared. The ice of the harbour, seven feet thick, though afloat, was held in place by northerly winds, and soundings showed that the bay was full of shoals which retarded its outward drift. 'A combination of the most favourable circumstances,' said Armstrong, was needed to clear the bay, and that combination never occurred in the summer of 1852.

On 9 September, after weeks of fading hope, McClure assembled the crew and 'in a solemn and impressive speech' warned the men that they must brace themselves for another winter, and announced another slight reduction in rations. He implored the men not to lose heart, and affirmed his own 'unshakeable conviction that not one of us would be left behind, but that all would safely reach their fatherland . . . One could observe many gloomy and anxious faces, but in this situation there was nothing to do but to submit,' says Miertsching.

For some weeks a seaman named Bradbury had been in a state of harmless idiocy. In October Mr Wyniatt became noisily and violently insane. In daylight hours, or what passed for such in the Arctic winter, he would walk about the ship whistling and bellowing. By night he made an uproar in his cabin which robbed others of their sleep. He would permit no one to approach him except his servant and Miertsching. The latter begged him 'in the most affectionate terms' to sleep at night, or at least to let others sleep, without making him comprehend. The poor young man could still respond to kindness. In his quieter hours he would visit the interpreter in his cabin and talk almost rationally. At other times he raged against the captain and Armstrong, made more than one murderous attack on McClure, and threatened to set fire to the ship. At such times he was of necessity kept in irons.

All winter McClure must have been tormented with the fear that the plague of madness would spread, or that the crew would revolt against the half ration he so rigidly enforced. Late in October his authority was challenged in a manner variously reported by Armstrong and Miertsching. The surgeon states briefly that the men 'came on the quarter-deck in a body to ask for more food – to their application Captain McClure refused to accede'. Miertsching's version is more circumstantial and more creditable to both captain and crew. The men, he says, gathered on the upper deck and through the officer of the watch sought speech with the captain. When he appeared, four spokesmen only approached him, apologized for their irregular assembly and, complaining that they could not sleep for hunger, asked for a small increase in ration, which the captain after an earnest conference promised to grant. He may have redeemed this pledge by occasional handouts, but the standard ration seems to have been unchanged.

Low temperatures and winter winds were driving the caribou from the highlands down to sheltered valleys within easy reach of the hunters. The bulk of any kill was turned into the common stock, but the successful hunter received for his own use the head of a caribou, the feet, liver, heart, lungs, kidneys, and a pound of meat in addition. Miertsching thinks that the hunters were not too few but too many, and complains of the misguided exertions of poor shots, who obtained nothing themselves, frightened the game away from good hunters, and by their wasted exertions, 'brought back stomachs fairly shrieking with hunger'.

The wolves were another nuisance. They frightened the caribou and sometimes devoured a carcass before the hunter could get help to bring it to the ship. They were too wary to be shot or trapped; two only were killed in a period of twenty months.

The efficient hunters – the officers, Sergeant Woon, and a number of seamen, among whom was Miertsching's disciple, James Nelson – suffered not a little in their zealous exertions. The good hunter, according to Armstrong, could always be recognized by his discoloured and frost-scarred features. In hot pursuit of a hare, Miertsching tumbled into a rocky hollow and sprained his ankle. He was not long immobilized, for nine days later he reports that his fingers have grown so raw from repeated frostbite that he cannot bear to carry his gun. Sailors accompanied him as caddies and were rewarded, when a caribou was shot, by a share of the blood and of the undigested grasses in the first stomach. In the intense cold of the third winter – more severe than its predecessors – cheaper firearms were unusable. Trigger springs would snap and barrels crack in the intense frost. Armstrong escaped what might have been a serious injury. With frozen fingers he failed to ram the bullet properly home in his muzzle-loader, and the gun burst on discharge. By these painful exertions a weekly average of three pounds of meat *per capita* was obtained. As this replaced, instead of supplemented, the assigned ration, the only gain was the advantage of fresh meat over salted, and the crew was failing fast. Armstrong found that the average loss of weight per man in the twelve months of 1852 was no less than thirty-five pounds. Twenty men, nearly a third of the crew, were on the sick list, and scurvy was affecting almost everyone. 'All were feeble, depressed, with a dull haggard stare,' wrote Miertsching.

Even the cruel economy thus practised ensured food for no further than the coming autumn; and there was no guarantee that the ship would be released in that period. On 3 March, McClure assembled the crew and stated how he intended to deal with the crisis. He himself with twenty of the strongest men would stay with the ship, in the hope of freeing her in the coming summer. The remainder, the less fit, would quit the ship on 15 April in two detachments. Cresswell and Miertsching were to head a party of ten, travelling by sledge to the Princess Royal Islands, where supplies and a boat had been stored; in the latter they would sail to the continent, up the Mackenzie to the fur posts, and so, by way of Montreal or New York, to Europe. Haswell would take Wyniatt and 30 men 500 miles to Port Leopold, where Sir James Ross had left a food cache and a boat, and sail into the track of the Greenland whalers.

Though strengthening himself with thoughts of the Divine Goodness, Miertsching could find no rational hope of survival by such means. 'Twenty-one men are now in hospital,' and 'in six weeks we must, with those judged unfit to remain longer with the ship, harness ourselves to sledges laden with supplies, and drag them through snow and ice for hundreds of miles. How many of us will in this way see Europe? The answer is: "No one".'

Both classes of men were dissatisfied: 'The men chosen to stay with the ship were disappointed and downcast at the lot assigned to them, while many of those appointed to travel have visions of their corpses lying on the ice, a prey for wolves and foxes.' Professional opinion was wholly opposed to the captain's plan. The surgeons had already made an official report that the men were incapable of heavy labour; Armstrong now made urgent representation to the captain that the men were utterly unfit for travel. McClure refused to alter his plan. He later asserted that he was sending the sick away because they could not hope to survive another winter in the north. He may sincerely have believed that he was giving them the better of two extremely poor chances – it was not then known how rapidly Franklin's scurvy-stricken crews had collapsed when subjected to the labour of travel. Yet McClure was strangely lacking in imagination not to have perceived that if he divided his crew he should have joined himself to the weaker portion. Supposing that he had carried out his purpose, and that by lucky circumstance the *Investigator* and her twenty sound fellows had reached home to inform the public that their weaker comrades had been turned adrift to perish, in all likelihood, on ice pack and tundra, no reasoned statement of probabilities would have saved him from the execration of the whole civilized world. His plan cannot be positively condemned, for, failing help from outside, all the men of the *Investigator* were doomed alike, but it was a lucky circumstance for him that in the very week in which he announced his purpose, a party left Melville Island to bring him word that desperate measures were uncalled for and that help was near at hand.

8 The Belcher Expedition and the Rescue of McClure

The return of Austin and Penny to report the utter failure of their mission and Austin's opinion that no purpose was to be served by continuing the search were received with dissatisfaction by the public at home. A committee was appointed to inquire into the management of the search; its proceedings were marked by disagreement between the two captains – passionate on the part of the worthy Penny. The committee placidly concluded that both officers had done their duty, and dismissed them with a clean bill, but with their differences unresolved. Penny applied for re-employment and was briefly informed that the Admiralty had no further need for his services.

Penny was hurt, and with good reason, at this snub. His had been the most useful work done, for McClintock's journey, magnificent as a feat, had opened up no new territory; the old whaler's discoveries exceeded in extent those of Ommaney and, as then appeared, were probably in the right direction. Osborn, who had his own grievance against Austin, having been disappointed of his expected promotion, eagerly espoused the cause of his friend. 'I hope,' he wrote, 'soon to see your protest and remarks upon the evidence. The report of the Committee is most unfair, and not borne out by the evidence adduced. I have been as you see left [off the promotion list] ... do not, however, my dear Penny, think that the omission has arisen from any part taken by me in the question between you and Austin, and believe me I am prouder of your friendship than half a dozen pieces of parchment could make me ... besides I am young yet and have room [?] and time enough to win a Post-Captain's commission in spite of Captain Austin or any other Liar in buttons.' On learning that Dr Peter Sutherland is bringing out a book on Penny's voyage, he writes: 'Encourage Mr S. to put a little more ginger into what he writes; he is rather long-winded and has the bump of venera-

tion for Post Captains and Admirals more developed than I
have.' (This wholesome advice, if passed on, went unheeded, for
Dr Sutherland is everywhere civil to the Royal Navy and nowhere
concise except where he transcribes Penny's admirably clear and
matter-of-fact account of his boat journey.)

Post captains and admirals were the only persons who could
aid in Osborn's promotion, yet the young sailor incites civilians to
show them disrespect, reserving his honeyed words for an obscure
and unfairly discredited whaling skipper. In another letter to
Penny he says: 'Many thanks to yourself and second self for your
kind invitation. Aberdeen is, however, too far off for me, *young*
and *inexperienced* [he underlines these adjectives; doubtless they
had been applied to him by Captain Austin], to carry a wife and
Band Boxes. Some future day we shall both meet and my Helen
will, no doubt, be as fond of your Margaret as I am of you, my
dear old friend.' Clements Markham spoke the truth: 'There
never was a truer friend than Sherard Osborn.'

When Osborn wrote these letters he evidently supposed that
his discourtesies to Captain Austin had cost him not only
advancement to a higher rank but continuance of employment in
his former one as well. He speaks of putting an engine in Lady
Franklin's *Prince Albert* and making a voyage on his own. He
mistook the judgment of his superiors, for the Admiralty was to
appoint him to command the *Pioneer* on a second cruise – the
only one of Austin's captains to be so noticed. Their lordships
of the Admiralty, though disposed, like Austin, to think further
quest useless, yielded to popular opinion by mounting another
expedition in 1852, and, again in deference to public demand,
sending it up Wellington Channel. Penny had the country with
him though he gained nothing thereby.

The Admiralty took advice from the Arctic Council and from
the officers of the most recent expedition. Now, McClintock had
found no trace of Franklin to the west and was sure that he could
not have got past Cape Dundas. Ommaney stated that only under
unusual conditions could he have gone southwest from Cape
Walker. Lieutenant Browne was equally positive that he had not
gone down Peel Sound. Penny had found open water up Wellington Channel, marking it as Franklin's only probable route. So up
Wellington the new expedition was to go, and none of the Royal
Navy's modern critics, with the same data, would have ordered it

otherwise. As it happened, Franklin *did* go up Wellington Channel. The Admiralty could not have guessed that, taking advantage of what must have been two favourable seasons, Franklin had doubled around Cornwallis Island back to Barrow Strait and in 1846 had shot down the very Peel Sound which Willy Browne had declared impassable. There was no reason for detaching a ship down Regent's Inlet to visit the Boothia Eskimos. Kennedy and Bellot had that assignment, and their ill success was not known until the new expedition was far on its way.

Nonetheless its orders, as originally drafted, were marked by an omission which, if uncorrected, would have brought death to the crew of the *Investigator* and, consequently, no small gratification to Dr King, who had been predicting some such catastrophe if the search was not conducted according to the methods he prescribed. All four ships were assigned to Wellington Channel. Mr Cresswell, father of the *Investigator*'s second lieutenant, wrote to the Admiralty pointing out that Collinson and McClure had been aiming for Banks Land, that the latter was unreported for more than a year and, if in trouble, would head for the landmark of Winter Harbour – as he did do in that very spring of 1852. The elder Cresswell urged the sending of a relief ship to Melville Island. The Admiralty acknowledged the soundness of this advice and altered its orders – one large ship with its steam tender was to ascend Wellington Channel; the other pair was to steer west and leave boats and supplies at Parry's old anchorage of Winter Harbour.

Another prudent measure was the addition to the squadron of a fifth ship to act as an Arctic depot. There was a danger that the over-zealous commander of a rescue ship might become as irretrievably lost as the *Erebus* and the *Terror*. To lessen this risk, the *North Star* was commissioned to accompany the squadron to Beechey Island and berth there to provide a point of retreat for any crew whose ship might be crushed or permanently beset. Commander Pullen, now returned from his Alaskan boat voyage, was appointed to her command.

Less judgment was used in the choice of the over-all commander. The Admiralty has been censured for not giving charge of one detachment to McClintock and of the other to Osborn. The objection to McClintock was that such advancement for a newly made commander would cause much dissatisfaction to unemployed officers of senior rank. In Osborn's case the authorities probably felt that they were doing enough by retaining in his former appointment a young officer who had been wanting in respect to his superiors. An admirable choice, both on account of his character and recent Arctic experience, would have been Kellett, who had just brought his *Herald* home from the Pacific. He was passed over in favour of Captain Sir Edward Belcher.

With his wonted hysteria, Dr King vowed that Belcher had spent his entire life in proving his total unfitness for so honourable an appointment. This was not wholly untrue, though a fairer appreciation is that of J. K. Laughton, that 'perhaps no officer of equal ability has ever succeeded in inspiring so much personal dislike'. Belcher *did* have ability. He was a marine surveyor of great competence, had served with distinction and won a knighthood in the China wars. But he had a certain resemblance to the notorious Captain Bligh. Like Bligh, he appears to have been careful and humane in the handling of his men. But, even more than Bligh, he aroused the hatred of his officers. He was coarse, meddling, tactless, and fearfully egotistical. This last was a prime disqualification for a special service in which several junior officers had more experience and were better fitted to direct operations than himself. Years before on the China station he had objected to Admiral Sir William Parker for acknowledging civilian help rendered to Belcher's *Samarang* in Borneo: 'The admiral's reply was in a tone of sadness mixed with anger: "You may be a skilful navigator and a clever seaman, but a great officer you can never be with that narrow mind".' That narrow mind still possessed Edward Belcher: so envious was he of the Arctic veterans serving under him that he asserted that no officer or seaman should be sent a second time on that service, for it was ruinous to discipline. Although his disqualifications were known, his rank and services entitled him to employment, and Their Lordships, who had authorized the expedition with reluctance and had no faith in its success, took the opportunity of obliging him.

Belcher, therefore, headed the squadron in the *Assistance;* Kellett commissioned the *Resolute,* and McClintock, now a commander, the *Intrepid.* Osborn remained with the *Pioneer.* Mecham was posted to the *Resolute,* as was a former mate on the *Herald* who had spent a winter with the *Plover* in Kotzebue Sound,

Lieutenant Bedford Pim. Belcher, in company with Osborn – not to prove one of those matches made in heaven – was to conduct the main search up and beyond Wellington Channel. Kellett, supported by McClintock, was assigned the duty of placing boats and supplies at Winter Harbour and, as he was certain to be detained for the winter, to direct spring journeys in whatever directions he deemed proper.

The story of the western expedition has been told in a manner detailed and graphic, if not always well-digested, by the sailing master of the *Resolute,* George F. McDougall. His title is a far cry from the brief flashy captions of our own day:

'The Eventful voyage of H.M. Discovery Ship *Resolute* to the Arctic Regions in Search of Sir John Franklin and the missing crews of H.M. Discovery Ships *Erebus* and *Terror,* to which is added an account of her being fallen in with by an American whaler after her abandonment in Barrow Strait, and of her presentation to Queen Victoria by the government of the United States.'

Stormy weather was the lot of the travellers on the voyage to Greenland. With the deeply laden *Resolute* rolling in a cross sea under reefed storm sails, McDougall listened to and copied down mournful yarns of shipwreck and starvation in the ice from an old whaler, ice master Collins.

On the way up Baffin Bay, the squadron put in at Godhavn, where the *Pioneer* tangled with an iceberg and was almost rammed by the following *Resolute.* Members of the expedition were entertained at a dance by the ladies of the settlement, Danish and Eskimo, among whom nieces of Penny's interpreter Carl Petersen, Sophy and Marie, were conspicuous by their charm. McDougall glanced a little censoriously at their Eskimo breeches; the practical McClintock, with his eye for logistics, thought trousers more appropriate than crinolines when fifteen couples were dancing in a room fifteen feet square.

Again at sea, they sailed northward, sometimes through fog so dense that a consort nearby was invisible, though orders given on her deck were clearly heard and the speaker identified by his voice. At other times, when they were icebound and motionless, officers and men would mingle to play cricket on a floe or go sliding down the side of an iceberg on barrel staves, confirming the sour Belcher in his disapproval of the discipline of the Arctic

199

service. Off the Devil's Thumb, the *Resolute* was heavily nipped and thrown over. She righted without damage, and along with the rest of the squadron secured herself in an ice dock.

Farther up the margin of Melville Bay, Sir Edward Belcher was able to display in a most creditable manner the spirit of order and discipline which he prized so much. His own ships and a number of whalers were held up in ice, when the American *McLellan* (whose captain had driven so hard a bargain with the distressed crews of De Haven) was crushed in a nip and abandoned by her crew. Custom decreed that in such an event her stores became common property, and all that was portable, especially the wines and spirits, was looted by her own and neighbouring crews. Rather than witness so disorderly a proceeding, Belcher, after obtaining the captain's permission, hoisted the British ensign on the wreck, posted a guard of marines, and transferred what he could of her stores and equipment to the ships of his own squadron, furnishing the captain of the *McLellan* with bills on the British Government for the goods obtained. It is to be hoped that Sir Edward received the thanks of the uninsured owners for this piece of salvage, for he was roundly cursed by the whaling population for 'having prevented their usual privilege of plundering the wreck and holding a drunken soirée on the ice'. After thirty-eight days in the ice of Melville Bay, Belcher emerged into the North Water and drew inshore to speak to the Cape York Eskimos.

This settlement was found to contain only twenty persons, accommodated in three sealskin tents. McDougall, who with some of the bolder and more inquisitive of his shipmates entered one of these shelters, paints a most repulsive picture of its filthy interior. The floor, he says, was carpeted with seal intestine. 'We of course considered this to be the refuse in which the dogs were fed, but were soon enlightened by seeing one of the ancient ladies take a portion of the entrails, and swallow a quantity of it as Italians do macaroni. Being a few yards in length, she was unable to swallow the whole, and therefore contented herself with a foot or two, which was severed with a knife.'

The entire squadron passed through Lancaster Sound and mustered at Beechey Island. There the *North Star* was secured as depot ship, and the supplies of the others topped off. From that point, the *Assistance* and the *Pioneer* were to go north up Well-

ington Channel, the *Resolute* and the *Intrepid* west along Barrow
Strait. The parting was soured by a quarrel between Sir Edward
Belcher and Robert McCormick, the extremely tough and aggressive Irish naval surgeon who had come along with the special
mission of taking a boat up the east side of Wellington Channel
to seek an outlet into Jones Sound. Kellett coaxed his countryman
to accept an invitation to a farewell dinner on the commodore's
ship; McCormick, with more honesty than tact, refused.

For the first stage of his westward voyage, Kellett found
Barrow Strait badly ice-infested and was reduced to tiptoeing
along the shore in a sea so shallow that when his ship was in tow
through calm water the sea bottom could be seen, sometimes
barely a foot beneath the keel. Near Assistance Harbour the sea
shoaled suddenly; the *Resolute*, in putting about, lost headway
and was driven by the current on to a ridge of gravel, where the
receding tide left her leaning on her port bilge. To lighten the
ship and take full advantage of the tide when it returned, orders
were given to transfer supplies to the *Intrepid*.

While the crews were thus engaged, it was observed that the
inner edge of an eastward-moving floe measuring $2\frac{1}{2}$ by $1\frac{1}{2}$ miles,
as was afterwards learned, had caught on a sandspit and was
swinging the ice sheet inshore towards the ships. The *Intrepid*
steamed out into the clear before it was too late. The *Resolute*,
stranded and now top-heavy, lay helpless in a shallow pool.

'About seven the edge of the ice took the ship under the lee
gangway, shaking her throughout. A moment had scarcely
elapsed ere we became sensible of the ship's lifting and instinctively each man grasped a rope, as he became aware that she
would inevitably be thrown over. Yielding inch by inch before
such a powerful lever, the ship at length rested on her keel, but
it was but momentary, for in a second she was thrown over on her
starboard side with a shock sufficient to bring every mast by the
board.

'As it was, the very topmasts bent like whalebone, bringing a
fearful strain on the weather shrouds; but not a rope was
stranded, not a single spar injured by this unprecedented occur-
rence.

'Would the ship be borne before the ice? or remain immovable
on the ground? were questions which naturally suggested themselves. Supposing the first to be the case, she would be forced

nearer the shore, into small water, which would lessen the chance of getting off, and if the latter, she would in all probability be overrun and buried beneath the ice, as many a gallant ship had been under somewhat similar circumstances in Melville Bay.

'. . . As the pressure increased, huge pieces of ice scaled the side, and would have fallen in board had not men been stationed on the gunwale with poles to repel these formidable boarders . . . For two hours we remained in this trying position; at the end of that time the floe was observed to be moving more out of the bay, when the pressure decreased considerably.'

In an effort to refloat the ship, hawsers were carried out to the retreating floe. The *Resolute* righted in response to the pull; then the anchors jumped. But now the *Intrepid* had rounded the floe and was approaching from its western end. At flood water she tugged her consort afloat.

With the *Intrepid* standing by and the *North Star* not many miles distant, the *Resolute* only, not her crew, had been in serious danger. But the men of the *Investigator*, lying icebound 400 miles to the west, did not dream of how narrow an escape they had on that August afternoon – a crippled *Resolute* spelled doom for them. Passing through somewhat freer waters to the west, Kellett's ships came in sight of Melville Island on 1 September, the first since Parry's *Hecla* and *Griper* to do so. A few days later they were off Winter Harbour.

Parry's sandstone 'monument' showed up clear against a background of fresh snow, but six miles of pack lay between the ships and the shore. McClintock had been there the year before by sledge and found no notice of Franklin. If the possibility of the monument's sheltering a recent message from McClure or Collinson occurred to Kellett, it was outweighed in his mind by the certainty that, unless he made haste to find another harbour, he must winter in the pack. So he coasted back on his tracks, leaving McClure's notice lying unsuspected on the sandstone rock. Forty miles to the east, Kellett turned into Bridport Inlet. On 9 September his men began to saw their way into a berth inside Dealy Island. On that very day, on the other side of Viscount Melville Sound, McClure was warning his men that they must brace themselves for a second winter of privation at Mercy Bay.

Though McClure's luck brought him into the direst peril it never wholly deserted him. As soon as Kellett's ships were

berthed, various parties set out to advance depots for the spring
sledge journeys. With cart and sledge, McClintock left for Hecla
and Griper Bay on Melville Island's north shore, while Lieutenants Mecham, Hamilton, and Pim travelled west to advance supplies for Mecham's extended journey in that quarter and for
Pim's passage over to Banks Land – to search for Franklin, as
there was no thought of McClure having come so far. Mecham
carried his depot overland to Liddon's Gulf, and on the way
back casually turned aside to examine the 'monument' at Winter
Harbour. A metal cylinder tumbled out of a pile of small stones
on the top of the rock. This he expected. It had been placed
there by McClintock. But to his astonishment, on opening it he
found the charts and Journal of Proceedings of the *Investigator*,
summarizing the events of her cruise down to 12 April of the
present year. At that date she had been lying on the north
shore of Banks Land in a harbour shown on her chart as the Bay
of Mercy. McClure did not disguise how critical that situation
was. ' If we should not again be heard of,' he wrote, ' in all probability we shall have been carried into the Polar pack, or to the
westward of Melville Island; in either case any attempt to send
succour would be to increase the evil, as any ship that enters the
Polar pack would be inevitably crushed; therefore a depot of provisions, or a ship at Winter Harbour, is the best and only certainty for the safety of the surviving crews.' McClure added that,
if released in the summer of 1852, he would not revisit Melville
Island but make all haste to escape to the east.

The lively discussion which this intelligence caused on the
Resolute could end only one way – in the unanimous decision
that no help could be sent to McClure that autumn. Thin ice –
Lieutenant Pim had observed a large body of open water off Cape
Providence – and increasing cold and darkness made the journey
too dangerous. There was also the possibility that the *Investigator*
had made her escape that summer and passed her rescuers unobserved on her eastward course – they knew now from Wyniatt's
chart how wide Viscount Melville Sound really was. Nonetheless,
this forced inactivity caused Kellett much uneasiness: McClure's
supplies must be nearly exhausted, and he was almost certain to
attempt escape on foot southward at the very dawn of spring
unless he could be warned in time.

Musk oxen and bears were plentiful around Dealy Island and,

while light permitted, kept the hunters busy. When darkness restricted them to the neighbourhood of the ships, they put school and theatre into operation. With none of McClure's aloofness, Kellett accepted election as chairman of the theatrical committee, with McDougall and Dr Domville as his aides. Their theatrical properties included parts of ladies' apparel; for the rest, McDougall was appointed dress designer with the ship's carpenter as his executive assistant. Petticoats were fashioned out of canvas; a quilt, stuffed with oakum, formed the bustle, making what McDougall bashfully calls the 'after part' of the actress to 'resemble a miniature St Paul's dome'. The sailors contributed a sentimental comedy on their own. Though intended to be serious, it turned out a burlesque, which, says McDougall, would have brought down 'roars of applause' if presented as such in a London theatre. The leading lady was 'perfections' self – barring the ankles'. The part of the second lady was well interpreted but for a 'certain swagger and rolling in her gait' and a habit of 'hitching up the frock with both hands, as sailors occasionally do to the waistband of their trousers'. The hot grog that was served to all theatre-goers after the performance must have ensured a full house.

These festivities and the celebration of Christmas and New Year's did not interfere with more serious pursuits. As a substitute for leather boots, cause of many crippling frostbites, Kellett set the men to sew canvas shoes large enough to allow several pairs of socks. Meteorological and magnetic observations were kept up regularly. A quartermaster, taking readings on the ice at dead of night, heard heavy breathing behind him and turned to see a polar bear within a few feet. He threw the glare of his bull's-eye lamp in the eyes of the beast, which shrank back and disappeared among the neighbouring hummocks.

Kellett's conviction that McClure would abandon ship in April impelled him to order the earliest spring journey yet undertaken. Lieutenant Pim, who had been appointed to search Banks Land for Franklin, now undertook the same duty on behalf of McClure. As his journey would be of indefinite duration – for if he found no men at Mercy Bay, it would be his task to overtake, if possible, and bring back the retreating crew – he was provided with a supporting sledge. To free the ships' officers for the long journeys, Dr Domville volunteered to take charge of this.

Two sledges, one man-hauled and one drawn by dogs, left the ships on 10 March in intense cold. This was the winter which bore so heavily on the starving men of the *Investigator*. The rescue party made very heavy going down the Melville Island shore, sometimes being confined to the tent for whole days by wind and cold. Twenty-five miles short of Cape Dundas, the jumping-off point for Banks Land, the large sledge broke down beyond the possibility of repair on the spot. Delay was impossible because McClure might even then be starting on the journey that would put his men beyond the reach of aid. Ordering Domville to transport reserve supplies to Cape Dundas and await his return, Pim set off across the sound with the dog sledge and two men only. The surgeon was left with his damaged sledge to relay nearly a ton of supplies to Cape Dundas, where he tented in extreme discomfort. His vigil was to be shorter than he expected. Pim and his companions, Robert Hoyle and Thomas Bidgood (Armstrong, ever the sailor's friend, is the only chronicler who notes their names), had the sharper pain of crossing eighty miles of wind-swept ice, harassed by the fear that their labour would be in vain. On 6 April they were approaching a breach in the rockbound coast that could only be Mercy Bay. By the afternoon, with Point Back receding to the left as they advanced, the far shore of the bay was opening up. Then the hulk of the *Investigator* came into sight, shorn of her topmast, wrapped in her housing and looking like a snowbound Noah's Ark. Moving figures on the ice assured them that they had come in time.

The men of the *Investigator* had been busied in preparation for the partial desertion of their ship. Miertsching, who had proved his manual skill by making boots for the captain, took over from the invalided armourer the task of making mess tins. All officers appointed to travel had turned in their journals to the captain. Miertsching gave up his treasured botanical and geological collections with the fear, too well justified, that he would never see them again. Full rations, issued to the travelling parties since 15 March, were restoring their health and cheer.

Sixth of April was one of those days of light overcast, intermittent snow, and raw air, which are the least agreeable features of declining winter. There was the usual stir around the ship and on the land nearby. The hunters were out as usual. Others were exercising on the ice. And four men on land were digging a grave for a comrade – the first casualty in forty months. McClure had inspected their work and was walking back with Miertsching when a sailor came running up to announce that some man or animal was crossing the ice from Point Back. Another rushed up to declare that there were three men – one man alone, followed by two more with a dog sledge. The lone man rapidly approached. Pim's features were so discoloured by the smoke of his blubber lamp that McClure took him for an Eskimo until he drew near and uttered a hoarse cry. 'In the name of God, who are you?' demanded McClure. 'I'm Lieutenant Pim, late of the *Herald*, now of the *Resolute*. Captain Kellett is with her at Dealy Island,' was the reply.

'These words proved,' McClure later wrote, 'that he was real English flesh and blood. To rush to him, to seize him by the hand was the work of a moment – our hearts were too full to speak, while the grimy stranger greeted us and told us who he was and whence he came. And what was it like on the ship when this was noised abroad? At the mention of the stranger the sick forgetting their pain, sprang from their beds, the healthy forgot their trials and despair, and in less time than it takes to tell it, all were on deck . . . All was surprise, joy, animation and uproar.'

'Many thankful prayers from joyful hearts were wafted up to the Throne of Grace,' adds Miertsching.

The miserable condition of the men of the *Investigator* had stolen on them by degrees, and they knew not how starved and haggard they appeared. The newcomers were more sensitive. 'The manly cheeks' of Hoyle and Bidgood 'were moistened with tears' at their wretched appearance. Pim, observing Armstrong and his mess sitting down to their meal, a dram of weak cocoa and a minute portion of bread, darted out to his sledge and brought back a packet of bacon to give them a meal that they would recall as long as memory lasted.

In the first frenzy of joy, men spoke as if their troubles were over and themselves at anchor in an English harbour. They could reasonably hope to be home by autumn if they joined Kellett's ships on the other side of the impenetrable polar pack. And this was the course Kellett expected McClure to follow. Still averse to giving an order to Collinson's officer, he had entrusted a letter to Pim in which he requested McClure to ascertain by medical examination whether or not his men were fit to risk another winter of detention in the Arctic. Knowing what the outcome of this would be and resolved to save his ship, or at least to make sure that if she was deserted it would be by Kellett's order, not his, McClure himself set out in company with Pim for Dealy Island to reason with his senior officer. To keep up the pretence that the ship could be got out by her crew and to preserve supplies for her voyage home, he gave the ruthless order that the ration of his starving men should not be altered until he could determine the fate of the ship. He also left orders that Cresswell, Miertsching, and twenty-four of the feeblest of the crew, including the two mental patients, Wyniatt and Bradbury, should leave as arranged on 15 April and follow him to Dealy Island.

Buoyed up as they were by the certainty of safety and comfort at the journey's end, Cresswell's party found it a hard one. Six of their four and twenty were unfit for sledge work and tottered behind, supporting themselves by resting a hand on a moving sledge. Before the trek ended two invalids were riding on a sledge, and probably, though Miertsching does not mention it, others had grown too weak to remain in harness. The ice was rugged, and some ridges were so steep that the burdened sledge haulers clambered up them on all fours. With perpetual daylight, they travelled in stretches of seven hours and rested for five. The work of setting up tents and putting the weaker ones to bed fell upon the few vigorous men. On the twenty-third they reached the Melville Island shore near Cape Dundas. A week later they passed Winter Harbour and were cheered by meeting an outward-bound sledge crew from the *Resolute*. On 1 May they entered Bridport Inlet, and Cresswell passed his telescope around to give his tired followers a glimpse of the masts of Kellett's ships on the skyline fifteen miles away. They set up camp and, now relaxed, slept ten hours instead of the accustomed five. A cheerful breakfast, mutual apologies and forgiveness for all the impatience and peevishness of the journey, a solemn religious service, and the sledges were put in motion for the last time. 'Upon rounding a rock we see the two ships. They, too, have seen *us*. They have hoisted a flag!' Kellett, McClure, and the few seamen left with the ships came hurrying over the ice to receive them. Amid the clamorous greetings of the seamen, Kellett went straight to the one stranger among them, shook hands with Miertsching and led him to his cabin, where soap, water, and clean linen awaited him. 'They offer me coffee, real hot coffee. What a delight is this also! I have not tasted it for two and a half years.' Overcome with this hospitality, the interpreter sank to the cabin floor in a profound slumber, which neither Kellett nor his steward were inhuman enough to disturb.

The arrival of Cresswell's party decided the fate of the *Investigator*. Shocked at their faltering gait, shrunken frames, and hollow, staring eyes, Kellett informed McClure that his crew must be spared further labour by the immediate desertion of the ship. The latter repeated the Cape Lisburne formula, that 'he could not do it on his own responsibility'. So Kellett handed him a written order requiring him to abandon the *Investigator* unless twenty volunteers, declared fit by proper medical authority, could be found to work her. Upon McClure's objecting to Dr Armstrong's notorious hostility, Kellett appointed Dr Domville to assist in the inspection and ensure an impartial decision. The older officer must have resented McClure's refusal to take personal responsibility for the situation which his own headlong tactics had brought about. At the time, no doubt, he attributed it to professional pride. Two years later he was to think otherwise.

With McClure on his way back to Mercy Bay, Kellett scraped together a travelling crew from the few men available and appointed his mate, Mr Roche, to conduct Cresswell, Wyniatt, and the least fit *Investigator*'s men to the *North Star* depot at Beechey Island. From there the summer supply ship would take them home. Miertsching, much against his will, was required to stay with the expedition. If released that summer, Kellett planned to visit the Cape York Eskimos and inquire further into the story of Adam Beck. If detained for a second winter, he wished to send a party down Peel Sound on the mission which the *Prince Albert* had twice failed to carry out. Cresswell reached England in October with Captain Inglefield of the supply ship *Phoenix,* and then only did the British public learn of the discovery of the Northwest Passage made two years before.

While awaiting the return of the travelling parties under McClintock, Mecham, and Hamilton, the fit men at Dealy Island passed the time hunting. On 10 June Dr Domville returned from the Bay of Mercy with the news that the *Investigator* was to be deserted. Less than half of Kellett's required minimum of twenty volunteers could be mustered, he stated, and almost the entire crew had been found unfit for further service. McClure, with his thirty-odd remaining men, was not far behind. At 8 A.M. on the seventeenth they came in sight, five miles away, moving very slowly – at noon they were still three miles away. No help could be given, for no fit men were there to give it. At 1 P.M. Kellett and Miertsching went out to meet them: 'The melancholy sight they presented I will never in my life forget,' wrote Miertsching. A number were so feeble that they were supported by comrades or leaned on the moving sledges; eight of the worst cases were lashed on sledges drawn by men so weak that when they stumbled they had to be helped to their feet. 'The spectacle of this miserable throng brought to my mind the unfortunate Franklin expedition; and had not our gracious and merciful Lord and Saviour intervened, and by bringing these ships at the right time, cancelled our intended long journey, we must all have perished miserably on the frozen sea.' This testimony by Miertsching, which contradicts so pointedly McClure's subsequent claim that he could have brought his crew to safety without the aid of the *Resolute*, is confirmed by George McDougall. Macdonald, one of the men of the *Investigator*, was, he wrote, 'in a dreadful state: his flesh would retain an impression, if touched with the finger, like dough or putty; his legs were swollen to twice their natural size; whilst his teeth could be moved to and fro in their gums by the slightest movement of the tongue. He, however, recovered his health.'

While Pim was on his way to Mercy Bay, McClintock, Mecham, and Hamilton, supported respectively by Ensign De Bray of the French Navy, and the mates, Nares and Roche, had left Dealy Island. Their journeys, which along with the work of the Belcher division, were practically to complete the rough chart of the Canadian Arctic to latitude 77 degrees north. Although Miertsching mentions that these parties set out with very faint hope of finding what they sought, McClintock had introduced a new device for the thorough search of smaller coves and inlets. This was the satellite sledge, five feet long and fourteen pounds in weight, which, carrying food and fuel only, enabled two or three men to make a rapid circuit of a bay while the main party rested or occupied itself elsewhere.

Crossing Melville Island to Point Nias on Hecla and Griper Bay, McClintock followed the coast west around its northwestern angle. From there he sent back De Bray with three men judged unfit – Hood and Wilkie, his comrades on all previous journeys, and Coombes. De Bray was instructed to transfer supplies from the large depot at Point Nias west to Cape Fisher before rejoining the ship. Unluckily, Coombes died before this could be done, and his comrades persuaded De Bray that the body should be carried to the ship immediately for burial. The embarrassed young officer felt bound to conform to what they assured him was the custom of the British Navy. Kellett was not a little put out at this mistake, which could mean starvation to McClintock's returning crew. Pim, by now back from Mercy Bay, made a special trip to remedy this omission – for which, incidentally, the men were more blamed than the luckless De Bray.

McClintock, in the meantime, seeing new land to the west, crossed Fitzwilliam Strait to Prince Patrick Island and divided forces with his sledge captain Green to search Intrepid Bay and Green Bay before reuniting and crossing an arm of the sea to examine the north end of Eglinton Island. They then doubled back to Prince Patrick Island and made camp at Cape McClintock, its northern extremity. With the small sledge and two men, Giddy and Drew, McClintock followed the west shore of Prince Patrick Island, ending his journey at Satellite Bay. There they were caught in a gale with no shelter to be obtained except by cowering behind the little sledge turned up as a windbreak. The tramp back to Cape McClintock was made even harder by rain and rotting 'needle' ice.

The return journey was without incident, until at Point Nias on the Melville Island north shore, the seaman Hiccles became desperately ill and was placed on the sledge. The rest of the party were in sorry plight with rheumatic knees, swollen feet, and blistered heels; and McClintock afterwards declared that the next eighteen hours were more trying than all the hundred preceding days. Hiccles recovered sufficiently to walk – in good time, for the interior of Melville Island in the warmth of mid-July becomes a maze of bog and morass. They cached sledge, tent, and supplies, and for the last three days walked with knapsacks, burrowing in the snow – which must have been horribly damp – to sleep. They reached the ships on 18 July after an outing of 106 days. They had travelled 1,328 statute miles and had laid down 886 miles of new coast.

Like McClintock, Mecham began his journey on 4 April and, supported by Nares, followed the shore of Melville Island to the west and crossed Kellett Strait to explore the southern part of Eglinton Island. Sending Nares back, he continued along the west and south shores of Prince Patrick Island and on its west side came upon the 'stupendous' pack of the open Beaufort Sea. Scouting ahead to find a road for the sledge, Mecham, unnoticed by his toiling crew, fell into a snow-filled crevasse, and was almost smothered before he could clamber out. His northward survey ended some twenty miles south of McClintock's farthest point at Satellite Bay. This gap was filled in by Stefansson in 1915. Short of rations and 150 miles by the sea route from his last depot, Mecham took to the land and, hoisting a sail on his sledge, crossed Prince Patrick Island with northwest winds behind him. He made the interesting discovery of petrified wood 400 feet above sea level. On 6 July he was back at the ships, 94 days out, with a total mileage of 1,153 – 785 of that was new coast.

Lieutenant Hamilton of the *Resolute* crossed Melville Island to the north and went up the unexplored east side of Hecla and Griper Bay. On the tip of the Sabine Peninsula, on 17 May near Cape George Richards, he met the sledge party of that very George Richards (commander under Belcher on the *Assistance*), bound in the opposite direction. Both officers found their intended journeys suddenly curtailed.

Richards described the fortunes of the Belcher detachment up to his departure from the ships on 10 April. In the previous autumn, the *Assistance* and the *Pioneer* had ascended Wellington Channel and Penny Strait to find their winter anchorage on the tip of Grinnell Peninsula, where Penny Strait merges with Belcher Channel to the north. As the sea was still unfrozen, Belcher was able to cross Belcher Channel with boat and sledge to make the discovery of North Cornwall Island. In the spring, Richards set out to cross Penny Strait with Osborn, Lieutenant Walter May, and fifty-five men, drawing six sledges and two boats – for the strait would probably be open sea again before the main party returned. Sending May back when the supplies he carried were expended, Richards, with Osborn, traversed the north shore of Bathurst Island, crossed Byam Martin Channel, and had sent the other supporting sledges back with Osborn when he met Hamilton and learned that the work in that quarter was already done.

Hamilton went off in pursuit of Osborn, who had gone back only a short distance, and secured the help of his carpenter, Sam Walker, for the repair of a damaged sledge. Richards nonchalantly added 150 miles to his return journey by crossing Melville Island and calling on the *Resolute*.

May got his detachment back to the ships over a still-frozen sea. Osborn, with the second supporting party, found Penny Strait broken up, and rather than stand idly by the boats awaiting the return of Richards from Dealy Island, he explored the west side of the strait by sea, though not far enough to make certain that Cornwallis and Bathurst were separate islands.

The extended journey east from the ships had been commanded by Sir Edward Belcher in person – a creditable effort for one of his age, though a generous captain would have entrusted it to the more experienced Osborn. He followed the north shore of Devon Island as far as Cardigan Strait and identified North Kent Island, beyond which lay the Hell's Gate channel of the later discoverer Otto Sverdrup. Together with the preceding Austin expedition, the sledge parties of Belcher and Kellett had given shape to the island chain extending from Devon Island in the east to Prince Patrick Island in the far west.

With all travelling parties back and the sea open, Belcher embarked on the homeward voyage. Like Penny before him, he found the lower stretch of Wellington Channel obstructed with southward-drifting ice. By his stubborn refusal to heed advice – so says Osborn – his ships were icebound and forced to winter in a windy, desolate anchorage, fifty miles north of Beechey Island.

Kellett's detachment met with no better luck. Until the middle of August the ice inside Dealy Island lay as it had in Mercy Bay, an unbroken sheet. On 17 August a furious gale drove it, still unshattered, into the open sea, with the heads of the imprisoned ships pointing now this way, now that, as the floe wheeled them about. They freed themselves and made sail to the east only to discover that westerly winds had caused a congestion in Barrow Strait. The weather grew cold and dead calm; the ships were not beset but froze gradually in thickening young ice. ' The prospect from the crow's-nest was disheartening,' writes

McDougall on 11 September, 'for with the exception of an occasional thread of water, nothing but ice met our view; and we could not conceal from ourselves that in all probability we were doomed to pass the dreary months of the approaching winter in the pack.' On the eighteenth they gave up hope. For the men of the *Investigator* it was the fourth winter in the ice.

As only 400 yards separated the two ships, the winter was enlivened by interchange of visits and by lectures and plays. To keep up communication in bad weather, Lieutenant Hamilton connected them with that novelty, the electromagnetic telegraph. Officers played chess by this means, possibly the first instance of chess by telegraph in the history of the game. In the broad sea south of Cape Cockburn they were spared the torturing pressures which Back's *Terror* had undergone; and the crews were well fed, though the crowding caused by the presence of the *Investigator* and the consequent shortage of bedding provoked much discontent.

Mr Sainsbury of the *Investigator*, long in poor health, died on 14 November. 'On the eve of his death he asked to see the captain and the officers; one after another he took leave of them, asking pardon for his faults, and receiving from each a clasp of the hand in token of sympathy.' On the sixteenth his funeral procession 'wended its way to the grave, a hole in the ice, about 250 yards from the ship. The day was cold (−20) and misty, and never shall I forget the scene on the ice as the body sewn in canvas, with weights attached, was launched through the narrow opening and disappeared to our view. Within an hour Nature had placed a slab over the grave of our departed shipmate.'

Miertsching, berthed on the *Intrepid,* was separated by a canvas curtain only from the hospital where the marine Hood lay dying. McClintock, whose comrade he had been on three extended journeys, had drawn up his will, in which he bequeathed all his belongings to a sister except for a £5 legacy to his sledge mate Shaw. A good soldier, though irreligious, he gave his attention to the prayers prescribed by the rules of the service, but would have none of Miertsching's ministrations. 'At eleven o'clock, thinking to hear the death-rattle, I sprang up again to tell him for the last time of the love of Christ, but he lay rigid and would not look at me. I could only kneel and commend him to the love of God. Towards two o'clock I could no longer hear anything. I got up again, but the sentry made a sign to me that all was over. He was a marine of the *Intrepid*.'

As the *Resolute* and the *Intrepid* had passed the winter not much more than a hundred miles east of Dealy Island, Kellett sent Lieutenant Mecham and Mr Krabbé, sailing master of the *Intrepid*, to Banks Land, the former to search Prince of Wales Strait for a record of Collinson, now unreported for three years; the latter to visit the *Investigator* and bring away the journals of her officers. At the same time (early in April), Hamilton was dispatched to the *North Star* to inquire for Belcher, of whose whereabouts Kellett was now ignorant. Hamilton soon came back bearing dispatches and a private letter of very singular content.

Belcher had passed a disagreeable winter. The consciousness that he had neither the confidence nor the regard of his officers provoked the bully in him, and he made a special butt of his first lieutenant, Walter May. May, a sensitive young man who later left the Navy for painting and sculpture, shuddered at his captain's obscenities – not without cause, for the one sample of Belcher's wit which May permitted himself to insert in his diary was, by any code, unworthy of a commanding officer in his fifties. May was accused of holding subversive language behind his captain's back, and threatened with court-martial. On learning that his bad relations with his officers were the subject of derisive comment on the *Pioneer*, Belcher threatened to sever communications between the two ships (merely to provoke Osborn, says May.) Ill temper was one of the hazards of a polar winter, and Belcher aggravated instead of trying to allay it. In the end, May found himself relieved of his duties. The less submissive Osborn was put under arrest. Unpopular with his officers and in poor health, the commodore resolved to make sure of ending the expedition in the coming summer, even if it meant deserting the ships and packing all crews on the *North Star*.

He therefore prepared a dispatch for Kellett, whom he supposed like himself to have been detained for the second winter, to 'meet me at Beechey Island, with the crews of all vessels, before the 26th of August.' As Kellett could not be sure of freeing his ships by that date, the implied meaning was that he was to desert them and bring the crews out on foot. It was a strange way of requiring a subordinate to do what he must account for before a court-martial. Nor were matters much helped by a private – or what Belcher chose to call a 'demi-official' letter – in which he mentions, 'I have sent you orders to abandon' the *Resolute* and the *Intrepid*. This ambiguity may not have been meant to entrap Kellett into an act which his superior officer could disown; it more probably expressed Belcher's reluctance to state openly that he would rather sacrifice his ships than risk another winter in the ice.

These letters, carried to the *North Star* and from there to the *Resolute*, must have caused Kellett no little embarrassment. McClure had forced him to order the desertion of one ship. Now Belcher seemed to be trying by more subtle means to make him shoulder responsibility for two more. He opened his official reply in a tone of good-humoured expostulation as if addressing a dim-witted woman or a child, apologizing in the politest manner for refusing compliance, but 'you really have given me no orders that I could act on'. He must have 'final, decided, and most unmistakeable orders' before he would desert H.M. vessels under his command. In a private letter, he assured Belcher that it was the unanimous opinion of his officers that the ships would not be endangered by the summer break-up as they were in ice of one year's growth only. McClintock, the dean of the expedition in polar experience, was sent by dog sledge to carry these dispatches to Belcher and, if necessary, amplify their content.

Though Belcher was not pleased at this reply – in his published account he appears distressed by Kellett's obtuseness – he was not the man to withdraw when he had committed himself. McClintock brought back an unambiguous order for the abandonment of the ships. By the end of May the entire crews of the *Resolute*, the *Intrepid*, and the *Investigator* were encamped on or around the *North Star* at Beechey Island.

There Mecham and Krabbé, whose homeward journey had thus been unexpectedly lengthened, overtook them. Mecham had visited the Princess Royal Islands and found two records left by Collinson. From these it was learned that the *Enterprise* had been safe in the summer of 1852. Krabbé had found the *Investigator* with her cable slack but still fast frozen in Mercy Bay. He had made diligent search, but had found only one journal, that of First Lieutenant Haswell. This was a perplexing and somewhat sinister circumstance, giving rise to the suspicion that McClure, in order to exalt his own character and minimize the sufferings of his men, had wished to suppress all personal accounts except his own. Dr Armstrong got his journal out – doubtless through the agency of Dr Domville – and Miertsching reconstructed his from memory, pencilled notes, and McClure's personal record. These two have placed the grimmer aspects of the voyage of the *Investigator* on record; but Armstrong's *Narrative* appeared two years after McClure had won the honours he coveted, and the English version of Miertsching's *Reisebeschreibung* was not published until 1967.

Sir Edward Belcher, having resolved to abandon the *Assistance* and the *Pioneer* also, rather than face possible detention for another winter, brought his men down to Beechey Island, and the crews of six vessels were clustered on and around the *North Star*. The timely arrival of Captain Inglefield with the supply ships *Phoenix* and *Talbot* permitted their evacuation without excessive crowding. Miertsching and the *Investigator* took passage with the veteran Pullen on the *North Star*.

Miertsching gives a lively description of the reaction to milder latitudes of men who had spent almost five years in the frozen north. They found the air of the North Atlantic warm and muggy; they suffered from headaches, seasickness, and a restless malaise which made them incapable of serious occupation. Every passing merchant ship was noted. On 7 October 1854, the ocean voyage was over, and the *North Star* was being tugged up the Thames.

'It will be long before I forget that day, favoured as it was by the grandest weather; the banks of the river were adorned with green trees and beautiful houses, and in the green meadows were no savage musk-ox or reindeer – but real, tame, useful animals were grazing and men were going about, busy with their various tasks; railway trains thundered by, and, in a word, we saw, full of life and activity, the fruitful, cultivated world to which we had become strangers. We stood and gazed like delighted children. . . . From the 4th of July 1850 to the present day we have seen neither tree nor bush. . . . It is almost too much for us seafarers, long inured to loneliness and deserts,' writes Miertsching. When the ship docked late in the evening, the pious missionary, his passionate prayers for a safe return granted at last, did not go into an ecstasy of thanksgiving: he pooled his

resources with those of the naval gentlemen and sent ashore for
beer.

'The newspapers had announced the arrival of the *North Star*,
and the next morning found the dock crowded with the wives of
officers and men with their children. In the midst of their pure
family joys, of their hugging, embracing and rapturous outcries,
there were the bitterest tears. Poor women had come full of hope
with children clinging to them to whom during the long years of
separation they had always talked of their father. Alas! that
father, that husband, lies far away in his lonely and icy tomb.
And the heart-broken widow goes away clasping her bereaved
orphans to her. May God comfort and sustain them,' notes
Miertsching.

Miertsching, only by courtesy a naval officer, obtained an immediate discharge and bade his friends of the *Investigator* an
affectionate farewell. Others were detained to face the court-
martial convened to inquire into the loss of the ships.

McClure produced the written orders of his senior officer,
Captain Kellett, requiring him to abandon the *Investigator*, and
was acquitted with a few words of formal compliment.

Kellett, it appears, was not called up to justify his action with
regard to the *Investigator* – a circumstance from which McClure
may have profited at a later date. The written orders of *his*
superior officer, Captain Sir Edward Belcher, freed him from
responsibility for the loss of *Resolute* and the *Intrepid*. He was
granted acquittal, and the president of the court added cordially
that it gave him great pleasure to return his sword to an officer
who had worn it so much to the honour and profit of his country.

Belcher, upon whom the whole burden now descended, pleaded
that, since his expedition had fulfilled its mission, he judged it
better to give up the ships than to expose their crews to possible
detention for another winter. It was an arguable but not a good
case. The ships were in no danger that was not ordinary in the
Arctic service, and the risk to their crews was hardly such as to
warrant a hasty desertion, which set an undesirable precedent,
was bad for naval morale, and looked somewhat ridiculous to the
world at large. After deliberation, the court concluded that in
view of the confidence reposed by the Admiralty in Captain Sir
Edward Belcher, he was authorized to act as he had done, but
regretted that he had not consulted with Captain Kellett and his

officers before giving up the *Resolute* and her tender. Actually there had been consultation, but the court apparently did not admit as evidence private communications between the two captains. Belcher was declared acquitted, and the president of court handed him his sword in chilling silence.

Dr Richard King feared that the cold rebuke expressed by the tone of his acquittal must have gone over Belcher's head: it was 'a lesson too refined for the organization of the man.' Sherard Osborn apparently thought so too: in the first edition of his *Discovery of the North-West Passage* he reflected on his former commander in terms so harsh that his friends prevailed on him to amend them. Belcher gained little from their intervention, for the adroit journalist substituted the needle for the bludgeon, and in his second edition described the humiliation of Belcher's 'bare acquittal' in language of unctuous sympathy which, unless Belcher was as stupid as King would have him, must have been more galling than downright abuse.

As soon as the expedition returned, Osborn demanded a court-martial before which Belcher might justify his action in placing him under arrest. The Admiralty refused to grant the trial, but administered a snub to Belcher by advancing to the rank of commander Osborn and May, on whom also he had adversely reported. They sent the pugnacious Osborn to fight the Russians in the Black Sea, where he achieved by valour the post captaincy which he would never have won by tact.

Yet another rebuke was in store for the unlucky Belcher. The icebound *Resolute* was carried by wind and current from Cape Cockburn through Barrow Strait and Lancaster Sound out into Baffin Bay. She drifted southward and on 10 September 1855 was picked up by Captain James Buddington of the American whaler *George Henry* and carried to New London, Connecticut. The Congress of the United States purchased her for $40,000 and sent her back refitted to the British Admiralty. When the *Resolute* was broken up, a British official sent President Chester A. Arthur of the United States an oak table made from her timbers. For many years this token of American generosity and British gratitude lay unused in a storage room. During the Presidency of John F. Kennedy it was found by Mrs Kennedy and restored to a place of honour in the White House.

About the time that McClure was released with formal praise

by the court-martial, humbler but better-deserved tributes were paid to two of his officers. When Miertsching took leave of his shipmates, 'several seamen, their features hardened by storm and foul weather, were not ashamed to shed tears.' Probably just after the court-martial (the only source for this is an undated newspaper clipping in the Grinnell Scrapbook in the Stefansson Collection), Dr Armstrong, along with Lieutenant Pim, was invited to a gathering of the petty officers, seamen, and marines of the *Investigator* to receive a chronometer 'as a testimony of their sincere respect and gratitude for his unwearied skill and humanity during the unparalleled Arctic Service which resulted in the Discovery of the North-West Passage'. The spokesman, James Nelson, addressing Armstrong, said, 'There are few, if any of us, who have not experienced your kindness at the sick bed ...' Turning to Pim, he added: 'Were it not for you, sir, many of us now present would never have seen old England again.' Pim, embarrassed at being suddenly brought into the programme, answered briefly, 'I thank you, my lads, I shall never forget our meeting.'

9 The Voyage of the *Enterprise* and the Committee's Award

At the date of Sir Edward Belcher's acquittal by court-martial, the fate of the *Enterprise*, the only British ship apart from the *Plover* which remained in the ice, was still uncertain. She might be anywhere in the vast waste that had swallowed up the *Erebus* and the *Terror*. Late in the autumn a dispatch from Alaska put an end to all anxiety. On 13 August 1854, two weeks before Belcher's crews made their getaway from Beechey Island, the crew of the *Enterprise*, in Bering Strait, was holding a service of thanksgiving for their deliverance after three whole years spent in the ice. Collinson had kept mobile twice as long as McClure, had made deeper penetration, and had come out in fine fettle under his own power. Towards the end of the century, Admiral Sir George Richards, viewing the search for Franklin in calm retrospect, wrote to General Collinson that his late brother's voyage was 'the most remarkable of them all'. It was doubly remarkable – for Collinson's superb technique in the care and handling of ship and men, and for the hard luck which denied him the original achievement needed to win the public recognition that he, more than any other, deserved.

Leaving Honolulu on 30 June 1850, Collinson had taken the safety route around the Aleutians, and in Bering Strait learned from the *Plover* that the *Investigator* had gone into the ice two weeks ahead of him. (General Collinson observes that but for the time he had lost in waiting for his consort in the Strait of Magellan and at Honolulu, Collinson, after making the circuit of the Aleutians, would have reached the rendezvous as soon as his junior.) Like McClure, Collinson tried to set a course through the ocean pack straight for Banks Land – with the same lack of success. By then it was too late in the season to attempt the shore route. He left Lieutenant Barnard, Assistant Surgeon Adams, and a seaman with the *Plover* and went south to winter at Hong

Kong. In the course of the winter, Barnard travelled abroad to make inquiries among the natives, and was mortally wounded in an Indian raid on a Russian trading-post where he was a guest. His death was a blow to the expedition, for he had had sledging experience with Sir James Ross and, with his easy-going disposition, might have averted the bitterness that was to arise between the captain and the other officers.

In the summer of 1851 Collinson returned to the north and followed the continental shore past Alaska and the Mackenzie River into Franklin Bay, and there with a favourable wind steered for Banks Land. He passed Nelson's Head (to which he gave the name Cape Erebus) and entered Prince of Wales Strait on 26 August, ten days after McClure had emerged from it to attempt the circumnavigation of Banks Land. He was going up the strait, hoping confidently to complete the Northwest Passage, when a beacon on one of the Princess Royal Islands was observed, and examined – the *Investigator*, it was found, had anticipated him. Collinson held his course to the top of the strait, where he concluded, as McClintock and McClure had done, that the ice of Viscount Melville Sound was no place for a ship. Reversing his course, he went down the strait and began to circle Banks Land. At Point Kellett a barrel hung from a pole notified him that he was still on the track of the *Investigator*. On 7 September, when that ship was lying in her ice crate at Ballast Beach, the *Enterprise* was only 100 miles behind her. But the appearance to port of the monstrous polar pack, slanting shorewards as the sea grew deeper ahead, conveyed a warning which Collinson could understand. He sheered off, with no misgivings for McClure, whom he supposed to have taken the same prudent course as himself, coasted back along the south Banks Land shore, and found a safe winter berth in Walker Bay on the southeast side of Prince of Wales Strait. In one season the *Enterprise* had almost matched the record made by the *Investigator* in two, and was fit as ever for duty.

Her crew exerted themselves during the winter to maintain that fitness by a wholesome diet. They obtained fish from a freshwater lake, and waged ruthless war on wolves and foxes to secure for themselves a monopoly of the flesh of the Arctic hare. In the spring, Lieutenant Jago took a sledge party along the north shore of Prince Albert Sound – to learn from a cairn that Lieutenant

Haswell of the *Investigator* had preceded him by twelve months. Collinson and Lieutenant Parks sledged up Prince of Wales Strait and separated, Collinson remaining to search the Victoria Island shore, while Parks crossed the sound to Melville Island. Owing to ration shortage he did not reach Winter Harbour where McClure and Court had left the record of their voyage a few days before. On his way back, Parks came across their sledge tracks, but supposed them to be those of Eskimos. In the long run, it was lucky for McClure that he thus narrowly eluded his chief. Had they met, Collinson would have repossessed the command and done his best to get the men of the *Investigator* out of their dangerous situation. In that event, McClure's discoveries would have been credited jointly to both ships, of which Collinson, not he, was supreme commander. In the journey back down the strait, two of Collinson's crew robbed the cache on Princess Royal Island and made themselves drunk, earning the only floggings administered to a crew of sixty during a cruise of five and a half years.

When the ship was released he sailed up Prince Albert Sound and, by proving it a bay, established that Prince Albert, Wollaston, and Victoria lands were united to compose one island. Emerging from the Sound, he turned left, passed through Dolphin and Union and Dease Straits and, directed by Simpson's chart (he knew nothing of Rae's boat voyage), berthed his ship for the winter in Cambridge Bay.

Collinson's navigation of Dease Strait was to be enthusiastically praised by Amundsen, who had trouble in getting his *Gjoa*, one-tenth of the *Enterprise*'s size and aided by mechanical power, through its shallow, irregular, and rocky channels. He admires the pains taken to fix and describe landmarks for the guidance of future pilots, and finds Collinson 'one of the most capable and enterprising sailors the world has produced'. No less praiseworthy were the measures he took to provide exercise and healthy diet for his crew during the winter months. McClure had been in the habit of turning his men out on the ice to exercise in whatever manner they chose. Collinson provided recreation by setting up a skittle alley under the housing on the upper deck and, finding that insufficient, made a billiard table of snow blocks, with a smooth surface of ice, and added cushions of walrus hide stuffed with oakum. As round shot proved too heavy for billiard balls, the carpenter shaped some out of the hardwood lignum vitae, 'which, considering he had no turning-lathe, quite surprised me'. Collinson adds: 'The thing took admirably, and gave them what I wanted, occupation off the lower deck of their own accord.' Fish, which they caught in abundance, and the venison obtained from nearby Eskimos, preserved the crew from scurvy. The one boast which the matter-of-fact captain permits himself was to state that of the six deaths (one per year) that occurred on the cruise not one could be attributed to the conditions of service in the Arctic. Collinson *was* perpetually at odds with his officers, almost all of whom were at one time or another under arrest for long periods, and that does not enhance his general character. But it does add to the credit he deserves for the management of his men under these difficult conditions.

Collinson's splendid thrust through 300 miles of channel, until then believed to be navigable by boat only, had brought him, like Rae, to the threshold of success, and unlike Rae, with the time and resources needed to exploit his favourable position. The researches of Sir James Ross in 1830 and of Thomas Simpson gave him a general idea of the pattern of land and sea that lay ahead. A hundred miles to the east was the King William Land shore and on it, capes Victory and Herschel, fixed on the chart and marked with cairns, and so the natural repository for records of crews wrecked in that area. The observations of his predecessors made it reasonably certain that a strait divided King William Land from the opposite shore of Victoria Island. Guided by this knowledge and with the means for mounting two extended sledge journeys, Collinson had planned to send one sledge up the east shore of Victoria Island and the other up the west shore of King William Land. On observing the intensely rugged character of the pack in Victoria Strait – the pack where Franklin had come to grief – he cancelled one half of his programme to keep the two long-range sledges together for mutual assistance. He elected to examine the east shore of Victoria Island – not suspecting that Rae had already traversed it – and lost the prize that lay within his grasp.

Collinson is more to be pitied than blamed for neglecting the one hint he received of the true state of the case. The crew of the *Enterprise* had frequent dealings with the Eskimos of the region, but could not speak to them with any ease. An officer,

223

Mr Arbuthnot, 'succeeded in inducing some of them [the Eskimos] to draw a chart of the coast to the eastward [evidently of Victoria Island] which was several times repeated, agreeing very well with each other, but were totally unlike the coast afterwards travelled over by me. He also appeared to think that they indicated a ship being there, but in my opinion it was a repetition of his questions.'

Collinson was too much a sceptic to alter his proposed route on the strength of the Eskimos' replies to leading questions which they imperfectly understood. This tragic error leads Admiral Wright to suspect that 'Captain Collinson's reasoning faculty became numbed by the conditions of cold'. It could more justly be attributed to the normal action of a mind that was naturally sceptical. Collinson was in exactly the same situation as Rae a year later, when he received first word of the castaways from the Eskimos of Pelly Bay. Both men were invited to alter a plan on the strength of a vague report of doubtful authenticity. Both, with inborn North Country caution, refused to do so. Only a natural gambler would have taken the Eskimos' advice – and would have achieved a stunning success. But he would no more merit praise for his lucky guess than Collinson and Rae deserved censure for their perfectly reasonable scepticism.

In April 1853, Captain Collinson, with two main and one supporting sledge, rounded De Haven Point and went up the west shore of Victoria Strait. The condition of the ice more than justified his determination to keep the sledges together for 'double-manning'. At one point he notes: 'Here there was scarcely such a thing as a level spot to be seen, but a most confused jumble of angular pieces, many of which were upwards of twenty feet high, while the snow between them laid [sic] so loose that we frequently sank up to the middle, and only extricated ourselves by our hands.' After a laborious struggle of many days, they came upon a cairn and record – on the Victoria Island shore near the John Halkett islet – and learned from it that Dr John Rae had been up that shore by boat in the summer of 1851 and had found no trace of the Franklin expedition.

Few men have suffered ill luck so relentless and persistent. If he had found Rae's record earlier, he would have had time to cross Victoria Strait to King William Land, where the clue to the mystery lay. If McClure had not broken away from him, he would have had two ships in company at Cambridge Bay and could have searched both sides of Victoria Strait and so achieved success. If he had only had Miertsching – indulgently allowed to stay on the *Investigator* so that he would not get his clothes wet – he would have had the Eskimo report clearly interpreted, and he would have learned the scene of the disaster. Mortifying too was the realization that the discoveries which he had made in a voyage successful without parallel in the history of the American Arctic were not his – he had almost everywhere been anticipated by McClure or by Rae. Collinson and his sledges kept on going. In the jungle of hummocks they strayed away from the land and made their farthest on Gateshead Island. The sheet of paper that told of Franklin's fate lay fifty miles to the southeast in a pile of stones on the King William Land shore.

Later in the spring a clue was found to the south of Cambridge Bay, a fragment of a hatchway or of the door-frame of an observatory. It bore no mark of identification, and if it had, it could have made no difference. The crew of the *Enterprise* had been out for three and a half years, and, though other necessities were in good supply, they were dangerously short of fuel.

The *Enterprise* sailed out by the way she had come. In the narrow seas south of Victoria Island she was hampered by ice and contrary winds and was overtaken by winter at Camden Bay on the Alaskan shore a little to the east of Franklin's Return Reef. Driftwood along the shore supplied the needed fuel for the winter; and in the summer of 1854 the men of the *Enterprise* emerged from the Arctic in excellent health and cheered the long-suffering crew of the *Plover* with one of the plays in which the Arctic winters had made them so proficient. They then sailed for home. The *Plover* was soon to follow. The official search for Franklin was over.

The rejoicing over the safe arrival of the *Enterprise* in England in May 1855 was soured by her captain's insistence that some of her officers should be court-martialled for the disorders of which they had been guilty. The Admiralty, sympathetic to the nervous strain of prolonged Arctic service, knew that the squabbles bound to arise among a small group of men penned up for months of darkness and discomfort, if aired in court, might make both prosecutor and accused appear ridiculous, and did its best to pacify him. When Collinson consented to soften his charges,

H

Their Lordships absent-mindedly took them as withdrawn and, by immediate promotion of the offending officers, put judicial proceedings out of the question. Hurt by this treatment or offended at the scanty acknowledgment of his services, Collinson never again applied for an appointment, although he remained on the active list and reached the rank of admiral. While living in retirement with his mother and sisters, he still busied himself with maritime affairs; he relieved Lady Franklin of the business management of the *Fox* expedition and edited the *Voyages* of Martin Frobisher. In 1875 he was granted the long overdue honour of knighthood.

If Collinson had had the good luck to be first with either the discovery of the Northwest Passage or the finding of the Franklin relics, some popular writer such as Sherard Osborn would have compiled its history while the memory of participants was still fresh, and given it the place it deserves as one of the greatest voyages in the maritime history of Great Britain. Collinson's own matter-of-fact journal does his voyage less than justice, and it suffers by comparison with the story of the *Investigator,* which owes much of its dramatic appeal to dangers and hardships which Collinson had the wit to avoid. His severity to his officers arose less from malice than from his strict sense of discipline. He had the uncompromising morality of the North Countryman; and, it should be added, his sense of justice, if aggressive and unyielding, was wholly impartial. He had no reason to love McClure, but when he saw him unfairly attacked he defended him in the press; his brother and biographer, Major-General T. B. Collinson, censured Dr Armstrong for the liberties he took in criticizing his captain. Collinson's journal, plain and unvarnished as it is, reveals a man lacking neither in humour nor good nature; the expressive portrait contained in his brother's memoir suggests kindness more than stubbornness, though both characteristics are there. In retirement, according to a family tradition, the autocrat of the quarterdeck was meekly submissive to his sisters. He was a fine old master-mariner of the last days of sail, whose merits far exceeded their reward.

With the return of Collinson, McClure's titular commander, arose the question of a Parliamentary reward for the discovery of the Northwest Passage. The promise of £20,000 made in the days of James Cook to the crew that accomplished this, had been withdrawn; but there was no thought of withholding generous reward from those who had achieved a national ambition which dated back for centuries. The proper distribution of the grant was not quite so clear. Should it be assigned to McClure and his crew alone, or shared with Collinson, his commanding officer, and Kellett, his rescuer? McClure could be made the stainless hero of a great exploit, or he could be represented as a selfish adventurer, who had run away from his captain, charged recklessly into danger, and had, at the last moment, been saved by Kellett from the hopeless situation in which his own rashness had placed him. There were insinuations (quite unjust) that in his haste to complete the Northwest Passage, he had neglected his mission to search for Franklin. A committee of the House of Commons was set up to obtain testimony and decide on the proper award.

This award was to be made to the discoverers of *a,* not of *the* Northwest Passage. For since the previous October it had been known through Rae's report that the lost crews of Franklin had probably discovered an alternative passage before starvation overtook them – not later than 1850.

Appearing before the committee, Collinson in answer to a question testified curtly that McClure had acted in accordance with his orders by entering the pack alone. This unqualified affirmative was more generous than McClure had any right to expect. He had barely conformed to the letter, and violated the spirit of his orders, and had acted contrary to the advice of Kellett, his senior in rank. Collinson's undeviating adherence to the letter of the law, which his officers and the Admiralty had found so trying, was working in McClure's favour. And Collinson was without envy. 'Heaven knows,' he said later, 'I would not rob him of one atom of his well-won honours.'

At the opposite end of the spectrum, Kellett and Domville gave evidence that in their opinion the crew of the *Investigator* would have perished but for the arrival of the *Resolute.*

McClure testified smoothly, plausibly, and at some length that the help of the *Resolute* had not been essential to the survival of his crew. He could, he said, have got the ship out in the summer of 1853 or, failing that, have conveyed her crew on foot to Port Leopold with the loss of only four of its invalid members. This was bold for a man without medical background, and Armstrong would not have endorsed his words; luckily for McClure, Dr Armstrong was then at sea with the Baltic squadron. McClure's extravagant claims seemed to find support in the actions he had taken – by keeping the men on short rations, he declared his intention of staying with the ship, and having taken care that the *Investigator* had been abandoned by Kellett's order, not his own, he was able to pretend that her desertion had not been absolutely required.

The impudence of McClure's testimony was not lost on the committee. One of its members asked him if, instead of confidently asserting that he could have preserved his crew, it would not be fairer to admit that the arrival of the *Resolute* had converted a mere *possibility* of survival into a *certainty*. McClure civilly accepted the amendment, without expressly renouncing his own arrogant claim.

In its finding, the committee awarded £10,000 to the officers and men of the *Investigator,* and to those of the *Resolute* and the *Intrepid* an expression of commendation phrased as only a Parliamentary committee knows how to phrase it.

The brave old Kellett was deeply hurt. He saw himself robbed of credit for the rescue of sixty men, and his crew of the grant which they had well deserved. Kellett declared that he would willingly subscribe £50 to a fund for their benefit. If the grant was intended for the discoverers of the Northwest Passage only, to the exclusion of those who brought the discoverers back alive, why, he might have asked, was he required to testify at all. The Committee's verdict certainly calls for explanation. There was no reason for taking the evidence of Kellett and Domville unless it contemplated dividing the grant among the discoverers of the passage and those who found them and brought them back alive. That purpose cannot have been altered by McClure's testimony, for it is evident that the committee was not deceived by it. Its motive was probably political. The Franklin search, like the contemporary war with Russia, had been a 'soldiers' battle', in which the splendid work of junior officers and men had not been matched by the wisdom and enterprise of the High Command. The public badly needed a hero, and this, McClure, with a little grooming – at Kellett's expense – was able to provide. His reputation was enhanced by the history of his voyage, compiled by Sherard Osborn from the captain's journal. It went through several editions, being the sort of adventure story which the Victorians loved, full of the dramatic incident and scenic description that Osborn was so well fitted to produce, and, in detail, no more realistic than an election address.

McClure's character may not have stood so high in his own professional circle. In his memoirs Dr Robert McCormick states that a Mr Mackinnon, M.P. 'told me that in Captain Maclure's [sic] case, had he not succeeded with it in the Commons, Maclure would have been forever done at the Admiralty.' This appears to mean that the Admiralty were dissastified with McClure's conduct, and, had their hand not been forced by the Parliamentary honours bestowed on him, would have refused him further employment and consigned him perforce to the semi-retirement which Collinson had adopted by choice.

Those best acquainted with McClure knew that he had personal and professional qualities of a high order. He was shy, but Miertsching, whom he freely admitted to his society, found him kind and considerate. He was a skilful and enterprising navigator and, despite his aloofness, could appeal to his men with effect and command their abiding respect. It was no small feat, with officers who appear to have been somewhat mediocre, to keep perfect control over sixty men incited to mutiny by perpetual hunger. He made the 'half a hundred devils' with whom Miertsching embarked into a decent, orderly unit. Kellett gave him a letter testifying to the uniform good conduct of the *Investigator* when jammed on board the *Resolute* under the most irritating conditions. His ruthless maintenance of the short ration before the desertion of the *Investigator* and his ingratitude to Kellett are repulsive, though some small indulgence may be granted an officer who, deprived by lack of 'interest' of advancement in the service until past the age of forty, seizes the offered opportunity with both hands!

The search for Franklin was now almost over. But two men – one American, the other British – remained to confer dignity and a touch of greatness on its closing phases.

10 The Americans in Smith Sound

In August 1854, Collinson departed from the American Arctic by its western, and Sir Edward Belcher by its eastern outlet. The *Plover,* not yet recalled, lay dormant in her Alaskan anchorage. The Americans were last in the field. Elisha Kent Kane's *Advance* was still active in newly-discovered seas beyond Smith Sound.

The chain of circumstances that took him there reaches back to the fictitious narrative of Adam Beck. Captains Austin and Ommaney, both in a hurry, had concluded it was false but the British public, especially relatives of the lost crews, were dissatisfied and desired further inquiry.

Another motive for a search in Baffin Bay was furnished by the brig *Renovation,* whose captain reported that in April 1850, not far from Newfoundland, he had seen two ships embedded in a large mass of ice, one upright near the water's edge, the other lying on her side at a higher level. They were not whalers – no whaling ships were missing. Their description fitted the *Erebus* and the *Terror.* It was speculated that Franklin's ships, while on their way home, had been beset in Baffin Bay and deserted by their crews, who might even then be starving on the Baffin Island shore.

In 1852, to resolve these doubts, Lady Franklin put Commander Edward Inglefield of the Royal Navy in charge of her 150-ton schooner *Isabel* with instructions to visit the scene of Adam Beck's supposed massacre and make every effort to get at the truth. On his way back he was to coast along the Baffin Island east shore, keeping a lookout for signals of distress. Inglefield carried out the first part of his commission and, like Sherard Osborn, cursed Adam Beck as a liar. That his far northern excursion might not be wholly wasted he swung up for a quick survey of Smith Sound.

This body of water, which William Baffin had supposed to be

230

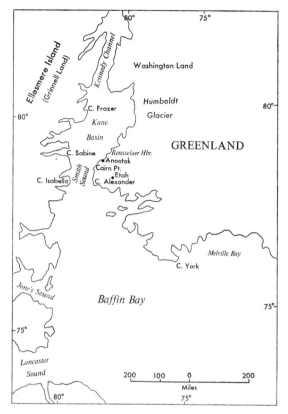

Smith Sound and Kane Basin

a bay and Sir John Ross had certified as such, lay between two great headlands, Cape Isabella on the left and Cape Alexander on the right. Coasting up the Greenland shore, the *Isabel* approached Cape Alexander in the late evening of 26 August, her captain busily wondering what lay behind the cape – the dead end of Ross, or a channel leading to far northern latitudes. Inglefield wrote:

'On rounding Cape Alexander the full glory of being actually in the Polar Sea burst upon my thoughts, for then I beheld the open sea stretching through seven points of the compass and apparently unencumbered with ice, though bounded on east and

231

west by two distinct headlands [Cairn Point on the east, Cape Herschel or perhaps Cape Sabine on the west].

' . . . We pushed on while the weather was fair, and beautiful indeed was the prospect before us; the sun had just sheltered himself for an hour below the horizon, and still shot his rays far into the northern sky, tinging the snows on the western land with crimson hues, and throwing a glow over nature which ill accorded with the biting cold.'

As the *Isabel* sailed up the Sound, the sea ahead broadened out. She was travelling close to the Greenland shore. Cairn Point was blocking the view to the right. To the left, the Ellesmere Island shore could be seen stretching away to the north, a wall of rock bulging out into bold headlands. The farthest point visible, probably Cape Fraser, lay at a distance estimated as eighty miles.

The young captain, engaged in a minor operation in a British enterprise, was inaugurating a whole era of United States polar discovery. He was afloat on the narrow sea where all the American journeyings were to converge. Beyond Cairn Point lay the Rensselaer Harbour of Dr Kane. Nearby was Littleton Island, where Charles Francis Hall's navigating officer, Tyson, and eighteen others were to begin their winter-long drift on the ice down Baffin Bay and almost to Newfoundland. Less than fifteen miles straight ahead protruded the rocky tongue of Cape Sabine, where eighteen of Adolphus Greely's party of twenty-five were to die of famine. Behind and to the right was the entrance to Inglefield Gulf, Admiral Robert E. Peary's base for his Greenland foot-journeys. And just around Cairn Point was Anoatok, where in the dark days of February 1908, Dr Frederick A. Cook *began* his northward journey towards the Pole, a journey whose precise *end* is indeterminate and – sixty years after – still a matter of fierce debate.

The *Isabel* had drawn nearly level with Cairn Point when her advance was halted by contrary winds. The ensuing gale drove her back, 100 miles to the south – Inglefield barely got his engines going in time to fight his way off the surf-beaten pack on the Ellesmere shore. To return north was no part of his duty. He went some distance into Jones Sound to examine the north shore of Devon Island, ran up Lancaster Sound to report his discoveries to Commander Pullen at Beechey Island, and followed the Baffin coast southwards until storm and growing darkness compelled him to haul off and set a course for home. It is a pity that so capable and popular an officer had been passed by in appointments to the Arctic service. For the next two seasons the Admiralty put him in command of the *Phoenix,* supply ship to Belcher's *North Star,* and the extension of his exciting discovery in Smith Sound was left to adventurers from the American side of the Atlantic Ocean.

Kane's purpose, already formed, of carrying the search into Smith Sound was strengthened by Inglefield's sensational discovery. How far he was moved by humane impulses and how far by the desire to promote his own honour, as well as his country's, is uncertain. Franklin's presence at the upper end of Baffin Bay was to the last degree improbable. He was known to have been at Beechey Island, and the odds were that by the time he had tested all possible leads from that point his supplies and the stamina of his crews would have been too far spent for him to make a fresh effort in an area even less promising than the one in which he had just failed. Still, the possibility had been recognized by others besides Kane. When Willy Browne 'closed' Peel Sound, Osborn, who had favoured that route, told Penny that Franklin could be found only up Wellington Channel or in Baffin Bay, and the headstrong Dr McCormick had wished to take a boat into Smith Sound, a project that the Admiralty, quite properly, refused to allow. Franklin's name lent glamour to Kane's proposed voyage. The merchant Henry Grinnell again furnished a ship, the brig *Advance,* and the United States Navy gave ten men to a crew numbering only nineteen, after the addition of Carl Petersen and the Greenland Eskimo Hans Hendrick. Except in courage and endurance they were ill fitted for the venture. Kane, a naval surgeon, was in command; early on the voyage he found his first officer incompetent and advanced the Navy boatswain Brooks to that post. The ship's surgeon, the newly qualified Dr Isaac Hayes, was too shrewd to be completely subordinate. Kane, Brooks, and the seaman William Morton had been in the ice with De Haven; Carl Petersen, a longtime resident of Greenland, had been Penny's Eskimo interpreter; the others were going north for the first time. Their supplies and equipment, procured from public contribution and the proceeds of lectures by Kane, were, in McClintock's opinion, quite inadequate. The substantial discoveries they were to effect and their return with no more than normal casualties shows the measure of Kane's greatness.

In the summer of 1853 the *Advance* passed up Baffin Bay calling at Greenland ports and adding Petersen and the Eskimo Hans to her complement, along with a team of dogs, and entered Smith Sound. There, on the mainland behind Littleton Island, Kane cached a boat and supplies, against an emergency – with 'reluctant liberality', for he had not the abundant stores of an Admiralty discovery ship. Rounding Cairn Point, he passed from Smith Sound into the broader waters of Kane Basin.

The sea, which Inglefield had found ice-free, was now badly choked, and the *Advance* was obliged to make progress by crawling along the eastward-tending shoreline. On 18 August she sought refuge from a gale behind a narrow projection from the cliffs, Godsend Ledge, and anchored with three hawsers. On the twentieth the wind was blowing with hurricane force.

'Still it came on heavier and heavier,' wrote Kane, 'and the ice began to drive more wildly than I thought I had ever seen it. I had just turned in to warm and dry myself during a momentary lull, and was stretching myself out in my bunk, when I heard the sharp twanging snap of a cord. Our six-inch hawser had parted, and we were swinging by the two others; the gale roaring like a lion to the southward.

'Half a minute more, and "twang, twang!" came a second report. I knew it to be the whale-line from the shrillness of the ring. Our noble ten-inch manilla still held on. I was hurrying my last sock into its sealskin boot, when McGary came waddling down the companion-ladders: – "Captain Kane, she won't hold on much longer; it's blowing the devil himself, and I am afraid to surge."

'The manilla cable was proving its excellence when I reached the deck; and the crew, as they gathered around me, were loud in its praises. We could hear its deep Eolian chant, swelling through all the rattle of the running-gear and the moaning of the shrouds. It was the death-song! The strands gave way with the noise of a shotted gun; and, in the smoke that followed their recoil, we were dragged out by the wild ice at its mercy.'

The *Advance* was driving up a channel a quarter of a mile wide with solid pack on one side and the cliffs on the other. She was approaching a cluster of bergs when the wind, eddying under the cliffs, took her aback without steering way. Second Officer Mc-Gary anchored her to a large drifting piece, which ground its way around the bergs with the brig in its wake. She crept into the lee of another berg and was nipped against it by a revolving floe, which forced the brig up a sloping face of ice: 'she rose slowly and as if with convulsive efforts along the sloping wall . . . At one time I expected to see her carried bodily up its face and tumbled over on her side. But one of those mysterious relaxations, which I have elsewhere called the pulses of the ice, lowered us quite gradually down again into the rubbish, and we were forced out of the line of pressure towards the shore . . . there was a deep-breathing silence, as though all were waiting for some signal before the clamour of congratulation and comment could burst forth.'

When the storm died down, the crew of the *Advance,* lacking the opportunity or perhaps the nerve to trust her again to the pack, mounted the 'ice-foot', the fast ice at the foot of the cliffs, and tracked the ship upshore to the shelter of Rensselaer Harbour, and there, after some deliberation, she was laid up for the winter.

Kane at once set out by boat and then on foot to extend his knowledge of the coast ahead. He reached a point where he could see the land trending again to the north, blotted out for many miles by the face of the Humboldt Glacier, and reappearing to the far north in the rocks of Washington Land. Later in September, McGary and Amos Bonsall, the photographer, took a sledge party out to plant a depot on the east shore of Kane Basin. After travelling for more than two weeks over ice sheet and water lane, they made camp on 5 October off the Humboldt ice stream. In the night a gigantic slab detached itself from the face of the glacier, shattered the frozen sea, and almost capsized McGary and his mates in the tidal wave caused by its descent. They laid their depot on the nearest available islet and hastened back to the ship.

The winter of 1853-4 bore hard upon the crew of the *Advance.* Kane depended upon persuasion, not authority, to enforce the anti-scorbutic diet which experience prescribed, and all but one or two of his party suffered from scurvy. This condition heightened the rashness of the depot journey which set out in the middle of March. Its purpose was to plant a cache on Washington

Land north of the Humboldt Glacier for the use of the party that was to travel far up the east side of Kane Basin later in the season. Petersen, who understood the climate and sledging operations better than anyone else on board, opposed the journey, but allowed himself to be overruled. On 19 March the party of seven men under the command of Mr Brooks left the ship, setting a course northeast directly over the frozen sea. In a temperature of 44 degrees below zero, the sledge grated over the snow as if it were sand. It is possible that Petersen, who must have been familiar with the Eskimo practice of icing the runners, did not reveal it in order that the catastrophe which he foresaw might occur not too far from the ship. If so, he achieved his purpose. Two days later, Mr McGary could still see the travellers from the masthead, not more than twelve miles on their way. On the third day they were out of sight.

On 31 March, Petersen and the carpenter, Mr Ohlsen, came back to the brig, exhausted, frostbitten, and almost speechless with the cold. They had tramped in forty miles, leaving Tom Hickey, the cabin boy, to care for the other four, who lay disabled with frozen feet in the perishing cold of a tent.

Kane was at his best in coping with such a crisis. Courage and resolution never failed him, and for the moment he had unquestioned authority. He had Ohlsen wrapped in furs and placed on the sledge with a tent and a little pemmican to act as guide for Kane and his rescue party of eight. The carpenter grew delirious towards the journey's end and could give no help. In any case, as Kane observes, the icebergs, which 'in form and colour endlessly repeated themselves,' were worthless as landmarks. It was the lucky discovery of an undrifted sledge track which guided them to the tents concealed by the hummocks and almost hidden in drifts.

The four crippled men were sewn in caribou skin, rolled in buffalo robes, and seated on the sledge. The return journey was made in a temperature of 55 degrees below with a slight wind. The sledge haulers were almost spent when the brig came in sight. 'Bonsall was sent staggering ahead, and reached the brig, God knows how, for he had fallen repeatedly at the track-lines; but he delivered with punctilious accuracy the messages I had sent by him to Dr Hayes.' Two men with a dog-sledge met the party two miles out and brought them in. Two men died a few days after the rescue. Brooks and another had to undergo amputations.

Kane was still resolved not to go back without making certain whether his basin was closed at its upper end or provided a salt-water outlet to regions farther north. He took charge of a travelling party himself but, weakened with scurvy, collapsed and was carried back to the ship. The sturdy seaman William Morton was then given the dog-sledge, and with the Eskimo Hans as his only companion he passed the Humboldt Glacier and, following the ice-foot, now crumbling in the summer sun, traced the Greenland shore many miles beyond to Cape Constitution, about latitude 80° 30'. Though his view was narrowed by that massive headland – too steep to be climbed – he could make out the opposite Ellesmere shore reaching far to the north. He had extended Inglefield's observations by some eighty miles and had discovered Kennedy Channel, by way of which Charles Francis Hall's *Polaris,* two decades latter, was to break through to the great ocean which lay beyond.

By the time Morton got back to the ship another crisis was taking shape. The break-up of the ice in Kane Basin was alarmingly slow that summer, and the fear was becoming acute that the brig might not be released that season. As his diminished and sickly crew was unequal to the task of conveying boats, supplies, and invalids to the open water of Smith Sound, Kane had one boat hauled to the Sound and set out with McGary and a crew down Baffin Bay, to ask help of Sir Edward Belcher's *North Star,* which he supposed correctly still to be lying at Beechey Island. They had an easy passage through Smith Sound into the North Water. But there they were overtaken by a storm so furious that for twenty-two hours they were in momentary danger of swamping. Only McGary's skill, says Kane, kept them afloat: 'There is no better boatman in the world than he.' Eventually, they were able to creep behind a piece of ice and lay there still deluged by the weather surf, until the storm subsided. This escape was all the luck granted them, for the storm had swept up the loose ice into a barrier to the south that no boat could penetrate.

On getting back to the brig, Kane found himself confronted by an anxious and divided crew. Some thought that the open water of the sound had extended near enough up the basin to make evacuation by boat possible. Petersen and Hayes favoured this, and were backed by a number of those who had suffered from scurvy in the first winter and feared a severer outbreak in the second. Kane chose to stay with the ship. His plea that he could not give up the vessel which Mr Grinnell had entrusted to him was pure rationalization: he knew that his first responsibility was for the lives of his men. But though Petersen had the advantage of him in local knowledge, Kane felt instinctively that a boat journey of 700 miles in late August was rash and likely to end in disaster. Grim as was the prospect of a second winter in the deep Arctic, it was the better alternative. The matter was left to individual choice. Six men accompanied Petersen and Hayes in the voyage to Upernavik; eight remained with the commander on the *Advance*.

The odds are that neither group would have survived without the help of the natives. At Etah, within Hartstene Bay a little to the north of Cape Alexander, was a small settlement of Eskimos whose hunting excursions occasionally took them up the east side of Smith Sound and into Kane Basin. They had first visited the brig briefly early in April, established friendly relations, and, along with Hans, provided the fresh meat that freed the crew from the plague of scurvy in the summer months. Helpless as his little party was, Kane had the courage and good sense steadily to discourage the Eskimos' practice of thieving, and in the autumn, shortly after the departure of the boat party, he concluded a treaty with the headman of Etah by which the Eskimos undertook to refrain from theft, to help the Europeans with fresh meat and guidance in hunting, and to lend them dogs. For their part, the Europeans bound themselves to do the natives no injury by sorcery, to aid in the hunt with firearms, and to give tools, instruments, and wood in exchange for meat. During the period of autumn, white men and brown hunted together frequently. Kane gave his new friends the benefit of his medical skill and completely won their respect and confidence.

As deep winter came on, this friendly intercourse ended and, with it, the wholesome walrus meat it helped to provide. Scurvy reappeared, and the ever reliable Morton was disabled by a frozen heel. Kane's entry in his journal for 2 December 1854 – *before* the middle of the winter – tells a tale so woeful that his feat in bringing all through alive is astonishing:

'Had to put Mr McGary and Riley under active treatment

for scurvy. Gums retracted, ankles swollen, and bad lumbago. Mr Wilson's case, a still worse one, has been brought under. Morton's is a saddening one: I cannot afford to lose him. He is not only one of my most intelligent men, but he is daring, cool, and everyway trustworthy. His tendon Achilles has been completely perforated, and the surface of the heel-bone exposed. An operation in cold, darkness, and privation would probably bring on locked-jaw. Brooks grows discouraged: the poor fellow has scurvy in his stump, and his leg is drawn up by the contraction of the flexors at the knee-joint. This is the third case on board – the fourth, if I include my own – of contracted tendons.' The burdens and anxieties of the captain-physician were doubled when on 12 December the eight men who had left the ship almost four months before came back escorted by Eskimos from Etah.

Kane's warnings had been more than justified by the event. Stretches of rotting ice, over which the boat was dragged with difficulty and loss of time, sludge in the pools, and, as the nights grew longer and darker, the growth of young ice, had forced the travellers to end their voyage on the south shore of Whale Sound, barely a third of the way to Upernavik. They had no supplies. The Eskimos of Netelik, an encampment nearby, had soon tired of feeding them, and even refused them transport back to the ship by dog-sledge. The travellers believed that the Eskimos were plotting their murder. Hayes tried to get possession of some teams by drugging the owners. Though the attempt was thwarted, the natives were so impressed with the magic powers of the strangers that they did consent to carry their troublesome guests to Etah, turning them over to their countrymen for delivery to the ship. The adventurous Hayes returned to his captain disabled by frostbite, and had to lose some toes by amputation.

Four of the eight who returned were added to the list of invalids, and, as Hayes was one of them, the entire load of responsibility rested on Kane. Only his spirit supported him. He, too, was suffering from scurvy, and he was physically the frailest man on board. Dreading the effect of the death of one man on the spirits of the rest, he concentrated on the worst cases, but 'as fast as I partially build up one, another is stricken down.' At one time thirteen of the seventeen on board were disabled. The healthy minority was strengthened by the return of Carl Petersen, and as daylight began to creep back he joined the Eskimo Hans in the hunt for foxes, hare, and ptarmigan. Early in March, Hans took the dog-sledge to Etah and came back with a load of walrus meat. Later in the month he went back on the same errand. Thus men gained strength for the now inevitable evacuation.

There was no longer any thought of saving the brig, already partially taken apart for fuel. Boats, supplies, and the four disabled men must be sledged ninety miles to Etah, where open water was assured, in order to take boat there for Danish settlements at the earliest possible date.

As there was a possibility that the brig might be driven out to sea before this operation was completed, the four sick men were carried forward and lodged in a stone hut at Anoatok, while stage by stage the others relayed their sledge loads along the shore of the basin and into Smith Sound. The Etah Eskimos came out to help them in over the last stage, which was particularly dangerous owing to a strong current working from below on the rotting ice. The runner of a sledge broke through the ice, and the sledge would have been lost with its cargo if the carpenter Ohlsen had not run a capstan bar under it and supported it until it was dragged clear. By so doing he suffered internal injuries of which he died three days later. Of his nineteen men, Kane brought sixteen out alive.

Near Etah the boats were hauled up for repair and caulking. The surf of an open sea was breaking on Cape Alexander three miles to the south. On 17 June, the sixteen Europeans distributed among the natives those belongings which they could not carry with them, and bade their kindly allies a last farewell. 'Poor creatures!' wrote Kane. 'It is only six months ago that starvation was among them: many of the faces around me have not yet lost the lines of wasting suspense. The walrus-season is again of doubtful productiveness, they are cut off from their brethren to the south at Netelik and Appah until winter rebuilds the avenue of ice. With all this, no thoughts of the future cross them. Babies squall, and women chatter, and the men weave their long yarns with peals of rattling laughter between.'

Like Back, Kane sympathized with the natives more readily than with those of his own blood. They, for their part, were full of gratitude for the kindness he had shown their sick. 'You have done us good,' one Eskimo told him, '... we are friends.'

In three boats, the men of the *Advance* rounded Cape Alexander and, not daring to risk a passage over the open sea, followed the windings of the coast, The shore ice was a ready refuge in case of storm, and the eggs of the eider duck were a means of eking out the rations of which they were fearfully short. Both these resources were lost in the 200 miles traversed past Melville Bay. Petersen afterwards told McClintock that, but for the providential killing of a seal, all must have starved. This fate was happily averted, and on 3 August Kane brought the fifteen men for whose lives he had laboured so hard safe into the port of Upernavik. A trading vessel carried them south to Godhavn. There Lieutenant Hartstene, U.S.N., who had been sent with two ships for their rescue, found them and carried them home.

The cruise of the *Advance* stands by itself in the history of the search for Franklin. Her crew had entered a new field of polar discovery. After adventures more varied than even those of the *Investigator*, they had come out under their own power, and had endured terrible want and hardship without a death caused by sickness alone. This record was due to the courage and devotion of a captain whose personality most of all distinguishes the voyage he commanded. Kane lacked some of the qualities of the good commander, for he had had no experience as a junior executive officer, and he was oversensitive to grumbling and discontent. He had formed dislikes of some of the men he commanded, including Petersen, who had served Penny well and was to do the same for McClintock. But his exertions to preserve health and morale during that second awful winter, with his own vital powers failing – he barely outlived the expedition sixteen months – with little moral support except from the dumbly loyal Morton, were heroic to the highest degree.

Kane's narrative of the expedition has the same unique quality as its author. The journal from which it was compiled was, unlike those of British contemporaries, obviously written with a view to publication, and though touched with romantic affectation, it is in general straightforward and graphic. For the critical periods, notably when the *Advance* was driving in the pack off Godsend Ledge and in the rescue of Brooks and his travelling party, the description is vivid and powerful. The sketches of Eskimo life show sympathy and penetration. The first edition of Kane's *Arctic Explorations* contained no fewer than *three hun-*

dred engravings of Arctic scenery, based on sketches by the author himself. That Kane should produce these, along with his journal, at a time when it seemed likely that both drawings and narrative would perish in the ice with their creator, speaks for the man's extraordinary courage, industry, and vitality. He was a striking and heroic figure.

11　Success at Last

In the autumn of 1854, the efforts to rescue Franklin seemed to be dissolving in utter failure. Collinson was in the Pacific on his way home. Beyond Smith Sound, Kane was striving for survival only. Belcher's court-martial had put an end to official British effort. Within two days of his acquittal, chance, which had so often given a wrong direction to the search or halted the searcher on the brink of success, suddenly and in the most unexpected manner gave away the secret.

On the completion of his 1851 commission, Rae had resumed his duties as a fur trader with the Hudson's Bay Company. But still hankering after travel and discovery, he set forth a plan for completion of the chart in the region of Boothia, east and north from the mouth of the Great Fish River. He wished to carry on the work of Simpson and Dease, by extending their chart from their farthest at the mouth of the Castor and Pollux River, north up the shore of Boothia Isthmus to the western outlet of Bellot Strait. His motivation was purely scientific. As he himself said, there was not the least likelihood of finding word or trace of Franklin in his suggested area of search.

On receiving authorization from the Hudson's Bay Company, Rae and his Eskimo partners went up to his old base of Fort Hope on Repulse Bay, and there spent the winter of 1853-4.

In late winter he set out by his former route past Committee Bay, across Simpson Peninsula to Pelly Bay, met a party of Eskimos, and, after an exchange of greetings, passed on. The next day he met a native hauling a load of meat on a sledge who had a most communicative companion. Conversing with him, Rae put the routine question: Did he know of any white men in the region? The man answered, No, but he had heard that a number of white men had died four years before (it was actually six) beyond the mouth of a great river, many days' journey to the west. In this simple manner the solution was found to the mystery which for years had been a matter of hot debate among scholars and scientists at home, and that had brought toil and suffering to hundreds of men in the icy wastes of the north.

The Eskimo's casual manner in giving this information was matched by Rae's nonchalance in receiving it. He did not alter his plan or permit this news to divert him from his appointed journey. He purchased a gilt cap band – the badge of a naval officer – from his informant. The Scottish fur trader advised the native that he would pay handsomely for similar relics delivered to him on his journey or brought to him at Repulse Bay. Then he continued on his way to the Castor and Pollux River.

Many have found this apparent indifference not only surprising but blameworthy. Certainly it was unfortunate. Had Rae gone directly in search of the 'great river', he might have found relics that were lost by the time McClintock reached the spot five years later – perhaps journals and logbooks recording the two brilliant summer voyages that preceded the final catastrophe. Rae's conduct is to be explained by his temperament: applause and glory meant less to him than to most men. His dispatches are factual and without self-advertisement. On the other hand, he was proud, like Collinson, averse to being made ridiculous, as he would have been, had he been misled by the fictitious story of some Adam Beck. Furthermore, this hearsay information had not enabled him to identify the river mentioned with that explored by Back; he got the impression that it was farther away. Even if the story were true, he might fail to verify it. Considering the tremendous interest and importance attaching to the Eskimo's story, Rae's conduct is surprising, but it *is* understandable.

It so happened that by adhering to his orders he made a discovery which *did* have a bearing on both the Franklin disaster and the subsequent navigation of the Northwest Passage by Roald Amundsen. Marching from the mouth of the Castor and Pollux River up the west shore of Boothia, he found that the isthmus connecting it with the land to the west did not exist, that King William *Land* was an *island*, separated from Boothia by an ocean channel – Ross and Rae Straits. This channel was free from heavy old ice, as the island shielded it from the polar stream coming in from Banks Land and piling up on the northwest shore of King William Island. Perhaps doubting the wisdom of his decision, Rae did not attempt to reach Bellot Strait. He ended his journey shortly after making his discovery, and on his way back and at Repulse Bay he gathered information and relics which if obtained earlier would certainly have prompted him to make the search for their former owners: coins, watches, Sir John Franklin's Hanoverian Order of Merit, a spoon bearing Crozier's initials, other spoons and forks identifiable by their names or by the crests of their owners – all officers of the missing crews.

According to the Eskimos' story, four years before, in 1850 – McClintock later proved the correct date to be 1848 – a party of Europeans had been seen dragging sledges down the west shore of King William Island. All were hauling except a tall, middle-aged man, probably Crozier, as Franklin and Gore, we now know, had died before the desertion of the ships. All looked thin and hungry. Later in the season, but before the disruption of the ice, thirty-five to forty bodies had been found on the seashore a long day's journey to the northwest of the mouth of a large river, evidently the Great Fish River, as the description of the spot matched Point Ogle. Some bodies lay in tents, and some lay huddled together under a boat. Other bodies were strewn up and down the beach. One man, with a telescope strapped over his shoulders, was lying on his gun. Shots had been heard in the area, and the sight of clean-picked bones showed that some had survived until the wildfowl migration in early June. There were also signs that the starving survivors had prolonged their lives by cannibalism.

Back at Repulse Bay, Rae again had a critical decision to make. Should he remain in the north for a second season in order to visit the scene of the tragedy, or go home immediately with the information and evidence already gathered? He chose the latter alternative, with the result, which he cannot have foreseen, that effective search was postponed for another five years. He was criticized for this action also: he was in a hurry, so it was alleged, to claim the £10,000 offered for a solution of the mystery. Rae's answer to this was plain and ought to have been convincing: he had not been aware of the promised reward and felt it urgent to bring home the news that would terminate costly and now wasted effort elsewhere.

But the crews of the *Erebus* and the *Terror* had been missing for nine years and had been officially presumed dead as of March

1854, and the substance of Rae's report caused little sensation. Its details aroused distress and anger. People asserted that the dead men had been the victims of a murderous Eskimo attack: no man would *lie* on his gun unless he had been struck down from behind. Rae gave offence by stolidly defending the natives against this charge. He was also censured for making known the evidence of cannibalism. Distressed relatives and friends attacked him, as guilty of slander on the dead men and on the venerable Franklin himself. Charles Dickens had the fair-mindedness to point out that Rae was in duty absolutely bound to state *all* the facts exactly as they had been presented to him. The fault, if any, Dickens said, rested with the Admiralty for giving his report unedited to the press. In an article that says more for his humane instincts than for his logic, Dickens tried to persuade his readers that the horrible rumour could not be true.

With all his talent and goodwill, Dickens could not defend Rae half as fervently as he was assailed by Dr King. One would have expected that unpredictable person positively to hail the man who had proved him right and enabled him to hurl exulting taunts at the Navy brass which had spurned him. Instead, perhaps moved by angry disappointment that another had made the discovery which he coveted for himself, King, after one or two preliminary growls in the press, began to bite and worry Rae as mercilessly as he ever had Barrow or Ross. He ridiculed Rae's conduct, denied his conclusions, and in a passage that was comic to the point of absurdity King, who had barely set foot on the Arctic shore, corrected the veteran and much-travelled Rae on the topography and animal life of the King William Island region and on the customs of the natives who inhabited it. ' I can assure Dr Rae that he is wrong in all his premises,' King exclaimed.

With almost libellous insolence he questioned Rae's capacity and hinted that he was an impostor: 'Although I had always my misgivings of Dr Rae's ability as a traveller, I always gave him credit for enterprise and manly bearing ... I only hope he made the journey to Castor and Pollux River and hence to Cape Porter. ... The means by which Dr Rae became possessed of the relics of the Franklin expedition will ever be a matter of doubt in my mind.' Rae was civilly but not cordially received by Lady Franklin. He had offended her by applying for the Admiralty reward, which, she declared, belonged to no one until further intensive search had been made into the circumstances of her husband's fate.

This was fair and reasonable, but the nation had been at enormous expense over the Franklin affair, the Crimean War was on, and naval resources fully employed elsewhere. The Admiralty applied to the Hudson's Bay Company to send a party down the Great Fish River and make further investigations. In 1855, Chief Factor Anderson and a company man named Stewart went by canoe – a safer conveyance than boats in Back's turbulent waterway – down to the estuary and gathered from the natives relics, chiefly wood, the plunder of ships and boats. Without an interpreter they could not find the beach where the bodies lay. Their canoes were too frail and damaged to make the crossing to King William Island. All they accomplished was to establish beyond doubt the identity of the river near which the men had perished.

King poured forth another flood of his inexhaustible rhetoric in deriding the folly of such an expedition, equipped with neither Eskimo interpreter nor trustworthy seagoing transport. His offer to lead another party himself was endorsed by three polar men of repute who, like himself, had something of the rebel in their make-up: Captain Sherard Osborn, home from the Black Sea, and still affectionately corresponding with William Penny; Lieutenant Bedford Pim, who volunteered to serve under King; and Dr McCormick.

But neither public nor private funds were available for King's project. In truth, Anderson's voyage, while proving King right in placing the tragedy near the mouth of the Great Fish River, had proved Sir James Ross equally right in denying that a boat was the proper means of getting there. The river rapids were not easily navigated by boats sturdy enough to stand buffeting in the open sea. Such craft had low cargo capacity and could barely supply their crews for the journey down and up the river. Only a week or two would be available for search in and beyond the estuary, barring the expedient, suicidal for those not versed in Eskimo ways, of living off the country and wintering over. Lady Franklin had steadily advocated the only reliable course – that of carrying as near as possible to the search area a ship which could support travelling parties for two seasons if necessary, and provide secure quarters for the intervening winter. She had attempted this twice, from her own resources, only to be foiled by the irresolution of those she employed for the work.

King's extravagant attacks upon highly-placed officials doubtless cost him the reward or public testimonial that was his due for directing the search to the quarter that proved to be right. The only published acknowledgment he received was in a footnote to the Introduction written by the geologist Sir Roderick Murchison for McClintock's *Voyage of the Fox*. The tribute is not Murchison's – he would have put it in the body of his Introduction. Nor would McClintock be disposed to speak well of the man who had slandered Sir James Ross. So the compliment paid Dr King must be credited to the man who prepared McClintock's journal for the press, that unwearying friend of the underdog, Captain Sherard Osborn. King's excitability and eccentricity were a handicap in his own profession also. Notwithstanding his gifts and reputation, he died in obscurity.

Though King found little support for this journey by river, the public still demanded a further quest by more reliable means. At the end of the Crimean War, the Admiralty was harassed by requests for a naval expedition, which, now that the scene of the disaster was fixed, had good prospects of success. A memorial dated 5 June 1856 was presented to the government, bearing the signatures of many distinguished naval officers and past presidents of the Royal Society who urged another expedition ' to satisfy the honour of our country, and clear up a mystery which has excited the sympathy of the civilized world '. When this application had remained ineffective for six months, Lady Franklin added an eloquent appeal of her own, stressing the public disgrace of letting the matter drop, especially when the return of the *Resolute,* refitted *as an Arctic ship,* made this neglect an act of churlish ingratitude to the Congress of the United States.

The Prime Minister, Lord Palmerston, Irish, warm-hearted, and at all times a strenuous maintainer of the public credit, was more than willing, but he was thwarted by his official advisers, Sir Charles Wood, First Lord of the Admiralty, and Sir Maurice Berkeley, First Sea Lord. They demurred at the expense, an objection which the Prime Minister received with contempt. They then complained of the risk to life – an outdated plea, as it had been proved that with proper precautions the Arctic was a much healthier posting than some fever-ridden station in the tropics. The fact was that the rulers of the Queen's Navy were sick of the Arctic. Franklin's expedition had been no project of theirs. They had merely consented to it. They had incurred much worry and enormous expense in mounting rescue expeditions. They had suffered ridicule and abuse in the press for the misdirection of the search, which was not their fault but that of the specialists whom they had been bound to consult. And McClure had very nearly involved them in the scandal of a second disaster. 'I make no more such polar journeys,' Miertsching had declared when paid off from the *Investigator*. Sir Charles Wood felt the same way. In despair of overcoming his opposition, Lady Franklin gave up and, vowing that she would spend up to £20,000 on the project, set about organizing her own private expedition. She bought the 177-ton yacht *Fox* and had it fitted out for Arctic service at the port of Aberdeen. Lady Franklin's favourites, Dr Kane (who paid a visit to England in the autumn of 1856, only a matter of weeks before his death) and Sherard Osborn were both disabled for the command by ill health. She offered it to the most senior naval officer with polar experience, Collinson, who declined. Belcher's former officer, the sturdy G. H. Richards, was opportunely appointed to the British Columbia Boundary Commission, and the post reverted to the man who, by the length and quality of his service, was the best qualified to fill it, Captain Leopold McClintock.

If Lady Franklin found no help from the government, she at least was not neglected by private individuals and organizations. A subscription to defray part of her expenses brought in almost £3,000. The names of the contributors testify to the public interest. The novelist Thackeray was a subscriber; so was Sir Charles Trevelyan, brother-in-law to the historian Thomas Babington Macaulay. Miss Georgina Hornby, doubtless the sister of poor Hornby of the *Terror*, contributed £100 of her own and collected another £13. 'The brothers and sisters of the late John and Thomas Hartnell of H.M.S. *Erebus*,' added £5. By far the largest contribution, £500, was subscribed anonymously by 'A Commander in the Merchant Service'. It was an open secret that this was Captain Allen Young of the Merchant Navy, who resigned profitable employment and gave his services to the expedition without pay for two and a half years. Boats, food, tents, stoves, etc., were given free by dealers in those articles. Arms, ammunition, rockets, and three tons of pemmican were presented by the Admiralty. A brewery added a valuable anti-scorbutic – all the ale that could be stowed aboard. Their bounty was limited, however, for the tiny yacht was so crammed with more essential stores that five officers had to be accommodated in a wardroom measuring five feet by eight.

Lady Franklin had advocated a government expedition not only to spare herself expense, but – recalling Kennedy's disciplinary troubles – to have the crew subject to Navy regulations. But discipline was the least of McClintock's worries. In his crew of twenty-five he enrolled no fewer than seventeen old Arctic men, bound to him by ties of mutual trust and confidence. An old sledge-mate, Salmon, himself rejected on account of his age, wrote to Harvey, chief quartermaster of the *Fox*: 'You are sure to succeed this time, for you have got the captain that will not turn back before he finishes the work he goes out to do.' Lieutenant Hobson, formerly of the *Plover,* was second-in-command. Allen Young served as navigating officer. A young civilian, Dr David Walker, was appointed surgeon on the recommendation of McClintock's brother. He fitted in admirably, and was always spoken of by his captain with good-humoured affection. Carl Petersen, lately returned to Denmark, was enlisted as interpreter.

Lady Franklin defined the purposes of the expedition – the rescue of any possible survivors of the *Erebus* and the *Terror*, the recovery of the log-books and records, and – a point which the loyal widow stressed – proof that the men who died near the Great Fish River had come down from Beechey Island by sea, which would confer on her husband, not on McClure, the title of discoverer of the Northwest Passage. McClintock cherished a fourth purpose, which perhaps for fear of disappointment he did not care to disclose. Convinced that Franklin had gone down Peel Sound and come to grief in the heavy ice seen by Ross to the west of King William Island and believing that he could have got through if he had known of the channel found by Rae on its eastern side, he planned to take the *Fox* through by that route and win for Lady Franklin the honour of sending the first ship through the Northwest Passage.

Before the *Fox* sailed, her owner, who could never do enough for her friends, had McClintock presented to the Queen at a royal levee. In so doing, she contrived to stick the needle into a great man who had offended her. The obvious person to make the presentation would have been McClintock's official chief, Sir Charles Wood, but rather than confer a social distinction on the man who had thwarted her, Lady Franklin arranged to have the introduction made by the president of the Royal Society, to whom McClintock was known through his work in the geology of the American Arctic.

On 30 June 1857, Captain Maguire, formerly of the *Plover,* brought Lady Franklin on board the *Fox* to inspect her fittings and bid her crew farewell. 'Seeing how deeply agitated she was on leaving the ship, I endeavoured to repress the enthusiasm of my crew, but without avail; it found vent in three prolonged, hearty cheers. The strong feeling which prompted them was truly sincere, and this unbidden exhibition of it can hardly have gratified her for whom it was intended more than it did myself.'

It was fortunate that the *Fox* had as her captain one who never turned back, for she was destined to the ignominy, shared only with the transport *North Star,* in 1849, of not even crossing Baffin Bay in her first season. On his way up the west Greenland shore, McClintock called at Godhavn to recruit Eskimo dogs and a native driver. There he was told by two whaling skippers, whose ships had been nipped and sunk, that prospects were good for a passage past Melville Bay and through the North Water. In this he was disappointed. As he neared the upper end of Melville Bay he found that southerly winds had retarded the Southward drift of the pack which the whalers had predicted so confidently. The ice was not heavy. The lumbering old *Resolute* might have ploughed through it, but the featherweight yacht was quite outclassed in the encounter. Day after day she lay imprisoned with the season wasting away. On 20 August McClintock found himself worse situated than Sir James Ross had been on that date during his unlucky voyage of 1848. 'My frequent visits to the crow's nest are not inspiriting; how absolutely distressing this imprisonment is to me, no one without similar experience can form any idea.' Icebergs were visible seaward, grounded in eighty fathoms and hindering the normal southward drift of the pack. The signs of approaching winter were unmistakable – increasing darkness, the growth of young ice, and the southward flight of birds. 'The dismal prospect of a " winter in the pack " has scarcely begun to dawn upon the crew; however I do not think that they will be much upset.' Nor were they. Worrying was no part of *their* duty. They made the best of leisure seldom granted to the sailor at sea, played games and ran races on the ice until increasing cold and darkness put an end to outdoor recreation. Eight or nine of the least literate were then enrolled in a school under Dr Walker's direction. For the rest, after the men had banked the deck and sides of the ship with snow, they were kept moderately busy with drill in sledging and the building of snow houses. For recreation they had, among other things, a barrel organ, the gift of Albert, the Prince Consort.

To judge from the tone of the captain's journal, the dreaded 'winter in the pack' was passed more cheerfully than the succeeding winter would be in a stationary and secure anchorage. While tides and gales caused fearful ruptures in the ice nearby, the *Fox*, locked in the heart of a stout old floe, lay undisturbed behind her walls of snow. She was a 'happy ship'. Petersen, 'disheartened' and 'moping' to Kane, was to McClintock 'an agreeable companion . . . and always contented and sanguine '. The men took walks by moonlight and hunted seal on the smooth ice which lay not far from the ship, though such exercises could be dangerous. The ice broke under Young while he was watching a seal hole – 'he escaped with a ducking '. McClintock, out for a ramble, was cut off by a rift in the ice and walked some distance along its margin before he was able to cross it and make his way back to the ship.

The Protestant festival of 5 November was observed with an issue of rum and a plum pudding, the gift of Lady Franklin. In the evening a torchlight procession by painted and yelling figures lit up the ice around and terrified the dogs. 'It was school-night, but the men were out for fun, *so gave the doctor a holiday*.'

The cheerful routine was interrupted on 2 December by the death of the chief stoker, Robert Scott, who fatally injured himself by falling down a hatchway. In the dead stillness of the Arctic night the funeral procession, guided by lanterns and signposts, wound its way around hummocks to a hole cut in the ice, and there the body was committed to the deep. Scott, according to McClintock, 'was a steady, serious man; a widow and family will mourn his loss '.

On Christmas Day the officers were invited down to the men's mess to witness preparations for dinner. 'We were really astonished! The mess-tables were laid out like the counters in a confectioner's shop, with apple and gooseberry tarts, plum and sponge cakes in pyramids, besides various other unknown puffs, cakes, and loaves of all sizes and shapes. We bake our own bread, and excellent it is. . . . Rum and water in wine-glasses, and plum-cake were handed to us: we wished them a happy Christmas, and complimented them on their taste and spirit in getting up such a display.' Late in the evening the officers were enticed down again. 'I found them in the highest good humour with themselves and all the world. They were perfectly sober, and singing songs, each in his turn. I expressed great satisfaction at having seen them enjoying themselves so rationally. [The custom of the Navy gave the men almost unlimited freedom on this occasion, and old Harvey, the chief quartermaster, must have had both authority and tact to keep the festivities of twenty men so orderly.] We all joined in drinking the healths of Lady Franklin and Miss Cracroft, and amid the acclamations which followed I returned to my cabin immensely gratified by such an exhibition of genuine good feeling, such veneration for Lady Franklin, and such loyalty to the cause of the expedition. It was very pleasant that they had taken the most cheering view of our future prospects. I verily believe I was the happiest individual on board, that happy evening.'

Throughout the winter months, the *Fox*, like De Haven's ships before her, had been going down Baffin Bay in a drift which accelerated as the winter waned and they neared the spacious waters of the North Atlantic. On 7 March 1858, the glare of the sun was seen reflected from the hills above Godhavn, ninety miles away. On 12 April they drifted out of the Arctic Circle. A week later they were 100 miles south of it and near the latitude of Hudson Strait.

McClintock must have called to mind the assurance which he and Kellett had given Sir Edward Belcher four years before that the *Resolute* and the *Intrepid* were in no serious danger as they were surrounded by ice of 'one year's growth only'. The *Fox* was cradled in more ancient and heavier ice. Frequently, her captain ascended to the crow's nest, seeking the open lane that would give her passage to open sea nearby, before the ice broke up in a shattering gale. She was not to be so lucky. On the twenty-fourth the frozen surface began to stir and split in a heaving sea. McClintock wrote in his journal: 'The long ocean swell already

253

lifts its crest five feet above the hollow of the sea, causing its thick covering of icy fragments to dash against each other and against us with unpleasant violence. . . . A floe-piece near us, of 100 yards in diameter, was speedily cracked so as to resemble a sort of labyrinth, or still more a spider's web. In the course of half an hour the family resemblance was totally lost; they had so battered each other, and struggled out of their original regularity. The rolling sea can no longer be checked. . . . The swell increased; it had evidently been approaching for hours before it reached us, since it rose in proportion as the ice was broken into smaller pieces. . . . I knew that near the pack-edge the sea would be very heavy and dangerous but the wind was now fair, and having auxiliary steam-power, I resolved to push out of the ice if possible.

' Shortly after midnight the ship was under sail, slowly boring her way eastward; at two o'clock on Sunday morning we commenced steaming, the wind having failed. By eight o'clock we had advanced considerably to the eastward, and the swell had become dangerously high, the waves rising ten feet above the trough of the sea. The shocks of the ice against the ship were alarmingly heavy; it became necessary to steer exactly head-on to the swell [to protect propeller and rudder]. We slowly passed a small iceberg 60 or 70 feet high; the swell forced it crashing through the pack, leaving a small water-space in its wake, but sufficient to allow the seas to break against its cliffs, and throw the spray in heavy showers quite over its summit.

' The day wore on without change, except that the snow and mists cleared off. Gradually the swell increased, and rolled along more swiftly, becoming in fact a very heavy regular sea, rather than a swell. . . . Much heavy hummocky ice and large berg-pieces lay dispersed through the pack; a single thump from any of them would have been instant destruction. By five o'clock the ice became more loose, and clear spaces of water could be seen ahead. We went faster, received fewer though still more severe shocks, until at length we had room to steer clear of the heaviest pieces; and at eight o'clock we emerged from the villainous " pack " and were running fast through straggling pieces into a clear sea. . . . After yesterday's experience I can understand how men's hair has turned gray in a few hours. . . . The ship and her machinery behaved most admirably in the struggle; should I ever pass through such an ice-covered, heaving ocean again, let me secure a passage in the *Fox*. . . . During our 242 days in the packed-ice of Baffin's Bay and Davis Straits we were drifted 1194 geographical or 1385 statute miles; it is the longest drift I know of. . . .'

Repressing the impulse to take his men to a Newfoundland port for rest and refreshment, McClintock steered for the Greenland harbour of Holsteinborg, where old Harvey with his flute set himself up as master of ceremonies and orchestra leader at a riotous ball held with the native population, while his commander prepared the European mail conveying to Lady Franklin the news that a whole season had been spent fruitlessly. He enrolled a second Eskimo driver and went up the Greenland shore again. On 30 May his ship was anchored to a berg near Upernavik, and McClintock himself was aboard a whaler, making 'furious attacks upon Captain Parker's beefstakes and porter'. The critical passage past Melville Bay was almost fatal at the very outset. While steaming along a narrow lane, the lookout failed to recognize the true nature of an ice-covered reef. The ship stuck fast and, with the receding tide, soon lay over on her side. Though her bow was fast, her stern was free, and the slightest jar from wind or ice would have capsized her. 'The dogs [affectionately noticed even in this crisis], after repeated ineffectual attempts to lie upon the deck, quietly coiled themselves up upon such parts of the lee gunwale as remained above water and went to sleep.' The night tide, luckily higher than the day tide, floated the ship off unharmed after she had been fast for eleven hours.

They made the crossing of the North Water in two weeks. After being marooned for some time in an ice lagoon, the *Fox* emerged from the pack off Jones Sound and turned her head to the south. A bald-headed Eskimo chief came off in his kayak, sent kind remembrances to Captain Inglefield and, possibly wishing his friends to stay longer, assured them that Lancaster Sound was still solidly frozen. Actually it was not, but an easterly gale had jammed it full of broken ice. So McClintock ran into Pond's Inlet and landed to question the natives. On his return, he learned that the pack had moved in on the anchored ship and that, by warping and blasting, Hobson and Young had got her clear a bare four minutes before the intruding ice had been crushed against the rocks. Still sound but with her coal supply much reduced by prolonged work in the ice, the *Fox* set a course for

Belcher's depot on Beechey Island. Lancaster Sound was now open but storm-swept. The ship sustained some damage to her rigging and was almost 'driven to leeward and dashed to pieces by the sea-beaten pack'. Yet McClintock's feelings on coming to anchor off the familiar Cape Riley were other than those of pure relief. 'These are only preliminaries,' he observes. The voyage just accomplished, though full of danger and uncertainty, he had now made for the fourth time. Ahead lay chances unknown and incalculable. The track of the *Erebus* and the *Terror* had been traversed only once – by those who had never come back.

With her coal replenished, the *Fox* put to sea again and fought her way against an adverse wind to within sight of Griffiths Island. Then the wind turned fair. Cape Walker reared its head above the horizon to the southwest, marking the entrance to Peel Sound, closed by Willy Browne, closed by Bellot and Kennedy, but down it Franklin *must* have sailed. McClintock's journal reflects his breathless excitement: 'We shot gallantly past Limestone Island [on the northwest corner of Somerset Island] and are now steering down Peel Strait; all of us in a wild state of excitement – a mingling of anxious hopes and fears.'

The fears had it! Twenty-five miles down, the sound was blocked by an unbroken barrier of ice extending from shore to shore. It was of one year's growth only, rotten, honeycombed, perhaps soon to dissolve, but the captain was too keyed up to await the uncertainties of wind and tide. Bellot Strait offered another entry into the sea lying west of Boothia. He put about to the east and began to circle Somerset Island, resolved to come back to Peel Sound if that hope failed him. He put in at Port Leopold, where he had spent his first polar winter ten years before, and examined the boat and stores cached there. They offered the means of life for his crew if the ship did not return from her perilous mission. Again at sea, a new doubt pressed in upon him: 'Does Bellot Strait exist?' Bellot and Kennedy were not in perfect agreement on what they had seen.

The eastern entrance to Bellot Strait lies at the bottom of Brentford Bay and is well masked by offshore islets. Sir John Ross had passed by without detecting it. It proved to be narrow – barely a mile across at its centre – and walled in by lofty cliffs, a partly submerged mountain gorge, in fact. After planting an emergency cache on land, McClintock took the ship in on 21

August. Halfway through and within sight of the sea breaking on the cape which marked the western outlet they were stopped by ice and realized that they were being carried back by the tide. The ship was swept with increasing velocity through clashing and rebounding ice pieces, past rocks barely 200 yards away, to Brentford Bay. Attempting it again they got clean through the strait only to find its outlet fenced by solid pack four miles in breadth. McClintock saw his hope of reaching King William Island or the estuary of the Great Fish River and carrying out his search within easy reach of the ship dashed to the ground. Nor could he any longer hope to sail the Northwest Passage. 'The fondly cherished hope of pushing further in our ship can no longer be entertained,' he wrote.

Along with Dr Walker, McClintock went by boat most of the way through the strait, and finding no passage by foot at the base of the cliff, he clambered with much difficulty to its top. Below and four miles to the west, he recognized Cape Bird, the farthest southward point seen by Sir James Ross and himself on their 1849 sledge journey. Fifty miles to the north he made out Four River Point, where that journey had ended. Had they but known it they were then on Franklin's track. Nine years had brought him only fifty miles nearer the object of his search.

The *Fox* was berthed for the winter at Port Kennedy at the east end of Bellot Strait, and her officers began to draw up plans for the long sledge journeys which they had hoped to avoid.

The vast exertions devoted to the rescue of Franklin, while utterly failing in their main purpose, had achieved the rough charting of the Canadian archipelago with the exception of certain stretches on the west shores of Boothia and Somerset Island, the south half of the Prince of Wales Island oval, and the northeast shore of Victoria Island from the farthest advance of Collinson and Rae to the farthest of Wyniatt. It was not then known that Victoria and Prince of Wales lands were separate, but McClintock, convinced that the heavy ice seen by Sir James Ross west of King William Island had drifted in from Banks Land, inferred the existence of the channel that later, at Lady Franklin's insistence, would be named after him. Determined to settle this point and, if possible, to fill all gaps in the map, he directed that in his spring journey Hobson should first go down the west shore of King William Island, where documents of the *Erebus* and the

I

Terror were most likely to be cached, and then cross Victoria Strait to extend the work of Rae on the Victoria Island shore. Thus, with a generosity in strong contrast to the egotism later displayed by Robert Peary in a similar situation, he yielded to his lieutenant the first chance of making the prized discovery of Franklin's record. McClintock himself was to follow the east shore of King William Island through the channel discovered by Rae, go on to the mouth of the Great Fish River, where the Eskimos stated a large number of bodies to be lying, and return by the west shore of the island to make a double search of the coast down which the lost men had travelled. To Young, who as a merchant officer could aspire to no naval honours, he assigned the charting of the Prince of Wales and Somerset shores, though he too was to be alert for cairns planted by Franklin on his voyage down Peel Sound.

As the journeys planned were long and the men too few to furnish crews for supporting sledges, both Hobson and Young went out in October to lay caches on their intended lines of march. This was a risky operation in autumn, when the sea was thinly frozen and liable to rupture, as Hobson was given good reason to know. He had carried his depot down the west Boothia shore to a distance ninety miles from the ship when he was halted by the open sea breaking against a headland. On his way back he camped on the sea ice. In the night the combination of a spring tide and a gale from the northeast detached him from the land ice and sent him with crew and equipment adrift in the still unfrozen sea. Luckily 'the gale was quickly followed by an intense frost, which in a single night formed ice sufficiently strong to bear them in safety to the land, although it bent fearfully beneath their weight.'

On 7 November, the engineer Brand died of apoplexy, casting a cloud over the little company just at the bleak commencement of winter. McClintock's journal for the months which followed is less buoyant and cheerful than his entries for the preceding season. Long separation from home was telling on their spirits, and the best of care and diet could not wholly offset the effects of cold, confinement, and idleness. 'The seeds of scurvy' were in all of them, wrote Walker. Fifty years later, Dr Walker praised the patience, tact and unwearying kindness with which McClintock kept a healthy and cheerful spirit among the crew, and especially his patience with the brashness of his newly qualified surgeon. McClintock gave no hint of such a fault in Walker. He speaks of him with fatherly kindness, praising his readiness to relieve the executive officers of short journeys in disagreeable weather. In deep Arctic darkness and with a northwester howling through the rigging, the crew of the *Fox* observed Christmas less boisterously than the year before, but with mutual good will. To give all hands twenty-four hours off, the officers relieved the quartermasters of the duty of taking the readings at the magnetic observatory 210 yards from the ship. How long a distance of 210 yards can be in a winter gale only dwellers in the far north can comprehend.

As soon as the returning sun gave some hours of daylight and a long period of bright twilight, McClintock sent the tenderfoot Young with four men and a dog sledge to set up a depot on Prince of Wales Island, while he, with Petersen and Alexander Thompson, an old Penny man, set out to visit the Eskimos whom Sir James Ross had found near the Magnetic Pole. (The Magnetic Pole moves about. Ross found the North Magnetic Pole on the West shore of Boothia, northeast from Cape Felix. It now stands in the Barrow Strait.) Bellot Strait was at no time safe for sledges owing to the violent tides sweeping back and forth under the ice; but just to the north it had an ' echo ', a false strait lying above sea level and partly filled with a lake, which gave the travellers easy passage through the half-submerged mountain chain of Somerset-Boothia. Leaving the ship on 17 February and passing through this false strait, they went south along the west shore of Boothia. On 2 March they arrived at the Eskimo settlement, 180 miles from the ship. The natives received them hospitably, inquired after Sir James Ross, whom the older inhabitants well remembered, and produced relics of the lost ships for barter. A silver medal was purchased, once the property of Dr MacDonald, assistant surgeon of the *Terror,* silver spoons and forks and buttons. Sledges and spear staffs were observed fashioned from wood of European origin. None of the Eskimos would admit having *seen* the men or ships from which these articles had come. One man had seen graves and unburied bones. Another reported from hearsay that a three-masted ship had been crushed in the ice to the west of King William Island, but had no idea of where she had come from. All her crew, he said, had landed safely. The chart which he drew at McClintock's

259

request was unintelligible. Assured that they were on the right track, the three men went back to the ship to prepare for the longer spring journey. This preliminary excursion marked an epoch in geography. By surveying the shore from Bellot Strait to the Magnetic Pole they had completed the coastal map of the North American mainland.

The spring travelling parties were off on 2 April 1859, Young to the west, McClintock and Hobson towards King William Island to the south. They called again at the settlement which they had visited in March, and there a young man told Petersen that *both* ships had been seen – one had been crushed and sunk while the other lay, and might still be lying, a wreck on shore. The Eskimos had boarded her and found a body – a large man with long teeth. He had been told this, for he was a child at the time.

A week later, McClintock and Hobson parted, Hobson to go round Cape Felix and follow the west shore of King William Island where the ships had been seen, McClintock to go through the channel on its eastern side where James Ross had made his tragic error twenty-nine years before. Ross and Rae straits were found covered with ice of a year's growth only, confirming the belief that there lay the navigable Northwest Passage, had Franklin only known it.

McClintock, with Petersen, four men, and two sledges, one drawn by dogs, went past Matty Island to the King William Island shore and there found an encampment of more than thirty persons, thievish, but otherwise the kindliest folk in the world. 'There was not a trace of fear, every countenance was lighted up with joy; even the children were not shy, not backward either, in crowding about us, and poking in everywhere,' McClintock recorded in his journal. The Eskimos sold the visitors pieces of plate bearing the names of Franklin, Crozier, and others, uniforms, buttons, and bows made of English wood. They confirmed the existence of the wreck, five days' journey away on the west shore. There had been many books, long destroyed by the weather. Though none would admit to having seen the hapless crews *alive,* one talkative old woman gave a graphic picture of the death march: 'They fell down and died as they walked along,' she said. Some were buried and some not. She was vague as to numbers. Leaving the wreck to be visited on his journey back,

McClintock crossed Simpson Strait and on 12 May was in the estuary which Back had discovered and Dr King had made famous.

A few fragments of iron, copper, and preserved meat were all that Montreal Island yielded. Fog, falling snow, and the sickness of one of the men greatly hindered extensive and effective search. A sad disappointment was the disappearance of the Eskimos whom Chief Factor Anderson had met at the river's mouth. They might have directed Petersen, who spoke their language, to the beach of the dead men described to Rae, where possibly records, cached and still legible, might be found. Deprived of this guidance, the searchers crossed Ogle Peninsula and turned northwards across the sea back to King William Island. They passed a little to the west of Point Richardson and Starvation Cove, where, as Lieutenant Frederick Schwatka was to learn more than two decades later, the forty sturdiest of Franklin's crews had barely reached the mainland and had lain down to die. On the morning of 24 May they landed on King William Island near the Peffer River and headed west to trace in reverse the very course travelled by the starving crews eleven years before.

The land was low, the beach windswept and bare. Before they had travelled very far, they found on a low gravel ridge a skeleton, 'lying upon its face, the limbs and smaller bones either dissevered or gnawed away by small animals'. Rags of a blue jacket and of a pilot-cloth great-coat identified the bones as those of a British seaman. A clothes brush and a horn comb lay nearby and a note-book frozen hard. This was later ascertained to belong to Harry Peglar, captain of the foretop in the *Terror*. The bones, McClintock thought, were those of a steward or officer's servant.

This find gave no further clue to the history of the expedition, and the area in which such a clue might be found was narrowing fast. With deepening anxiety, the little party resumed its journey. Abandoned snow huts were seen, but still no Eskimos, as they passed along the shore towards Cape Herschel.

This cape was a low stony point, heaped with ice hummocks and backed at a distance of a quarter of a mile by a hill 150 feet high. Here, in 1839, Simpson had built a massive cairn. The south face of this had been torn out and its central stones removed. The sledge crew quickly demolished the rest, and, with the tenacity of men who cannot give up a cherished hope, they hacked the frozen ground around with pickaxes. In vain. No trace of a record could be found.

McClintock felt sure that Franklin's men had placed a note in the cairn. The Eskimos had evidently tampered with it. They would have torn it down to the ground if they had not found its contents. Evidently, they *had* found something, which could only be a document relating to the lost expedition. McClintock described the moment: 'It was with a feeling of deep regret and much disappointment that I left this spot without finding some certain record of those martyrs to their country's fame. Perhaps in all the wide world there will be few spots more hallowed in the recollection of English seamen than this cairn of Cape Herschel.' The disheartened members of the little caravan got in motion again, reflecting that Hobson was on the west side of the island and might have had better luck.

The prize which McClintock had sought through eleven years of stress and toil was granted him in a manner so simple that it was an anti-climax. West of Cape Herschel the shore grew very flat and was lined by great hummocks, the ice which had baffled Rae and Collinson on the other side of Victoria Strait. Twelve miles from the cape they came upon a cairn, newly built, for the stones were unweathered and still soiled from the ground on which they had rested. It marked the end of Hobson's journey from the north and contained a note dated six days previously. Like McClintock, Hobson had met no Eskimos. He had seen no trace of the wreck. But in the ruins of a cairn on the south side of Point Victory he had found a metal cylinder, containing 'the record so ardently sought for, of the Franklin Expedition.' It was written on a printed Navy form and comprised two distinct entries.

The first read:

28 of May 1847. H.M. ships *Erebus* and *Terror* wintered in the ice in lat. 70 05 N.: long. 98 23 W. [a few miles northwest of Cape Felix].

Having wintered in 1846 – 7 [a mistake for 1845 – 6] at Beechey Island, in lat. 74 43 28 N.: long. 91 39 15 W., after having ascended Wellington Channel to lat. 77, and returned by the west side of Cornwallis Island.

Sir John Franklin commanding the expedition.

All well.

Party consisting of 2 officers and 6 men left the ships on Monday, 24 May, 1847.

Gm. [Graham] Gore, Lieut.

Chas. F. Les Voeux, Mate. 2

No other seaborne expedition of the period had equalled the success of Franklin in his first two seasons. Failing to get past Cape Walker, he had gone up Wellington Channel, found the strait which was later to elude Penny and Osborn, and come down between Cornwallis and Bathurst islands to winter (as was known) at Beechey Island. In the summer of 1846 he had gone down Peel Sound (or, as some believe, had rounded Cape Walker and gone south by McClintock Channel) and had been stopped by ice at Cape Felix. Cape Herschel lay only seventy miles farther south. Once there, on Simpson's track, he would have, in Sir John Richardson's phrase, 'forged the last link in the Northwest Passage,' by completing its chart from ocean to ocean. Gore's cheery note shows that they were confident of freeing the ships and passing down Victoria Strait in the coming summer.

How misplaced that confidence was, was made plain by the second entry:

25 April 1848 – H.M. Ships *Terror* and *Erebus* were deserted on the 22 April, 5 leagues N.N.W. of this, having been beset since 12 September, 1846. The officers and crews, consisting of 105 souls, under the command of Captain F. R. M. Crozier, landed here in lat. 69 37 42 N., long. 98 41 W. Sir John Franklin died on the 11 June 1847; and the total loss by deaths in the expedition has been to this date 9 officers and 15 men.

James Fitzjames,

Captain, H.M.S. *Erebus*.

and start tomorrow, 26, for Back's Fish River

F. R. M. Crozier,

Captain and Senior Officer.

'A sadder tale was never told in fewer words,' comments McClintock. Yet, for all its brevity, it was plain enough. Ice-bound, like the *Investigator*, for a third winter, the men of the *Erebus* and the *Terror* had begun the all but hopeless march to safety from which McClure's men had barely been delivered by the arrival of Kellett. They must have been in even worse condition than the men of the *Investigator* – their death rate in three winters had been four times as high. A third of their number did reach the continent near Back's Fish River. For the rest, a few graves and unburied skeletons have been found along the King William Island shore and on islets in Simpson Strait to prove that in those last days of misery and despair they did achieve the discovery of the Northwest Passage which they had so joyously undertaken.

During their last winter, the plight of those hapless men had been aggravated by their situation in the ice pack. They lay not in a snug anchorage like Mercy Bay on a shore that was the haunt of caribou, but in a jungle of hummocks thirteen miles from a coast virtually destitute of game. McClintock remarked upon its unusual barrenness. 'The coast we marched along was extremely low – a mere series of ridges of limestone shingle, almost destitute of fossils. The only tracks of animals seen were those of a bear and a few foxes – the only living creatures a few willow grouse. . . . The prospect to seaward was not less forbidding – a rugged surface of crushed-up pack, including much heavy ice. In these shallow ice-covered seas, seals are but seldom found: and it is highly probable that all animal life in them is as scarce as upon the land.'

In a bay a little to the north of Cape Crozier, McClintock came upon a boat – already found by Hobson – mounted upon a sledge and containing two skeletons, one of a slightly built youth, the other of a large, middle-aged man. The body of the man appeared to have been mauled by wolves. The boat was loaded with tools, weapons, and equipment, 'a mere accumulation of dead weight . . . very likely to break down the strength of the sledge-crews.' In addition, there were five or six small books, works of religious devotion and silverware. McClintock observed that plainly the officers had distributed their silverware among the men as the only means of saving it. 'Not a single iron spoon, such as sailors always use, has been found.'

From the circumstance that the head of the boat was pointing northeast, back towards the ships, McClintock inferred that a detachment had been sent back for an additional food supply and had left the boat and two of its feeblest members in the shelter of the bay, intending to pick them up later. The strength of the others must have failed also, for they had never returned to the boat.

The researches of the Americans Charles Francis Hall (in 1869) and Lieutenant Frederick Schwatka of the United States Army (in 1880) have confirmed and added a little detail to this reconstruction of the tragedy. From the number of corpses seen by Eskimos at Terror Bay, to the south of Cape Crozier, it is evident that many of the weaker men gave up at that point and chose to die on the spot. It may have been from there that a party returned to the icebound ships. The main body rounded Cape Herschel and followed the shore to the east, and thirty to forty of the strongest left the island near the Peffer River and crossed Simpson Strait, only to die in Starvation Cove to the west of Point Richardson. Records, which they had carried to the last, were lying on the beach. A number of graves and unburied skeletons have been found along their line of march. Near the Peffer River, Hall found a skeleton that was doubtfully identified by a gold-filled tooth as Lieutenant Le Vesconte of the *Erebus*. In a grave near Point Victory, Schwatka found bones positively recognized as those of John Irving, third lieutenant of the *Terror*. In 1931, Dr Gibson of the Hudson's Bay Company discovered parts of seven skeletons in Douglas Bay and four more on the nearby Todd Islets, the bones, evidently, of men who had come so far but did not feel equal to crossing Simpson Strait. Hall determined that the wreck Hobson and McClintock looked for in vain had been cast up not on King William Island but on one of the neighbouring O'Reilly Islets.

Though very short of provisions, McClintock gave his sledge crew a day's rest at Point Victory, while with the dogs he made the thirty-mile circuit of Collinson Inlet in the faint hope of obtaining a further record. He then made haste to arrive at his journey's end. He was more than 200 miles from the ship. It was early June, and melt from the sunlit heights was drenching the snow in the ravines and threatening to burst out and flood the surface of the still-frozen sea. Held up by water in the pass north of Bellot Strait, they abandoned dogs and sledges to tramp the last few miles to the ship. They came on board on 19 June after an outing of seventy-eight days and a journey of some 1,000 miles.

Hobson was in his berth seriously ill with scurvy. He had limped for most of his journey, finished it riding on a sledge, and had been carried on board. Young was still absent, and Dr Walker gave a disturbing report on him. As directed, he had crossed over to Prince of Wales Island, and found that a strait, which was to be named McClintock Channel, divided it from Victoria Island. To extend his search as far as possible, he had sent back the main sledge crew, and with the dogs and one seaman, George Hobday, had gone up the east side of McClintock Channel to the conical hills which marked Osborn's farthest from Barrow Strait. On 7 June he came back to the ship for medical treatment and, disregarding Dr Walker's protests, left again on the tenth to complete his assignment. Greatly alarmed, McClintock mustered the fittest of his own long-suffering sledge mates and set off to bring him back. He met the returning party twenty miles from the ship, Young disabled and riding on the ledge, old Harvey barely able to walk from scurvy, and all terribly reduced in weight. They had achieved their mission of charting the unknown parts of both sides of Peel Sound, and were greatly cheered by learning that the expedition had succeeded in its main purpose. Soon, all were on board and, in McClintock's words, 'indulging in such rapid consumption of eatables as only those can do who have been much reduced by long-continued fatigue and exposure to cold. Venison, ducks, beer and lemon-juice, daily; preserved apples and cranberries three times a week; and pickled whaleskin – a famous anti-scorbutic – *ad libitum* for all who liked it.' The wet, wind, and fog that had made the lives of the travellers miserable gave way to glorious unending sunlight. 'The carpenter's hammer, and the men's voices at their work, were new and animating sounds.' Hobson, still on the sick list, but doing duty, hobbled about to supervise the restowing of the ship. Young busied himself surveying the harbour. The doctor was 'perpetually in chase [of bird specimens] unless busily occupied in grubbing up plants ', while the captain, with pencil and protractor, began to digest his own and his officers' surveys and to lay down on the map the 800 miles of new coastline which they had brought to light.

With this addition and with the exception of the Victoria Island east shore from the end of Collinson's survey at Gateshead Island to the farthest of Wyniatt in 1851, the misdirected search for Franklin had unveiled the entire fantastic jigsaw of the Canadian archipelago up to latitude 77 degrees north, a marvellous achievement for ten years, and a worthy monument to the brave old seaman whose disappearance had brought it to pass. And that disappearance was now fully accounted for. Young's discovery of the heavily ice-infested McClintock Channel confirmed the theory, already held by McClintock himself, that a stream of the tremendous polar pack bred in the Beaufort Sea, fifty and even eighty feet in thickness, came grinding through McClure Strait, Viscount Melville Sound, and McClintock Channel to pile up against King William Island and establish an impenetrable barrier to navigation. Franklin, so McClintock declared, could have made the Northwest Passage only by passing east of King William Island by the obscure back alley of Ross and Rae straits. 'Had Sir John Franklin known that a channel existed eastward of King William's *Land* (so named by Sir James Ross), I do not think he would have risked the besetment of his ships in such very heavy ice to the west of it; but had he attempted the north-west passage by the *eastern* route he would probably have carried his ships safely through to Bering's Straits. But Franklin was furnished with charts which indicated no passage to the eastward of King William's Land, . . . and made that land a peninsula attached to the continent of North America; and he consequently had but one course open to him, and that was the one he adopted. . . . How very different the result *might* and probably *would* have been had he known of the existence of a ship-channel, sheltered by King William from this tremendous "polar pack"'. We cannot know whether Franklin deliberately put his ships into the heavy ice off Cape Felix. He may have regarded the pack at the top of Victoria Strait as a local accident and liable to disperse with the first change of wind. He did not know that it was fed by a continuous stream from the northwest, nor that its southward flow was retarded by the islets at the lower end of Victoria Strait. The expedition was foredoomed to failure by Ross's error in closing the eastern channel; chance then took a hand to make the catastrophe complete. The ice of Peel Sound had opened up to give the ships free passage into that part of the archipelago that was least accessible by sea and had then clamped them in behind a barrier of ice so far-reaching and solid that their would-be rescuers considered it impossible that they could have gone that way.

Had Captain Crozier directed the survivors' march north to Regent's Inlet instead of south to the Great Fish River, he would have found subsistence at the wreck cache of the *Fury*, and some of his men might have lived through the winter to be rescued by Lieutenant Robinson of the Ross expedition in the spring of 1849. But Crozier had not been promised a relief expedition, and he supposed wrongly that the cache had been rifled by whalers. So his natural course was to go south and seek fresh meat for his scurvy-ridden crews. Franklin and Crozier could have said, with their counterpart in the Antarctic, Robert Falcon Scott: 'We took risks, we know we took them; things have come out against us, and therefore we have no cause for complaint, but bow to the will of Providence.'

McClintock thanked the assembled crew for their great exertions and assured them that every part of the search had been 'fully and efficiently performed'. The relics of the lost expedition were shown to all, labelled, and packed away. Then began the most anxious period of the whole Arctic year. When the ice of Regent's Inlet broke up, easterly winds drove it against the Somerset Island shore and fenced the *Fox* in behind miles of shattered pack, condemning her crew to the same weary vigil as had fallen to the men of the *Investigator* at Mercy Bay. McClintock wrote in his journal: 'I went to a hill-top and saw that much ice had broken up in Brentford Bay, and that there were streaks of water along the land . . . this water, however, was not accessible to us. . . . Later in the day and from loftier hill-tops, a good deal of water was seen off Cape Garry, and a water-sky beyond. It now blows very strongly from the S.W., the most desirable quarter; and the anxious desire to escape has become oppressive.' The weary captain took stock to ascertain how he was supplied in the event of a third winter in the ice and eased his yearning for home by diving into packets of old letters.

On 9 August the ship was off at last, steaming up a three-mile lane between pack and shore. As both Engineer Brand and Chief Stoker Scott were dead, McClintock, on the strength of a course he had taken sixteen years before, installed himself as engineer. 'I experienced some little difficulty in the management of the engines and boiler; the latter primed so violently as to send the water over our top gallant yard . . . but eventually we got the engines to work well, and steamed across Cresswell Bay during the night.' Then the ship was caught in strong east winds and for four days kept offshore only by clinging to an ice piece of deeper draft than herself. She was at sea again on the fifteenth, and on the twenty-first we have a brief entry – a great sigh of relief: 'At sea – out of sight of land!' On the twenty-fifth: 'We are only 108 miles from Godhavn and the anxiety to clutch our letters has become intolerable.' Late on the night of the twenty-seventh, the *Fox* found a safe anchorage in that Greenland port, and the Franklin Search was over.

The inhabitants of the sleeping hamlet were awakened by Petersen demanding the mail for the *Fox*. 'It is rather a nervous thing opening the first letters *after a lapse of more than two years*,' admits McClintock – how things have changed in a century – but the news was all good. Lady Franklin and Miss Cracroft wrote to tell of their travels on the European continent. McClintock commented: 'They have travelled more than we have.'

He ends his *Fox* journal with a gracefulness and a touch of pathos fitting the sad but not inglorious epoch, which his labours had brought to a close. During the five days of his stay at Godhavn, the natives relieved the toilworn crew, the men watering and ballasting the ship, while 'a troop of Esquimaux girls' scrubbed her paintwork and decks. In return, the men with 'a very limited quantity of rum-punch for the ladies' went ashore every night to dance in an empty storehouse. Christian and Samuel, the Eskimo drivers, received their pay and discharge. 'I was gratified very much when I heard them say that the men had treated them well – "all the same as brothers"; and they really seemed sorry to leave the ship; they would come on board and look gravely about at everything as if regretting the coming separation. Even our poor dogs seemed to think the ship their natural abode; although landed at the settlement, they soon ran around the harbour to the point nearest the ship, and there, upon the rocks, spent the whole period of our stay.' Petersen's nieces, the Misses Marie and Sophia – the latter still obstinately wearing her Eskimo trousers – came on board once to give a concert. Other evenings the officers passed tranquilly with the three Danish gentlemen of the settlement. 'Nothing could exceed their kindness to us. . . . We shall always retain very agreeable recollections of Godhavn; twice it has been to us an Arctic home,' wrote McClintock.

On 1 September the *Fox* weighed anchor for the last time, and favouring gales bore her quickly home. McClintock winds up his stirring narrative with the quiet observation that after 'two years in the still water of the frozen North' his band of heroes suffered much from seasickness on the Atlantic rollers. The ship docked in the Thames on 23 September. On the twenty-seventh she was paid off and the Polar Medal was presented to the few crew members who did not already wear that decoration. Hobson received his promotion and McClintock a knighthood. Lady Franklin, whose devotion to her husband's memory was now crowned by success, was applauded in the press as a national heroine. While firmly refusing any public recompense for the fortune she had spent in the search, she urged the claims of the men who had served her. A grateful Parliament took the hint and voted a grant of £5,000 to the officers and men of the *Fox*.

Lady Franklin's fighting spirit was aroused once more and for the last time on her late husband's behalf by certain critics who disputed McClintock's assertion that 'to Franklin must be assigned the earliest discovery of the Northwest Passage.' Could that which not a single man had lived to report rightly be called a discovery? Lady Franklin vowed that it could, and that, if need be, she would demand a Parliamentary committee to rule on the question. It was *not* necessary. It was a point to be judged not by logic but by sentiment, and sentiment was more than ready to prefer Franklin's claim to that of the grasping McClure. In 1875, a few weeks after Lady Franklin's death, the aged Sir George Back unveiled a monument in Westminster Abbey to Sir John Franklin and those 'who perished with him in completing the discovery of the Northwest Passage '.

Thirty-two years later, a marble slab was placed at the foot of the monument in memory of Sir Leopold McClintock, the discoverer of Franklin's fate.

Bibliography

STANDARD SOURCES

ARMSTRONG, ALEXANDER, MD, *A personal Narrative of the Discovery of the North-West Passage*, London, 1857

BACK, SIR GEORGE, *Narrative of the Arctic Land Expedition to the Mouth of the Great Fish River*, London, 1836

BARROW, SIR JOHN, *Voyages of Discovery and Research in the Arctic Regions From the Year 1818 to the Present Time*, London 1846

BEAGLEHOLE, J. C., ED., *The Journals of Captain Cook: Vol III*

BELCHER, SIR EDWARD, *The Last of the Arctic Voyages*, London 1855

BELLOT, JOSEPH RENÉ, *Memoirs*, London, 1855

BROWN, JOHN, FRGS, *The North-West Passage and the Search for Sir John Franklin, with sequel including the Voyage of the 'Fox'*, London, 1860

COLLINSON, SIR RICHARD, *Journal of HMS 'Enterprise'* (edited by Major-General T. B. Collinson), London, 1889

FRANKLIN, SIR JOHN, *narrative of a journey to the Shores of the Polar Sea*, London, 1823; *Narrative of a Second Expedition to the Shores of the Polar Sea in the Years 1825, 1826 and 1827*

KANE, ELISHA KENT, MD, *The Grinnell Expedition*, London, 1854; *Arctic Explorations, the Second Grinnell Expedition*, New York, 1857

KING, RICHARD, MRCS, *Narrative of a Journey to the Shores of the Arctic Sea under the Command of Captain Back, RN*, London, 1836; *The Franklin Search from First to Last*

MARKHAM, SIR CLEMENTS, *Life of Admiral Sir Leopold McClintock*, London, 1909

MCCLINTOCK, SIR F. L., *The Voyage of the 'Fox' in the Arctic Seas, a Narrative of the Discovery of the Fate of Sir John Franklin and His Companions*, London, 1859

MCDOUGALL, GEO. F., *The Eventful Voyage of HM Discovery Ship 'Resolute', 1852 – 53 – 54*, London, 1857

MCCLURE, SIR ROBERT, *The Discovery of the North-West Passage* (edited by Captain Sherard Osborn, CB) 2nd Ed., London, 1857 (N.B. This book actually written by Osborn, using McClure's journal as his principal source. With questionable ethics McClure's name was put on the title page presumably to promote sales)

OSBORN, CAPTAIN SHERARD, CB, *Stray Leaves from an Arctic Journal*, Edinburgh and London, 1865

PARRY, SIR W. E., *Journal of a Voyage of Discovery of a North-West Passage from the Atlantic to the Pacific*, London, 1821

ROSS, SIR JOHN, *A Voyage of Discovery Made for the Purpose of Exploring Baffin Bay*, London, 1819; *Narrative of a Second Voyage in Search of a North-West Passage*, London, 1835

SIMPSON, THOMAS, *Narrative of Discoveries on the North Coast of North America During the years 1836–39*, London, 1843

SUTHERLAND, PETER C., MD, *Journal of a Voyage in Baffin's Bay and Barrow Strait in the years 1850-51*, London, 1852

TRAILL, H. D., *Life of Sir John Franklin*, London, 1896

MODERN SOURCES

The circumstances surrounding Franklin's fate are examined in the most painstaking way in *Sir John Franklin's Last Voyage* (the *Beaver*, June 1937) by William Gibson, FRGS, who knew the King William Island area well, and in R. J. Cyriax's *Sir John Franklin's Last Arctic Expedition*, London, 1939. In *Franklin, Happy Voyager*, (London, 1956) G. F. Lamb provides an excellent modern biography of the discoverer, and Rear Admiral Noel Wright's *Quest for Franklin*, (London, 1959) is both controversial and stimulating. A substantial primary document is J. A. Miertsching's *Frozen Ships*, (tr. L. H. Neatby) published by Macmillan of Canada in 1967. Frances J. Woodward's *Portrait of Jane – a Life of Lady Franklin*, (London, 1951) is also excellent.

UNPRINTED SOURCES

Sherard Osborn's correspondence with Captain William Penny in the Library of the Scott Polar Research Institute has been referred to as well as Osborn's letters to John Barrow, Jr in the British Museum. Also of great interest is the journal of W. W. May, first lieutenant of Sir Edward Belcher's *Assistance,* in the Canadian Archives. The Grinnell Scrap Book in the Stefansson Collection is full of miscellaneous information: in the same collection Mrs Dow's manuscript biography of Dr Kane, though incomplete, is a wealth of material for any future biographer of the American discoverer.

Index

Abbott, John, on *Pioneer*, 124, 136
Aberdeen, Port of, 122-3, 196, 249
Abernethy, ice-mate on *Victory*, 66, 69, 70
Adam, Indian *voyageur*, 53, 54
Adams, Assistant Surgeon, 220
Adams, John, of *Bounty*, 62
Adelaide, Cape, 72
Admiralty, the British, 26; organizes Arctic exploration, 26, 27, 30, 58, 92-3; withdraws, 42, 65, 76; pays for Ross, 74; sends rescue ships, 98, 101-2, 103, 113, 117, 119, 159, 196-8, 246-7, 248-9; courts martial, 217-18, 225-6; and McClure, 229
Advance, brig; with De Haven, 119, 127-8, 131, 133-4, 146-7; with Kane, 142, 230, 233-42
Ah-el-dezeth, River, 79-80
Akaitcho, Indian chief, 46-7, 51, 54, 55-6, 81
Akoull, Chukchee chief, 108, 109
Albany, on Hudson River, 20
Aldrich, Bob, 139
Aleutian Islands, 166, 167, 169
Alexander, Cape, 21, 29, 89, 115, 231, 240, 241
Alexander, barque, 28
Amlie Island, 167
Amundsen, Roald, 222, 244
Anderson, on *Investigator*, 162, 189
Anderson, on *Prince Albert*, 151, 152
Anderson, James, 247
Anderson Bay, 115
Anoatok, 232, 240
Antarctic exploration, 92
Arbuthnot, of *Enterprise*, 224
Arctic, maps of the, 19, 99; described, 23-4
'Arctic Council', the, 103, 196, *illus.*
Arctic Harbour, 49
Armstrong, Dr Alexander, 160-2, 163, 164, 165-6, 171-3, 175-80, 181-5, 187-94, 205-6, 216, 227-8;

given testimonial, 219
Artillery Lake, 79
Assistance Harbour, 131, 134, 137, 139, 142, 201
Assistance, HMS; with Austin, 121, 123, 125, 126, 128-9; with Belcher, 198, 200, 211; deserted, 2, 6
Athabaska Lake, 45-6
Augustus, Eskimo interpreter, 51, 59, 60
Austin, Capt. Horatio; commands *Resolute*, 114, 121, 122-7, 129, 131, 134-5, 137, 142; McClure misses, 190; return home, 195-6
Aylmer Lake, 79

Back, Capt. Sir George; on Franklin's 1st journey, 44, 45, 46, 47-8, 50, 51-4, 55; on 2nd, 58, 59, 60; leads rescue expedition down Great Fish River, 76-83; on *Terror* in Hudsons Bay, 84-6; retires, 86; and Dr King, 86-7; personality, 87-8; on Arctic Council, 103; mentioned, 66, 75, 76, 90, 96, 97, 101, 102, 112, 113, 115, 122, 132, 270
Back, Cape, 115
Back, Point, 188
Baffin, William, 20-2
Baffin Bay, map, 231; Bylot in, 20-2; Ross in, 29-31; Parry in, 33-5, 42; Osborn in, 123-4; De Haven in, 133; Kennedy in, 147; Inglefield, 230-1; Kane, 234, 237; McClintock, 253
Baffin Island, 17, 23, 34, 39
Baillie Hamilton Island, 140, 141
Ballast Beach, 184, *illus.*
Banks Land (Island), 39, 94, 96, 113; McClure at, 170, 171, 174, 177, 190; Cresswell at, 179, 180; Pim, 204-5; Collinson, 221
Baptiste, on Franklin's 2nd trip, 59

273

Baretto Junior, supply ship, 14, 15
Baring's Land, 174, 177
Barlow Inlet, 131
Barnard, Lt, on *Enterprise*, 106, 220-1
Barow, Sir John, 26, 29, 30, 31, 32, 39, 66, 74-5, 76, 90, 92, 93, 95-6, 97, 119
Barrow, Point, 62, 89, 111, 170
Barrow Strait, 24, 100, 106; map, 71; Parry in, 35; *1850-1* search in, 119, 128, 130, 132-9; Kellett, 201, 212
Bathurst, Cape, 62, 113, 114, 172
Bathurst Inlet, 49
Bathurst Island, 35, 139, 141, 211
Batty Bay, 73, 149, 151
Beaufort Sea, 23, 25, 211, 267
Beaulieu, Francois, 46, 62
Beck, Adam, 125-6, 230
Beechey, Capt., 39, 58, 62, 100, 103, 120
Beechey, Cape, 61
Beechey Island, 76, 106; discovered, 35; Franklin relics at, 127-30; depot ship at, 157, 197, 200, 216; *illus.*
Beechey Point, 112
Belanger, *voyageur*, 51-2
Belcher, Capt. Sir Edward; character, 198; commands rescue squadron, 157, 198-201, 211-12, 214; orders ships deserted, 214-15, 216; court-martial, 217-18
Bellerophon, 43
Bellot, Lt Joseph Réné, 47, 134; early career, 143-4; on *Prince Albert*, 144-57; on *Phoenix*, 157; death, 157-8
Bellot Cliff, 156
Bellot Strait, 68, 69; discovered, 155-7; McClintock in, 256-7, 259
Berens Point, 111, 112
Bering Strait, 22, 28-9, 33, 62, 98, 107, 162
Berkeley, Sir Maurice, 248
Bidgood, Thomas, 205-6
Bird, Capt., in *Investigator*, 104, 106
Bird, James, 91
Bird, Cape, 105, 257
Black Meat, Indian, 46, 65
Blanky, Thomas, 66, 67, 72
Blazer, tug-boat, 10
Bligh, Capt., 28, 198
Bloody Falls, 49, 62, 90
Blossom, 58, 62
Bonsall, Amos, 235, 236
Booth, Felix, 66
Boothia Isthmus, 75, 80; denied by Simpson, 90-1
Boothia Peninsula, 23-4, 68-9, 72,

93-4, 96, 97; Ross at, 68-9; Rae at, 243-4; McClintock, 258-9
Bounty, Cape, 37
Bounty, 28, 62
Bowden, Cape, 131
Bowen, Port, 42, 149
Bradbury, on *Investigator*, 191, 207
Bradford, Dr, 139
Brand, engineer on *Fox*, 258
Brentford Bay, 68, 154-5, 156, 257, 268
Bridport Inlet, 202, 207
Britannia, Cape, 89
Brooks, William, 233, 236, 237, 239
Brown, Robert, 43
Browne, Lt William, 106, 130, 137-8, 155, 196
Buchan, Capt. David, 28-9
Bushnan, Lt, 58
Bylot, Robert, 20, 21

Cabot, John, 17
Cabot, Sebastian, 10, 17
Cairn Point, 232
Cambridge Bay, 115, 222, 225
Camden Bay, 225
Cardigan Strait, 212
Carlton, Fort, 45
Castor and Pollux River, 89-90, 244
Cator, Lt B., 121, 123
Chantrey Inlet, 83, 89
Chipewyan, Fort, 46, 47, 48, 78
Chukchee (Tuski) tribe, 107-9
Churchill River, 44, 77
Clarence Islands, 75
Clayton, John M., 119
Clearwater River, 77, 78
Coburg Island, 21
Cockatrice, HMS, 165
Cockburn, Cape, 213
Collins, Ice Master on *Resolute*, 199
Collinson, Admiral Sir Richard, 115, 116, 229, 249; commands *Enterprise*, 159-70, 214, 215, 220-5; return, 225-6; character, 226; and N.W. Passage reward, 226-7; map, 19
Collinson, Maj.-Gen. T. B., 220, 226
Collinson Inlet, 265
Columbus, Christopher, 17
Committee Bay, 97
Confidence, Fort, 89, 90, 114
Constitution, Cape, 237
Cook, Dr Frederick, 97, 232
Cook, Capt. James, 22-3, 27, 29, 37, 168
Coombes, seaman, 210
Copper Indians, 46-7, 48-9, 53-4; rescue Franklin's party, 54; paid, 55-6; Back meets again, 80-1

Coppermine River, 22, 44, 46, 48-9, 50, 54, 62, 89; Rae down, 114-15
Cornwallis, Admiral William, 32
Cornwallis Island, 35, 141
Coronation Gulf, 115
Court, Stephen, 160, 177, 178 188, 190
Cracroft, Sophia, 144, 253, 269
Crédit, voyageur, 51
Cresswell, Father of Lt S., 197
Cresswell, Lt Samuel G., 160, 173, 177, 179, 180, 193, 207-8, illus.
Cresswell Bay, 42, 154, 268
Crozier, Capt. F. R. M., 11, 12, 14, 82, 92-3; takes command of Franklin's crew, 245, 263, 267-8
Crozier, Cape, 263-5
Cumberland Gulf, 19
Cumberland House, 45

Damley Bay, 62
Davis, John, 19-20
Davis Strait, 28-9, 146, 222, 255
De Bray, Enseigne, 209-10
De Haven, Lt Edwin J., 119, 128, 131-4, 147
De Haven Point, 224
De Long, Lt G. W., 110-11
Dealy Island, 130, 202-4, 212
Dease, Peter Warren, 58-9, 88-9
Dease Strait, 115
Demarcation Point, 60
Devil's Thumb, 124, 200
Devon Island, 34, 35, 128, 130, 132, 212
Dickens, Charles, 10, 13, 246
Diomede Islands, 167-8
Discovery, 20-1, 22
Dodge, Ernest S., 31
Dolphin, 60, 62
Dolphin and Union Strait, 62
Domville, Dr, 204-5, 208, 216, 227
Dorothea, 28
Douglas Bay, 265
Drew, sledge-mate to McClintock, 210
Dudley Digges, Cape, 29
Dundas, Cape, 139, 196, 205

East Cape (Cape Dezhnev), 110
Eglinton Island, 210, 211
Ellesmere Island, 21, 29, 232
Elson, mate of Blossom, 62
Enterprise, Fort, 46, 48, 49; found deserted 51, 53; relieved, 54; map, 36
Enterprise, HMS; with Ross, 104, 106; with Collinson, 118, 159, 160-3; without Investigator, 165, 168, 169, 215, 220-5

Equator, crossing the, 161
Erebus, HMS; with Ross, 92; with Franklin, 10, 11, 13-16, 92, 95-7, 141; sought, 100, 104, 106, 116, 117, 129, 155, 249-50, 256, 257-8; traced, 230, 245, 259-60, 262-5; illus.
Eskimos, 48, 154; 'Arctic High-landers', 29; of Winter Island, 40-1; of Cape York, 125-6, 200; of Kotzebue Sound, 168-9; and Franklin, 60, 61-2; and Ross, 68-9, 70; and Back, 82; and Pullen, 111-12; and Rae, 116, 243-4; and McClure, 170-2, 180-1; and Collinson, 223-4; and Kane's party, 238, 239, 240; and McClintock, 255, 259-60, 269
Etah, 238, 239, 240

Farquharson, Col., 166
Felix, Cape, 69, 263, 267
Felix Harbour, 68, 127
Felix, yacht, 119, 125, 126, 127
Finlayson Islands, 115
Fisher, Dr J., 38
Fitzjames, Commander James, 11, 12-15, 19, 92, 93, 96-7, 263
Fitzwilliam Strait, 210
Flinders, Capt. Matthew, 43
Foggy Island, 60
Forsyth, Commander, 125, 126-7, 129, 143
Fortescue Bay, 163
Four River Point, 105, 257
Fox, yacht, 121, 128, 249-70, illus.
foxes, 'Arctic postmen', 105, 135
Fram, 111
Franklin, Capt. Sir John, 9, 23, 28, 32, 76, 120; personality, 56-7; early carrer, 11, 42-3; marriages, 57-8, 65; 1st overland journey, 43-5; return, 49-54; map, 37; 2nd land journey, 58-63; appointed to find N.W. Passage, 92-5; voyage, 11-13, 96, 129-30, 227, 233, 243-4, 245-6, 256, 260-1, 262-8; map, 70; missing, 98-103; illus. Narrative . . . 55, 56, 57, 63-4
Franklin, Lady (née Jane Griffin), 12, 57, 65, 118, 270; personality, 119-21; attempts organize rescue, 102, 119, 120, 126, 143, 144, 145, 226, 230, 246, 247, 248; sends Fox, 249-51, 252, 253, 255, 269; illus.
Franklin Bay, 62, 173
Franklin, Fort, 59, 113
Franklin, Lake, 82

Franklin record, discovered, 15-16, 262-3; *illus.*
Frobisher, Sir Martin, 17, 19; *Voyages*, 226
Frobisher Bay, 17
Frozen Starit, 40
Fur traders, 44, 45, 46, 47-8; *see also* Hudson's Bay Co.
Fury, HMS, 39-42
Fury Beach, 67, 68, 72, 73, 77, 106, 127; cache stowed at, 42; Kennedy at, 148, 151, 154
Fury and Hecla Strait, 41, 90

Gateshead Island, 225
George Henry, U.S. whaler, 218
Gibson, William, 265, *illus.*
Giddy, sledge-mate of McClintock, 210
Gjoa, 222
Godhavn, 199, 241, 251, 269
Godsend Ledge, 234, 241
Goodsir, Dr H. D. S., 13
Goodsir, Dr (brother of above), 140
Gore, Lt Graham, 14, 245, 263
Gorgon, HMS, 122, 163
Great Bear Lake, 46, 58, 59, 62, 90
Great Fish River, 46, 65, 100, 117, 263; Back explores, 76, 77, 78, 79, 80-3; Anderson down, 247
Great Slave Lake, 22, 44, 46, 65, 77, 78-9, 80
Greely, Adolphus, 232
Green, sledge-captain, 210
Greenstockings, Indian girl, 47, 80-1
Grey, Earl, 100, 101, 102
Griffin, Jane, *see* Franklin, Lady
Griffin, Samuel P., 119, 128, 133
Griffiths Island, 131, 134, 136
Grinnell, Henry, 119, 132, 233
Grinnell Land (Peninsula), 132, 211
Griper, HMS, 33, 35, 37, 65

Halkett Island, 116
Hall, Charles Francis, 232, 237, 265
Hamilton, Lt, 203, 208, 211, 212, 213, 214 of *Resolute*
Hartnell, John and Thomas, 249
Hartstene, Lt, 241
Hartstene Bay, 238
Harvey, William, 157; on *Fox*, 250, 253, 255, 266
Haswell, Lt William H., on *Investigator*, 115, 160, 177, 193, 215, 222; under arrest, 164-5; sledge journey, 178, 180-1
Hawaii, 22, 122, 165
Hay, Cape, 39
Hayes, Dr Isaac, 19, 233, 236, 237-8, 239

Hayes River, 45
Hearne, Samuel, 22, 49, 77
Hecla, HMS, 33, 35, 38, 39, 42, 66, 94
Hecla and Griper Bay, 38, 210, 211
Hendrick, Hans, 233, 234, 237, 238, 240
Hepburn, John; with Franklin, 45, 46, 47, 51-2, 53, 54, 55, 56; on *Prince Albert*, 145, 146
Herald Island, 110
Herald HMS, 107, 110, 169-70
Hermione, 28
Herschel, Cape, 90, 223, 261-2, 265
Herschel Island, 112
Hewlett, on *Investigator*, 181, 182
Hiccles, sledge-mate, 210
Hickey, Tom, 236
Hoar Frost River, 78-9
Hobday, George, 266
Hobson, Lt W. R., 250, 255, 257-8, 260, 264, 265, 266; discovers Franklin record, 15, 262
Holsteinborg, 255
Honolulu, 165-6
Hood, Robert, 44, 45, 46, 47, 51, 52
Hood, T., on *Intrepid*, 210, 213-14
Hood's River, 49
Hooper, W. H., 107, 108-11, 112, 113, 114
Hope, Fort, 97, 243
Hoppner, Capt., 66, 75
Hornby, Georgina, 249
Hotham, Cape, 140
Hoyle, Robert, 205-6
Hudson, Henry, 20
Hudson Bay, 22, 43; Hudson in, 20; Parry in, 39-40; Back in, 84-6
Hudson Strait, 17, 18, 40
Hudson's Bay Co., 20, 22, 44, 46, 47, 58, 77, 86, 87-8, 243, 247
Humboldt Glacier, 235

Icy Cape, 23, 58, 61, 170
Igloolik, 41
Ile a la Crosse, 45, 48
Indians; of the Plains, 45; *see also* Copper Indians
Inglefield, Commander Edward; with *Isabel*, 230-3, 255; with *Phoenix*, 157, 208, 216
Inglefield Gulf, 21
Intrepid, HMS; with Austin, 121, 123, 126, 128, 142; with McClintock, 198, 201-2, 213-214; abandoned, 214-15
Investigator, HMS, 21; with Ross, 104-6; with McClure, 114, 118-19, 159-79, 203; in Mercy Bay, 188-94; relieved, 205-7; abandoned,

208; searched, 215; inquiries re, 217, 227-9; *illus.*
Irving, Lt J., 265
Isabel, 157, 230-3
Isabella, Cape (Boothia), 69
Isabella, Cape (Ellesmere Is.), 21, 29
Isabella, 28-30, 73-4

Jago, Lt, 221
Jeannette, 111
Jones Sound, 21, 29, 119, 127, 142, 232

Kairoluak, Eskimo chief, 171-2
Kamchatka, dispatch point, 33, 98
Kane, Dr Elisha Kent; with De Haven on *Advance*, 119, 127-9, 130-4, 147; leads own expedition, 233-42; *Arctic Explorations*, 241-2; mentioned, 19, 76, 110, 120, 230, 243; *illus.*
Kane Basin, 234-7; map, 231
Ka-oong-ah, Chukchee native, 109
Kellett, Capt. Henry, 198; with *Herald*, 107, 110, 169-70; with *Resolute*, 198-202; at Dealy Island, 202-4; rescues McClure, 205-9; deserts ships, 214-15; inquiries, 216, 227-8
Kellett, Cape, 189
Kellett Point, 221
Kellett Strait, 211
Kenualik, Eskimo chief, 172
Kendall, Ernest, 57, 58, 59, 60, 62
Kendall River, 115
Kennedy, Capt. William, 134, 143, 144, 145, 147-51, 153-7
Kennedy, bo'sun on *Investigator*, 184
Kennedy Channel, 237
Kennedy, Port, 257
King, Dr Richard; on Great Fish River, 76, 77, 78, 80, 82, 83-4; subsequent controversy, 84, 86-7, 88, 95-6, 97, 100-3, 104, 107, 115, 117, 118, 126, 197, 198, 218, 246, 247-8
King William Island (Land), 26, 83, 89, 90-1, 96, 116-17, 223, 257, 267; discovered by Ross, 69, 70, 72; Rae proves an island, 244; McClintock sledges round, 260-1; Franklin record found on, 262-4
Kotzebue, Otto, 27
Kotzebue Sound, 62, 110, 162, 168
Krabbé, sailing-master, 214, 215

Labrador, 26
Lady Franklin, 139
Lamb, G. F., 102

Lancaster Sound, 24, 126-7; discovered, 21; Ross closes, 29-31; Parry in, 32-5, 42; *Victory* in, 67, 94, 104, 106; De Haven in, 133; McClintock in, 255-6
Laughton, J. K., 198
Le Vesconte, H. D. T., 265
Leask, ice-master, 143, 145-6, 147, 148
Leopold, Port, 127, 156, 193, 256; Ross winters at, 104-6; Kennedy at, 148-50
Liddon, Lt M., 33
Liddon Gulf, 38, 139, 203
Lion, 60
Lisburne Cape, 169
Littleton Island, 232
Lord Mayor Bay, 68, 97
Lyon, Commander G. F., 39-41, 65, 120

McClintock, Lt Bunbury, 122
McClintock, Admiral Sir Leopold, 69, 72, 73, 197; with Ross, 69, 104, 105-6; with Austin, 122, 128-9, 130, 134, 136-7; journey to Winter Harbour, 139; commands *Intrepid*, 198-202, 213, 215; journey to Prince Patrick Island, 209-10; commands *Fox*, 249-70; *Voyages of the Fox*, 128-9, 228-9, 248; sledging innovations, 122, 136-7, 209; *illus.*
McClintock, Cape, 210
McClintock Channel, 24, 266, 267
McClure, Capt. Sir Robert, 25, 26, 69, 72, 73, 221, 222; early career, 121-2; with Ross, 104-6; commands *Investigator*, 114, 119, 159-94; parts from *Enterprise*, 164; goes into Arctic alone, 169-70; completes N.W. Passage, 177; sledge journey, 180-2; in Mercy Bay, 188-94; map, 19; message in Parry's monument, 190, 202-3; rescued by Kellett, 205-9; and officers' journals, 205, 215-16; court-martial, 217, 218; and N.W. Passage reward, 226-9; character, 229; *illus.*
McClure Strait, 185
McCormick, Dr Robert, 201, 229, 233, 247
Macdonald, on *Investigator*, 209
MacDonald, Dr A., 259
McDougall, George F., 199, 200, 204, 209, 213
McDougall, Lake, 82
McGary, on *Advance*, 234-8
Mackenzie, Alexander, 22, 44

Mackenzie River; Franklin on, 58, 59; Simpson on, 90; Pullen on, 113, 114
Mackinnon, British M.P., 229
McLellan, American whaling ship, 134, 200
McLeod, A. R., 77, 78, 80, 81, 83
McLeod Bay, 78
Mcmurdo Sound, 92
Magellan Strait, 163-4
Magnetic Pole, North, 72, 259
Maguire, Capt. R., 251
Markham, Sir Clement, 16, 122, 196
Martin, on Plover, 109-10
Mary, 125
Matty Island, 69, 70
Maufelly, Indian guide, 78-9
Maury Channel, 141, 142
May, Lt Walter W., 211, 212, 214, 218
Mecham, Lt G. F., 137; with Resolute, 198, 208, 214; finds McClure's record, 203; sledges to Prince Patrick, 209, 211; to Prince of Wales Strait, 214, 215
Melville Bay, 21, 29, 134, 146, 202; Austin in, 124-5; Belcher in, 200; McClintock in, 251, 255
Melville Island, 39, 100, 130, 210; Parry winters on, 35-8; McClintock's journey to, 139; Kellett on, 202-5
Melville Peninsula (Rae Isthmus), 41, 84
Melville Sound, 49
Merchant-backers of expeditions, 20
Mercy Bay, 188-94, 205, 215
Michel, Iroquois voyageur, 51-2
Miertsching, Johann August, 159-68, 170-3, 175, 177-81, 183, 185-7, 189-93, 205-9, 213-14, 216-17, 219, 229, 249, illus.
Miller, Capt. on Theseus, 28
Moldoyah, Chukchee guide, 109
Montreal, 77
Montreal Island, 83, 89, 261
Moore, Commander on Plover, 107-8, 168
Moore, Officer on Plover, 109
Moose Deer Fort, 46, 47, 54
Moose Factory, 114
Moravian Brotherhood, 159
Morton, William, 233, 237, 238-9, 241
Murchison, Sir Roderick, 248
Murdaugh, officer on Advance, 147
Muskox Lake, 80, 81

Nancy Dawson, yacht, 110, 111

Nansen, Dr F., 111
Nares, G. F., 209, 211
Navy Board Inlet, 73
Nelson, Admiral Horatio, 27, 28
Nelson, James, on Investigator, 192, 219
Nelson's Head (Cape Erebus), 174, 221
Netelik, Eskimo encampment, 239
New Orleans, attack on, 11, 43
New World, S.S., 163
Newton, William, 160, 173, 178
Nias Point, 210
North Cornwall Island, 211
North Kent Island, 212
North Somerset Land, 68, 156
North Star, HMS, 114, 126, 127, 251; depot ship at Beechey Island, 157, 197, 200, 202, 208, 214, 215, 237; return home, 216-17
North West Company, fur traders, 46, 47
Northwest Passage, completed, 177; dispute over reward, 226-7
Norway House, 77

Officers, naval, 27-8
Ogle, Point, 83, 89, 97, 245, 261
Ohlsen, C., 236, 240
Ommaney, Capt. Erasmus, 121, 125, 128-9, 137-8, 196
Ommaney Bay, 138, 156
Ooligbuck, Eskimo, 59, 88
O'Reilly Islets, 265
Orkney Islands, 44, 97, 143, 150
Osborn, Capt. Sherard, 233; character and career, 121; commands Pioneer under Austin, 121-6, 135-9; on bear hunt, 135-6; under Belcher, 196, 197-9, 211-12; under arrest, 214; and Austin and Penny, 122-3, 195-6; and Belcher, 218; subsequent carreer, 218, 247, 249; Discovery of the N.W. Passage, 165, 166, 185, 218, 228-9; edits McClintock's book, 248
Osmer, C. H., 13, 15

Paine, J. C., 178
Palmerston, Henry John, Viscount, 248
Parker, Admiral Sir William, 198
Parker Bay, 115, 116
Parks, Lt, 222
Parliament, House of, 22, 75, 227-9, 270
Parry, Caleb, 32
Parry, Capt. William Edward; early career, 32; with Ross in Baffin Bay, 28-31; leads Hecla and

Griper expedition, 33-9; Hudson's Bay expedition, 39-42; mentioned, 65, 66, 67, 68, 76, 92, 93, 94, 98, 105, 120, 128, 135, 139, 170, 178
Parry, Cape, 62, 174
Parry's Monument at Winter Harbour; carved, 38; McClintock at, 139; McClure at, 190; Mecham at, 203
Paynter, Commander, 163, 164
Peary, Admiral Robert, 21, 29, 136, 232, 258
Peel, Sir Robert, 75, 92
Peel River, 113
Peel Sound, 24, 104, 196; E. shore traced by Ross, 105; W. by Browne, 137-8; Kennedy at, 155; Franklin down, 197, 267; McClintock fails, 250, 256; Young charts, 266
Peglar, H., 261
Pelly Bay, 97, 224, 243
Peltier, *voyageur*, 56
Penny, William, 117, 122-3, 124, 125-6, 127, 129, 131, 132, 134, 135, 247; explores Wellington Channel, 139-42; return home, 195-6; and Osborn, 122-3, 196, 247
Penny Channel, 141
Penny Strait, 211, 212
Pepys, Samuel, 26
Petersen, Carl, interpreter with Penny, 125-6, 199; with Kane, 233, 234, 236, 237-8, 239-40, 241; with McClintock, 250, 251, 259-61, 269; nieces of, 199, 269
Phillips, Commander, 125, 127
Phoenix, HMS, 157, 208, 216, 233
Pigott, Capt., 28
Pim, Lt Bedford, 199, 203, 204-7, 210, 219, 247
Pioneer, H.M.S.; with Austin, 121, 123-4, 126, 129; with Belcher, 196, 198-9, 200; abandoned, 216
Pitcairn Island, 62
Plover, HMS, 98, 103; on Siberian shore 107-8; in Kotzebue Sound, 110, 162, 168-9, 220, 225, 230
Plymouth, Devon, 159-60
'Polar Basin' theory, 19, 22, 29
Pond's Inlet, 255
Polaris, U.S. discovery ship, 25
Porden, Eleanor (Franklin's first wife), 57-8
Portage La Loche, 77, 78
Prince Albert, 196; with Forsyth, 119, 125, 126-7; with Kennedy, 134, 143, 144-50
Prince Albert Land, 174, 176-7, 179, 222; Haswell explores, 180

Prince Albert Sound, 115, 180, 221, 222
Prince Alfred Bay, 140
Prince Alfred Cape, 183
Prince Patrick Island, 210, 211
Prince of Wales Island, 137-8, 155, 156, 257
Prince of Wales Strait, 19, 24; discovered by McClure, 177; *Investigator* winters in, 182; Collinson in, 221-2
Princess Royal Cape, 116
Princess Royal Islands, 175-6, 179, 182, 193, 215, 221
Proctes's Bay, 72
Providence, Fort, 46, 47, 51, 54, 55
Pruden, Mr, fur factor, 45
Prudhoe Bay, 63-4
Pullen, Commander W. J. S.; on *Plover*, 107, 110-14, 117; on *North Star*, 157, 197, 232
Punishments, naval, 38

Quail, Capt. on *McLellan*, 134

Rae, Dr John; early career, 114; *1846* shore survey, 97; *1849* rescue expedition, 106-7, 114; *1851*, 114-17; *1853-4*, 88, 243-5; and Hooper, 113; finds wreckage, 116-17; return home, 245-6; mentioned, 91, 103, 104, 223, 224, 258
Rae Isthmus, 97
Rae Strait, 260, 267
Rattler, tugboat, 10
Regent's Inlet, 23, 34, 41, 94, 143, 154, 268; map, 71; Parry in, 42; Ross in, 67, 68, 73; Franklin in, 126-7; Kennedy in, 148-55
Reid, James, 12, 13, 14-15
Reliance, Fort, 80, 83
Reliance, 60
Renovation, 230
Rensselaer Harbour, 235
Repulse Bay, 22, 23, 40, 65, 84; Rae at, 97, 243-5
Rescue, 119, 127, 128, 129, 131, 133
Resolute, H.M.S., 21; with Austin, 121, 123, 125, 126, 130, 131, 246; with Kellett, 198-203, 206-9, 211-12; at Melville Island, 201-3; icebound, 212-14; deserted, 214-15; salvaged, 218; court-martial re, 217-18
Resolution, H.M.S., 22
Return Reef, 60-1, 63, 112
Richards, Commander George, 211-12, 220, 249
Richardson, Sir John, 76, 84, 96-7, 103, 117, 263; on Franklin's 1st

land journey, 44-6, 50-5; on 2nd, 58-60, 62; with Rae seeks Franklin, 104, 106-7
Richardson, Point, 83, 261
Riley, Cape, 128, 256
Ripon Island (Cape Britannia), 83, 89
Robinson, Lt, on *Enterprise*, 106
Roche, mate on *Resolute*, 208, 209
Ross, George (father of James), 76
Ross, Capt. Sir James Clark; with Parry, 33; under John Ross, 66, 67, 69-72; sledges to King William, 69-70; map, 71; scientific repute, 75; claims King William joins Boothia, 70-1, 83, 90, 267; locates Pole, 72; in Antarctic, 92; and Franklin's voyage, 92, 93, 100, 101, 102, 103; with *Enterprise* seeks Franklin, 104-7; return, 118; mentioned, 76, 97, 122, 134, 137, 147, 159, 247, 248, 257, 259
Ross, Rear-Admiral Sir John, 76, 120; in Baffin Bay, 28-31; and Lancaster Sound, 30-1, 32, 76; leads *Victory* expedition, 65-74; map, 19; abandons ship, 72; rescued, 73-4; return home, 74-6; rescue team sent for, 76-7, 80; and Franklin, 96, 98, 103; on *Felix*, 119, 125-31, 134, 137; *Treatise on Steam Navigation*, 66
Ross Strait, 260, 267
Royal Geographical Society, 86, 87, 157
Royal Society, 27, 43, 75
Russell Island, 137
Russell Point, 177

Sabine, Col Edward, 33, 38, 103, 118
Sabine, Cape, 232
Sabine Peninsula, 211
Sachs Harbour, 183
Sainsbury, Hubert, 160, 165, 213
St Germain, Indian interpreter, 50
St Roch, police boat, 26
Salmon, sledge-mate of McClintock, 250
Samwell, Dr D., 168-9
Sanderson's Hope, Greenland Cliff, 20
Sandy Bay, 163
Saskatchewan River, 45
Satellite Bay, 210
Schwatka, Lt F., 261, 265
Scoresby, William, 132
Scott, Robert, on *Fox*, 252
Scott, Robert Falcon, 92, 268
Separation Point, 60, 61, 62

Sheddon, Robert, 110
Simpson, Alexander, 91
Simpson, George, 47-8, 56, 58, 77, 88-9, 91, 97
Simpson, Thomas, 88-91, 93, 94, 101; map, 71; cairn of, 261-2
Simpson, Fort, 90, 113
Simpson Strait, 89, 264-5
Sledging techniques, 69, 105-6, 122, 136-7, 209
Smith, John, on *Prince Albert*, 125, 149-51
Smith Sound, 21; closed by Ross, 29; Inglefield in, 230-2; Kane in, 233-40; map, 231
Smyth, Lt William, 85, 122
Snow, W. Parker, 125-7, 140, 143
Somerset Island (Land), 68, 156
Sophia, 139
Southampton Island, 84
Starvation Cove, 261, 265
Steam power, 66
Stewart, Alexander, with Penny, 140
Stewart, J. G., with Anderson, 247
Stromness, 123, 144-5
Sun, Baltimore, 132
Sussex Lake, 79
Sutherland, Dr Peter, 140-1, 195-6
Swift, HMS, 165
Swilly, Lough, 85

Talbot, supply ship, 216
Tasmania, Franklin governs, 12, 57, 93
Taylor, Zachary, U.S. President, 116, 119
Taylor Island, 115-16
Terror, HMS; *illus.*; with Back, 84-6; with Ross, 92, 94-5; with Franklin, 10-16, 92, 95-7, 141; then as *Erebus*, *q.v.*
Terror Bay, 265
Theseus, 28
Thompson, Alexander, 140, 259
Todd Islets, 265
Toolemak, Eskimo sorcerer, 40-1
Traders, *see* fur traders
Trafalgar, battle of, 9, 11, 42, 43
Trent, 28, 43
Tuktoyaktuk, Eskimo settlement, 171
Turnagain Point, 49, 89

Union, 60, 62
Upernavik, 124, 126, 238, 239, 255; Kane party reaches, 241
U.S. Congress, 218
U.S. Navy, 233

Vaillant, *voyageur*, 51

Venture Strait, 211
Victoria Harbour, 72
Victoria Headland, 82, 89
Victoria Land (Island), 90, 94, 96, 142, 181, 257-8; Rae at, 114-17; Collinson at, 223-4
Victoria Strait, 116, 223, 224-5, 267
Victory, Cape, 223, 262
Victory, Point, 70, 265
Victory, 66-8, 72, 76
Viscount Melville Sound, 35, 39, 175-7, 182, 203, 221

Walker, Dr David, 250, 252, 258-9, 265-6
Walker, Sam, carpenter, 212
Walker Bay, 221-2
Walker Cape; sighted by Parry, 35; key point in Franklin's orders, 94, 95, 98-100, 101, 104, 117, 135; reached by Ommaney, 137-8
Webb, Officer under Austin, 138
Wedderburn, Fort, 46, 47
Wellington Channel, 23, 104, 128, 130, 135, 142, 196-7, 211; discovered by Parry, 35; explored by Penny, 117, 140-1; De Haven driven up, 131-2; Belcher in, 212-15
Wentzel, Frederick, 46, 49, 52, 54-5
Whale Sound, 239
Wilkie, sledge-mate of McClintock, 210

William IV, King of England, 74, 75, 76
Winter Harbour, 37-8, 139, 190, 197, 199, 202-3; *see also* Parry's Monument
Winter Island, 40
Wollaston Land, 62, 90, 94, 96, 114-15, 222
Wolstenholme Sound, 21, 125, 126
Wood, Sir Charles, 248, 249, 251
Woodward, Frances J., 56-7
Woon, Sgt, Royal Marines, 189, 192
Woorel, Siberian village, 107-9
Wrangel Island, 110
Wright, Admiral, 224
Wrottesley, Cape, 185
Wyniatt, Robert J., on *Investigator*, 138, 160, 165; sledge journey, 178-9, 180; insane, 191, 193, 207-8

Yaneenga, Chukchee woman, 109
Yarborough Inlet, 63
Yellowknife River, 44, 46, 53-4
York, Cape, 29, 104; Penny at, 125-6; McDougall, 200
York Factory, 43, 44, 56, 97
Young, Allen, 121; on *Fox*, 249, 250, 252, 255; discovery work on sledge, 258-60, 265-6